Theological Exegesis of Scripture

Theological Exegesis of Scripture

Volume I: The Pentateuch

PAUL C. MCGLASSON

CASCADE *Books* · Eugene, Oregon

Cascade Books
An Imprint of Wipf and Stock Publishers
199 W. 8th Ave., Suite 3
Eugene, OR 97401

www.wipfandstock.com

PAPERBACK ISBN: 978-1-5326-4673-7
HARDCOVER ISBN: 978-1-5326-4674-4
EBOOK ISBN: 978-1-5326-4675-1

Cataloguing-in-Publication data:

Names: McGlasson, Paul C., author.

Title: Theological exegesis of Scripture : volume I: the Pentateuch / by Paul C. McGlasson.

Description: Eugene, OR: Cascade Books, 2022

Identifiers: ISBN 978-1-5326-4673-7 (paperback) | ISBN 978-1-5326-4674-4 (hardcover) | ISBN 978-1-5326-4675-1 (ebook)

Subjects: LCSH: Bible. Pentateuch—Criticism, intepretation, etc.

Classification: BS1225.4 M38 2022 (print) | BS1225.4 (ebook)

05/20/22

Contents

Preface

THE PRESENT BOOK IS the first in a projected six-volume *Theological Exegesis of Scripture*, covering both testaments of the Christian Bible. By theological exegesis I mean the interpretation of Scripture according to its theological shape as a witness to the living will and work of God in church and world. The book is based on careful study of the Hebrew text, in close consultation with commentaries ancient and modern, Jewish and Christian.

A few very brief comments are in order that will help to describe and delimit the scope of this volume, and the projected set as a whole. First, I have, out of necessity, chosen the method of *lectio selecta* (commentary on select passages) rather than *lectio continua* (commentary on whole books) in order to keep the project within manageable limits of both space and time. At times, my selections accord with those common to traditional lectionary readings (which lean toward Genesis and Exodus, within the Pentateuch); at others, I have worked with passages often neglected, but in my judgment worth closer inspection at the present time. At all times, I have endeavored to make selections useful to teachers, pastors, and students, for whom the book (and set) is primarily designed.

Second, I have decided against adding a scholarly apparatus. Doing so would likely double the size of the volume, without adding to its inherent value. And that is simply because so much of the information such an apparatus would include is readily available in the myriad biblical encyclopedias, dictionaries, handbooks, introductions, and so forth—both in print and online—that are now readily available. I thought it best to keep the present work laser-focused on the contribution it is intended to make, and resist the temptation to crowd the text with extraneous material.

Finally, this is a work *of* theological exegesis, not a work *about* theological exegesis. I do not for a moment deny the importance of careful reflection on the question of how to do theological interpretation of Scripture, and there are of course several fine books on the subject. This however is not one of them. At some point, it comes time simply to get on with the task, and that is the aim of the present volume, and the overall project of which it is a part.

This book was written during a time of national and indeed international crisis. A raging pandemic has, at the time of writing, already caused several million deaths worldwide. The rise of ethno-nationalism and authoritarianism has, both in the United States and globally, scarred the peaceful unity of peoples and nations, often with tacit or even explicit support from elements within the "Christian" church. Climate change is not only continuing, but accelerating, because of the unleashing of carbon dioxide and methane into the atmosphere, and humanity seems paralyzed to the threat it is both causing and facing as a result. Immigration is growing, yet the humane treatment of immigrants is diminishing. In short, the church of our time faces these and other challenges the church of the past has not faced, at least in the present form.

Yet we live now, by the same promise to the church of all ages, that the risen Christ guides us still through the witness of Holy Scripture. Theological exegesis of Scripture is based upon that promise alone, and upon no other foundation. Indeed, we first encounter that divine gift of promise in the book of Genesis. And so, we begin, at the beginning . . .

I. Genesis

1. The Morning Stars

Genesis 1:1–5

THE OPENING VERSES OF the Bible resound with a confident affirmation of faith. Not a word is missing; not a spare word is added. The declaration of God's sovereign act of creation is filled with a precise wonder. Indeed, the entire first chapter of Genesis reads like a long-circulated confession of faith, symmetrical in form, theocentric in vision. God is the grammatical subject of the first sentence of Holy Scripture; God is the one theological Subject of creation, who alone calls the world into being according to his own mysterious purpose.

The opening sentence contains a syntactical ambiguity, often referenced in modern translations. The traditional rendering is "In the beginning, God created . . ." Hebrew syntax would also allow the translation: "When God began to create . . ." While the syntax is indeed ambiguous, the theological content leaves the translation far from uncertain. The traditional rendering in fact captures the genuine sense of the text and should best be followed. In the beginning, God created the heavens and the earth. Such is the opening profession of faith with which the Bible begins. We can only understand it by recognizing that the word *God* in the text is in fact God of heaven and earth; and that the God of heaven and earth is even now our Creator who comes to find us in the word of Scripture.

In the beginning. There is no reference here to an abstract chronology by which time can be measured. The point is not to suggest: go back, year by year, and you will at such and such a date reach the "beginning." Various "short" and "long" chronologies have been introduced to "date" the creation. All must be cast aside as contrary to the biblical word. For the entire point of the opening passage of the Bible is that *time* itself came to be with creation. Time is a creature of God. He is not timeless; he has his own time, the eternity of his life in glory, which gathers all time, past,

present, and future, into a single moment. But his time is not our time, his
ways not our ways. Creation came into being with time; time came into
being with creation. It cannot be dated, for there is no reference point
outside of the existence of God's own act, which can be measured only in
reference to itself. The creation is new *absolutely*.

God, and God alone, created the world from nothing. As has often
been remarked, the Old Testament uses a special Hebrew word to describe
the divine act of creation, in order to make very clear the absolute difference between divine and human acts. God alone creates by using no
preexisting materials, no preexisting pattern or design. Human beings can
certainly be creative according to the Bible, but they use tools to hand,
often in unique and extraordinary ways. By sharp contrast, God alone,
without any analogy whatsoever, creates from nothing. Before the universe came to be, there was God alone, in the majesty of his eternal reality.
Not a monad, according to the fuller witness of Scripture, but a living
relationship of love, the triune God. For his own mysterious purpose, according to his own sovereign good pleasure, God in his own merciful love
created a world independent of himself.

And what did he create? The heavens and the earth. Hebrew often
uses the rhetorical figure of merism, in which two contrasting words are
used to refer to the whole. In this case the whole is . . . everything that is,
the cosmos. The scope of God's creative power and will reaches forth over
all reality. The remaining verses of the first chapter will unfold the beauty
of God's creation of the cosmos in two contrasting rows. On the one hand,
God will create a series of domains; today we would call them ecosystems:
the light, the sky (separating the waters above and below), the dry land
and plants. Then he will populate those domains with creatures: the sun,
moon, and stars; fish and birds; and finally land animals and humans. God
creates human beings in his own image; he creates them male and female.
God gives humankind the Sabbath as a gift. Notice, God does not invite
humanity to join his work of creation; he invites them to join his rest. From
beginning to end, there is an inviolable focus on the sovereign and creative
majesty of God alone, different in kind, not just degree, from all human effort. The Sabbath is described in the Bible as a "perpetual covenant" (Exod
31: 16). Creation is both the basis for the gracious covenant that provides
its true inner purpose; and it points forward from the very beginning.
God's creation of the universe is an eschatological act. The God of creation
is found always in the future, never in the past.

God and the cosmos, the cosmos and God. We are well on our way, it
would seem, along the unfolding story of creation. Until suddenly everything comes to a full stop as a new threat suddenly enters the picture: "the

earth was a formless void and darkness was upon the face of the deep." Now, we must unfortunately quickly depart from the traditional reading of this verse. Theological exegesis is not the same thing as retrieval of tradition, however much it is rooted in it. Traditional exegesis understood the formless void to be a reference to the *incomplete* nature of creation at the beginning. Usually on the analogy of Greek metaphysics, it was seen as the underlying *matter* of the universe, to which God in the subsequent "days" of creation would then give form. It is a logical, even compelling reading; but it is not true to the text of Scripture. We must dig deeper to find a fresh understanding of these remarkably fulsome theological texts in the opening verses of the Bible.

The creation is complete; God has created the cosmos. He will in the coming "days" of creation with the hand of a divine artist draw in the details of his beautiful world. But the formless void does not refer to the incomplete; it refers rather to a profound *threat* to creation, and that is the threat of chaos. No sooner does God make his cosmos than chaos threatens to undo it. We have two questions. What is the nature of this chaos, and where does it come from? We will get the answer to one, but be left to ponder in mystery the other.

The nature of chaos, here and elsewhere in the Bible, is the threat of total destruction, total annihilation, utter and complete assault on all blessed order in the universe. Since the time of Descartes, our own modern culture has been held captive to the question of existence: the opposite of being is simply not-being. *The* metaphysical question is thus: why is there anything at all, and how can I prove it? Not so the Bible. For biblical faith the opposite of existence is *chaos*. To live under the goodness of God the Creator is to enjoy blessings of life in his ordered universe. To lose our way, as individuals or societies, is to face the threat of chaos, which tears apart the fabric of creation, leaving us defenseless and hopeless against the powers of destruction. Chaos comes when a pandemic brings massive global disease and death, forcing to a full stop the entire world of modern social existence; when an authoritarian political movement defaces the architecture of civil society as a whole; when the climate itself turns against the world it otherwise nourishes. Chaos is not just an event, however unfortunate; it enfolds every other human occurrence within its grasp, calling humanity itself into question. So, the "why question" is different, and leads to our second question: why is there chaos?

And here we are left to ponder in mystery. As is often the case in the Bible, we are not left without guidance. Indeed, two points are very carefully made. First, chaos is not eternal. Before the world began, there was only one reality: God. Not God and chaos. There is no primordial dualism in the Bible.

But if chaos is not primordial, where did it come from? The other point is also clearly made: God did not create chaos. He created the cosmos; chaos threatens the world he made. So how are we to account for the presence of chaos so soon—indeed immediately—after the creation of the world?

We struggle to say the unsayable, but the struggle is worth it. There are not words for chaos, for chaos is the destruction of language, the destruction of order, the destruction of logic, the destruction of meaning. And so, we can only point with broken language. In creating order, God did not create chaos. It therefore lives as that which God did not intend, as that which God did not create; it is possible only as that which is impossible. In creating the cosmos God rejected chaos, and it lives as that which God rejected, always threatening to undo that which God chose to create. It exists as the power of bringing existence to an end, the power of sheer destruction. It has no life apart from God; yet it draws no life from God, but lives only as that which God grants no being at all. It is formless and void.

That it does not undo God's creation from the beginning is simply because of the action of God's Spirit. The verb is a participle, and should be kept a participle in translation, to catch the immediate and active force: "the Spirit sweeping [not *swept*] over the face of the waters." Only the moving of God's Spirit keeps chaos at bay. And indeed, as the remaining portions of Scripture confirm, God's Spirit can withdraw in judgment, and chaos again invades creation, wrecking and destroying lives, societies, epochs. Chaos here is held in check; but the threat remains. We pray to God's Creator Spirit even today to sweep away the chaos of our time.

We come to the first day. God brings the reality of his world into being by speaking. There is no gap in God between intention and speech; between speech and action. The text is precise: God speaks, and it is. "God said, "Let there be light"; and there was light. Once again, we must depart from much traditional exegesis, again in large measure based on Greek metaphysics. It was argued that God in speaking "caused" the world to exist. Indeed, because causality could be ascribed to God, a rational proof for God emerged. The chain of causality must have a First Cause; God is the First Cause of the universe. Now, the Bible will come to show a fine understanding of causes; why some things happen, why others do not. But the point to be stressed here is that the idea of causality is not only absent from the witness to creation, but inimical to it. The reason is not far to seek. Like time, causality is a creature of God. In creating the world, God created causality; but God is not subject to the laws of time and causation. The Bible does not say God's Word *caused* the world; it says, in the miracle of joyous affirmation, God spoke, and the world was. There is only God's word, and the cosmos he creates; there is no intermediary. We assign names to objects that already exist; God gives existence to objects simply by declaring their name. Creation is a miracle without any analogy whatsoever; it cannot be proved; it cannot only be believed.

God creates light. He not only creates it, he *sees* his creation, and calls it good. God in these opening verses of the Bible is creating a universe, filled eventually with earth and sky, plants and animals, and at long last humankind. But he not only creates; he sees what he creates, and affirms and embraces its existence. It is not just *there*; it is *good*. Creation itself is not a neutral fact, still less a harsh wilderness to be tamed, or from which we must ultimately escape in order to find our true being. Creation is a divine gift of grace and blessing. Creation is not the promise of salvation; but it is the necessary basis upon which the divine promise of redemptive love will be freely given. God sees all his works and calls them good, and we marvel at his handiwork.

He divides the light from the darkness, and calls the light day and the darkness night. Morning is broken on the first day. Notice that there is a rhythmic pattern built into creation. It is not all light; there is darkness and light, light and darkness. Of course, in the literal sense that is true of the beauty of sunlight and the sacred dark of night. Both fill heart and mind with wonder, with readiness for the day, giving way to the coming ease of the quiet night. But there is clearly a figurative sense. Life itself is light and darkness, darkness and light. We are not now referring to chaos and cosmos; rather, within the cosmos itself there is a dialectical pattern in human existence. There are times when life is light, and we step lightly. Yet there are times when shadows intrude, and we struggle forward with difficulty, looking—even blindly—for a way. Both make us more human, both make us more nearly the wondrous creature of God we are.

We consider now three points more carefully. First, as we have seen, God not only creates, he *rejoices* in what he creates. He makes; and he *sees* what he makes. There is an element of sheer divine pleasure in the glory of light and dark, sun and moon, field and ocean, plant and animal. The psalmist brings this divine joy in creation out most explicitly: "The Lord is good to all, and his compassion is over all that he has made. All your works shall give thanks to you, O Lord, and all your faithful shall bless you" (Ps 145:9–10). We are not allowed to be against creation, nor even indifferent in the face of the natural world. We are called by the glory of God to live with joy in the world he has made and called good. We do not wait for the joyous mysteries of creation to come to us; we seek them out, often finding them in the most unlikely places. The truth is they are everywhere; it is our calling to seek and find the joys of life that God himself freely gives to those who look where they may be found. The most astounding truth of all is that God, our Creator, takes delight in our joy in his blessed creation. We give God joy by our joy in his marvelous world; such is the miracle of his love.

A second point arises not so much from the text itself as from the ecological crisis in which we find ourselves. The Bible predates the modern industrialization that produces the crisis that now quite clearly threatens the health of our planet, the very planet described with such care and evident admiration in the first chapter of the Bible. While the Bible does not speak to a crisis, does it speak to a perspective from which the crisis can best be addressed? Indeed, the opening verses of the Bible offer the church and the world a quite distinctive alternative. We have heard far too much from those who feel that human beings have the right to exploit the world for human need and consumption. Clearly, exploitation is not a biblical option, nor is it a remotely attractive solution to the problem; indeed it is the problem. But nor does the common alternative of taking "responsibility" for creation, however well intended, reflect the awful majesty of the biblical word. Who are we—human beings—to take responsibility for God's universe, God's cosmos, God's earth? We made nothing; how can we be truly responsible for it? Rather, the Bible sounds a third option which needs to be heard. This is not our world; this is God's world: "The heavens are yours; the earth also is yours; the world and all that is in it—you have founded them" (Ps 89:11). Even the ground beneath our feet is not ours, but his: "The land shall not be sold in perpetuity, for the land is mine; with me you are but aliens and tenants" (Lev 25:23). The entire earth belongs to God alone, and we are all—all—immigrants, passing guests here but for a while. If that is the clear biblical witness, I question whether rushing to a notion of human "responsibility" for creation is quite the answer. Do we not need, on the basis of the Scriptural mandate, a new sense of frank humility in the face of the natural world? It is *not ours*; let us start with that as our first premise in every public and private decision made.

Thirdly, we reflect briefly on life under the dialectic of shadow and light. We love, and that love fills us with the light of life. But in daring to love we also risk, and suffer, loss. The loves are profound; the losses leave our emotions numbed and our sense of purpose exhausted. We strive for achievement, and using every ounce of imagination and creativity we arrive at our goal. But along the way there are mistakes, there are failures. We cherish our achievements; yet we can come close to breaking under the burden of our failure, and struggle to shake off the abiding effect of regret. Could we not just have light without shadow? God himself answers the question from the very beginning. He names the light and the dark. Both belong to him: "Yours is the day, yours also the night" (Ps 74:16). It is not a biblical faith which says: God is with us only in prosperity . . . so pray for the light! God's truest saints have long known that he draws nearest in the shadows of life: in loss, disappointment, grief, suffering, oppression. Only when we recognize his loving face in the shadow of night do we truly praise in the glorious light of day. Shadow and light converge on Easter morning, God's new Day.

2. Houses of Clay

Genesis 2:15–25

WHILE WE WILL FOCUS upon the final section of the chapter, it is helpful to begin with a few comments about the second chapter of Genesis as a whole. It is now quite common to see in modern Bibles a title or reference to this chapter something to the effect of "a second story of creation." And it is true that the second chapter of Genesis almost certainly derives from a quite different literary source than the first, though the history of how and when those sources were linked, and by whom, is much disputed. But we do not have two accounts of creation in the written word, whatever the origin of the traditions that make it up. The key to understanding the theological shape of these two chapters is 2:4: "These are the generations of the heavens and the earth when they were created." How does this help us understand the theological setting of chapter 2, in its relation to chapter 1?

This is the first of the ten "generations" formulas that provide one of the prominent elements of the theological structure of the book. These formulae not only tie the various stories of Genesis into one coherent whole; they structure that one theological framework around the concept of the divine promise. But we meet with the first such formula only to find an inviting anomaly. Throughout the remainder of the book of Genesis, the formula always stands at the head of a group of stories, which then tell the family history of the person referred to. The formula is always at the head of the stories to follow; and always points forward to progeny, never backward to ancestors. So, what does that tell us about the relation between Genesis 1, which focuses on the creation of the cosmos by God, and Genesis 2, which focuses on the creation of humankind? Why is the first "generations" formula put between the two so prominently and so counterintuitively, as no human person is involved?

First, the two passages are not two "accounts of creation," but rather the one story of creation in chapter 1, followed by its continuation in chapter 2. There is only one account of creation in the Bible, despite the insistence of modern editors. Second, the shift in focus is obvious to the alert reader or listener: chapter 1 portrays the grandeur of God in bringing the universe into beginning by his Word, while chapter 2 focuses on the special role of humanity within the patterned beauty of the earth. Indeed, verse 4 inverts the common merism: "heavens and earth" becomes "earth and heavens." We will now see the divine creation, no longer from the perspective of the cosmos, but from the special vantage point of earth, where humankind dwells. But third, and most remarkably, the account in chapter 2 is in some sense on the analogy of a child to a parent to chapter 1. That is to say, humankind is the child of creation. That is not to deny the spectacular assertion in chapter 1 that humanity is made in the image of God; nevertheless, the "generations" formula sets the human story going forward as, in some sense, a product of the universe. Darwin could not have said it any better.

Two more comments derive from the extraordinary declaration in 2:7: "then the Lord God formed man from the dust of the ground and breathed into his nostrils the breath of life; and the man became a living being." Humankind is made from dust, from clay, from a clod of dirt. The word for dust and the word for humanity sound very similar in Hebrew; a play on words in Hebrew is reminding us that from the beginning, dust is destiny. We are dust, and depend solely upon the breath of God for life itself. He breathes, and we live; he returns his breath, and we die. The resonance of this statement goes far in the Bible. Human beings are created mortal. They die as a result of the catastrophic sin in chapter 3; but clearly that death is not the introduction of mortality. We are dust, mortal from the very beginning. We are born into families; we live in communities, which shape our very identity. Our lives begin, then flourish, then sadly and inevitably decline. In death, we return to the dust from which we came. Along the way we are fragile creatures, profoundly susceptible to the threats of disease, attack, loss, unnamable fears, exile, verbal assault. We may indeed be created in the image of God, but that most certainly does not mean that we are accorded semidivine status. There is a sense of realism about humanity that is built into the biblical picture of creation, and is never abandoned. Humankind is never seen in the Bible as the great achiever of glorious goals, the great generator of life-changing worldviews. Dust is not an –ism; dust is dust. We are houses of clay.

Yet God makes us into living beings. The word used here in Hebrew was once commonly translated as "soul," as if the outer body was dust while the inner person, breathed by God, was an invisible and immortal substance. That is the Greek view; it is certainly not the biblical view. There are not substantial "parts" to the person in the Bible. The Bible sees human beings as whole creatures, right from the beginning. That we are dust is true of the whole person, not just the external body. We are dust, from the inside out, and from the outside in. We are also living beings, as whole persons. So, what does that mean, in distinction from the dust from which we come? As whole persons we have desires, longings, even cravings. Some of these may be to our own benefit; some, alas, may do us harm, such as the unchecked desire for vengeance. We feel alive, happy, hopeful, loving; but again, we just as easily turn to hate and despair. As living creatures in society we make laws; we also break those laws. In short, to speak of "life" (or the older formulation of "soul") is to see the whole person as one who desires, longs for, and decides. This is what God makes when he breathes into humanity his own breath. Keep in mind that all living creatures have the divine breath of life (1:30), as anyone who has ever loved a pet animal knows well. The church assault on Darwin was a mistake, unless we are ready to make the same assault upon the word of God, which is ultimate folly.

The first human being—we will not learn his name, Adam, until verse 20—is placed by God in a garden park in the paradise of Eden. The first home of humankind is a bountiful and beautiful garden. The garden is filled with luxurious trees, and fruit is abundant and available to the man. He must do minimal work to keep and cultivate the garden, but clearly it is God who provides the abundance. Two trees however stand out. The first is the tree of life, about which we will hear later. The second is the tree of the knowledge of good and evil, which now provides the setting for the drama to follow. God gives the first man freedom to eat of all the trees of the garden, with one exception: he must not eat of the tree of the knowledge of good and evil. Death—not mortality, but death—will follow if he does. Our first question concerns the nature of this tree: what is its significance? The issue is not rightly captured by the simplistic idea of moral choice, as if eating the fruit from this tree will confer such moral knowledge. Indeed, as we will see, the scene immediately determines the true nature of moral choice, the ability to decide between right and wrong (*liberum arbitrium*). Rather, eating from the tree of the knowledge of good and evil aggrandizes to humanity the supposed right to establish abstract moral norms—including religious norms—independent of the living will of God. The tree of the knowledge of good and evil would give humanity the correct *human* view of God and the world; what God offers, even demands, is the right *divine* view of humanity.

Why is this not then a tree of moral choice? Here we must observe a distinction. God makes it clear for the first time in this passage that true freedom comes only through service to his living command. An abstract system of moral and religious values—today we call it a religious world-view—not only fails to capture the biblical vision of truth, but in fact profoundly perverts and distorts it. Freedom is obedience to the divine will. It is certainly *spontaneous*, not coerced; but it is not the choice of one option among other options. God gives the first human person one option only: do not eat. That is one side of our freedom: to choose what God wills. On the other hand, God makes it clear that apart from this very defined prohibition, there is absolute freedom to enjoy the luscious fruits of every tree. The divine command *excludes* one possibility; but it also *includes* a vast range of options for human enjoyment. Obedience and enjoyment are certainly not mutually exclusive—far from it. In the obedience to the divine word, there is a limit that protects from the harmful that destroys true humanity, and a permission to relish the wide range of divine bounty. As to *why* God excludes this possibility, the question is not even here raised; only the serpent will first raise it. We only know that it is for our good.

The second chapter moves swiftly to a final scene that thrusts the story of humanity forward with profound consequence and beautiful rendering. God himself observes that ultimate human solitude is damaging; indeed, his words are emphatic, and stand in verbal contrast to the goodness of creation itself. He once called the universe "very good"; now God states that it is "not at all good" that the man is alone. God alone now takes the initiative to remedy human loneliness. It is a divine decision of grace for human benefit, yet carried out at first with human input. God aims to make for the man a helper that is fitting to him, indeed that corresponds to his existence. There is no hint of subordination in the notion of a helper, especially in the Bible, and most especially from the mouth of God; for God himself is the ultimate Helper of all humankind. It is a term of honor and respect. To be alone is quite simply to be helpless. So, God proceeds. He makes the various animals of earth, and birds of the sky. He brings them to the man, who names them one by one. The act of naming is here not an act of dominance, but an act of communion, an act of familiarity, an act of common ground. The man, the beasts, the birds, all stand in mutual relation under the rule of God.

But there is no mutual relation for Adam; notice once again that it is here for the first time that the word is vocalized by the ancient Hebrew scribes as a proper name. It is not a mistake, or an irrelevance. Adam, too, has a name; he too fits into the great harmony of creation. But he is still alone, and we see him alone best when we know his name. He is not just a person; he is *this* person, a real human being with a name, a unique personality, just as we are. So far, no fitting helper has been found for him. There is nothing in all the world of birds and animals that is so close to this human person, Adam, that he sees a likeness of his own face in a corresponding creature; that he sees in the other a genuine partner and companion to accompany him whatever trials lay ahead. God genuinely empathizes with the condition of human solitude; so God himself step into the breach. The man is put into a deep sleep. The purpose is not so much anesthetic related to the surgery, as it is to protect the mystery of God's miraculous power at work. We as readers are allowed to see it, if only through a brief glimpse; Adam himself will see nothing until the final result is revealed. It is a narrative technique we will encounter time and again in the Bible, where the reader is given information that the characters in the story do not have. The purpose is manifold; we are certainly to see the glory of God's new creation, but we are also to go through the miraculous mystery with our eyes shut, as if asleep with Adam. Both perspectives are necessary.

While the man is asleep, God takes a rib from his side, and from it creates a new creature, a woman. The wound in the side of the man is instantly healed by God. God himself "brings" the woman to the man, in words that echo the presentation of the bride in the wedding ceremony. The man, now awake, sees the woman. His short speech contains the first recorded words of a human being, according to the Bible. They are, quite simply, love poetry. The man is deeply moved, indeed stutters in ecstasy: "This . . . this . . . this . . ." There is a play on words in the name of this new creature, which comes across in English just as well as Hebrew: she is woman, for she is taken from man. The very definition of man and woman is now co-linked. Man is no longer man apart from woman; woman is no longer woman apart from man. Yet their mutual relation is not identity; they live in the freedom of self-possession, as indicated by the possession of a name. Man is man, not woman; woman is woman, not man. They are one as two; they are two as one. Notice that there is no mention of the bearing of children here; the woman is valued simply for her new existence in the beauty of creation.

The biblical narrator adds two further details that round out the picture of paradise. Because they came from one flesh, man and woman are destined to live as one flesh. The true pattern of life therefore is to leave family behind, and to join as husband and wife. There is without doubt here a reference to sexuality. Man and woman, woman and man, were created to live together in mutual sexual fulfillment. "One flesh" certainly has a sexual, even erotic edge. But the phrase carries multiple meanings that reach far into human experience. To leave home and live together as one means to build a new life together with shared experiences and ideas, shared goals and plans, shared hardships and triumphs, always in mutual encouragement and enjoyment. Woman and man, joined together in loyalty and affection as one, take on a new identity as a window through which God's own love and peace shine anew into the world. And secondly, in a remarkable statement, the narrator simply points out that they are naked together, and feel no shame in their nudity. The verb translated "to feel shame" is used once, only here, in the entire Pentateuch, and it is used in a rarely used reciprocal verbal form. We are, as it were, directed to consider a transcendent truth. To feel shame is to experience an inner contradiction through which we hide our true selves from the other, and indeed from our very selves. In shame, we live an inner self-contradiction; in shame, to be naked is to be *exposed*. We are led to consider that human beings joined together in love are created to live without fear of exposure in sheer vulnerability. The man and the woman in the garden of paradise did not choose their mutual vulnerability; they were quite simply unaware that any other alternative was a human possibility.

We reflect, as the Bible guides us, ever more deeply into our own humanity before God. We are dust. We are born of dust, and to dust we shall return. There is certainly a call to humility in this recognition. We who would shape history should perhaps first realize how deeply history has shaped us, both for good and ill. We who would break free of society should without doubt recognize that society is the womb in which we have found our very identity. We who would shatter the norms of the present in order to build a new future should most certainly realize that the norms of the present were once the new future of a distant past. We live within limits, both in ourselves, and in our times, and the first step of humility is to accept and embrace those limits. But humility does not rest with mere acquiescence; humility recognizes the unspeakable gifts of God that come precisely within those limits. There are goods in society all around us; there are hopes for the future that are well-founded; there are norms in the present worth keeping, and others worth dashing to the ground. We have work to do, and God in his mercy has given us talents and insights with which to do it. The second moment of humility is to do everything in our power to excel in the talents God has given to each, that we might make the best contribution to the common good. We know best which talents are worth exercising to the fullest, for it is those which fill us with the greatest joy and gratitude. And the third, and final, and most important moment of humility is to realize that, though we are dust, dirt, clay, that is not the last word of our existence. Over us, beyond us, yet altogether nearer to us than we are to ourselves, is the divine Potter. If we are clay, we are clay in *his* hands. If for a time, and for a season, we cannot begin to see the figure he is shaping our lives to be, much less the shape he is giving to the times in which we live, we put our absolute trust in him. He is the Potter; we are the clay. That is not spoken in resignation, but with a kind of exhilarating curiosity. We may never know the full meaning of our lives and of our times until we meet the Potter face-to-face. But remember: he himself became dust, dirt, clay, that he might shape us into his image. Even the risen Christ, transformed and exalted, yet has "flesh and bones" (Luke 24:39).

We begin to learn our freedom, even if in learning it we so often forsake it. It is often said that freedom is the ability to choose between several alternatives. However, that definition may or may not work in some contexts, it most certainly fails miserably in the overpowering truth of Holy Scripture. We encounter our freedom in the garden of Eden; we will lose it there as well. But as those who have received it back as a gift, we must reflect on what we have received. God *sets limits*; obedience to those limits is our freedom. The limit is not inhumane; the limit is grace. Outside of those limits is not freedom, but bondage. The "choice" to kill is not an act of free humanity, but an act of humanity in bondage. Only the service of God is perfect freedom. On the other hand, in some areas of life, God allows human personality to *roam free*. Adam and Eve may eat of any of the fruit trees in the garden except one. Obedience to God does not mean that every single dimension of life is determined by a rule, not at all; the rule of faith itself points to wide areas of life in which it is God's own will that we enjoy the largesse of his bountiful creation. Clearly the errors are twofold. Some will deny that God sets any limits whatsoever: anything and everything is allowed! Others will argue that everything is under the rule of God's explicit law, and will legislate a kind of divine legalism for all domains of life. The church of Jesus Christ avoids the one error with as much determination as it avoids the other. We serve God's will with steadfast obedience; yet we will not allow anyone to trample on the freedom that God himself gives in the many spheres of life. *Both* errors are involved in original sin, as we will soon discover.

The ancient Jewish scholars who vocalized the text of the Bible did not give Adam his name until a certain point in the story: when he realized that he could find no fitting helper. Humanity (which sounds like Adam in Hebrew) is described with loving detail; but not until his solitude is exposed is his name given, and the individual man Adam emerges as a true character in the story. We are not self-made. Indeed, we only first become fully human, fully an authentic self, when we recognize that fact. We live of course in a world supposedly full of "self-made" individuals, quite proud of their accomplishments. It is crucial to recognize that, from the point of view of Scripture, such "success" is the ultimate failure. To live the myth of self-possession, self-empowerment, self-achievement, is to live a lie. The best that can be attained in such a world is power; and that attainment of power is the loss of humanity, not its gain. We only become truly human when we recognize that our humanity is defined in encounter with the other. We do not live until we love, indeed until we give ourselves away to the other, without whom we cannot flourish and grow in the world. The most vital dimension of that encounter with the other is joy. To live in the enjoyment of our fellow humanity is to be truly human; to pursue the solitary path of power over others is to lose it. We hear much these days of toleration, and that is certainly a good thing. But who wants to be merely tolerated? To recognize a piece of myself in someone so utterly different than me; and far more important, to recognize in someone so utterly different than me a piece of myself, is the true poetry of human joy. Whoever cannot find it, and hides in fear and anger, loses everything worth having. Whoever finds in the other the joy of human connection has found the living Christ, who comes to us ever anew in the face of our neighbor.

3. The Human Paradox

Genesis 3:1–7

IT IS NO SECRET that humankind presents an astounding and disturbing paradox. At one and the same time humanity is capable of enormous accomplishment and profound destruction, often enough in the same realms of endeavor and even at the same points of time. Examples abound and need not long detain us. Human technology reaches a level of brilliance never attained, only to exceed it yet again; yet that same technology can and is used often enough to kill, to maim, to destroy innocent human life. Medical care has become the hope of countless persons; yet in our very recent past it has been used to conduct unspeakable experiments on the innocent. Human mastery of the natural world has enhanced the productivity of the earth, feeding millions and billions; yet that very mastery threatens the very viability of the biosphere that humankind inhabits. The list is endless and can easily be multiplied.

What is important however is the paradox itself, which seems to pervade human history. Now, the Bible does not offer a probative explanation of this dual determination of human existence. In fact, a number of explanations can be offered, many highly illuminating and useful. The Bible is a witness of faith, not one possible explanation among others, to be debated and proven or disproven. Rather, the Bible offers illumination, to those with eyes to see and ears to hear. While we will return to the twofold determination of humankind after our exegesis, a couple of points are necessary in advance.

Humankind lives in a *history* with God. That history is of course told in the Bible, which reaches back to the beginning, and points forward to the end. At both the beginning and end, the Bible shifts to a different level of speech. It is not a shift *away* from time and space, away from narrative sequence. But it is a shift *toward* imagination. Imaginative narration is not ahistorical, nor supra-historical. It is, rather, at the beginning of time, the

18

prehistory of our common humanity; and at the end of time the *post-history*, when time itself will give way to eternity. Prehistory here means *God's* beginning with us in our time; post-history means God's *goal*. The narrative of the fall is thus a moment in time and space; yet as God's beginning with us it is told with imaginative narration, and known in truth only by faith.

Adam and Eve are naked in the garden of Eden, and feel no shame. The story is not a derivation for the feeling of shame in sex, but there is no doubt that the disruption of sexual innocence is a victim of the fall. Sexual violence and abuse will become an all too familiar feature of the Bible; the biblical world is not an alternative pious universe, but the real world in which we live. They begin the story nude, and happily unaware, unashamed, of their nudity. It is pleasurable. What they are on the *outside*, and how they feel about themselves and toward each other on the *inside*, are at one. Yet there is already a hint of the disruption to come. The Hebrew word for naked, and the word for shrewd, sound similar. The listener is already made aware; what they cherish most is about to be threatened.

The identity of the serpent is made clear in the text, though traditional exegesis loses sight of it through needless theological speculation. It is always best to follow the plain sense of the text, especially when it is so clear. The serpent is not the devil, or Satan; the serpent is a creature of God. The distinction of the serpent is to be the shrewdest of all God's creatures. How can it talk? How does it know the information it claims to know? How is it in a position to argue with human persons so persuasively? The Bible of course does not answer. We are simply here to register a terrible and perplexing reality. The impossibility of chaos which God excluded from creation, and which stands only as an impossible reality threatening creation (Genesis 1:2), now enters creation itself. It comes from God only as that which God does not will for his creation. It is real only as that which God renders impossible. The serpent speaks with the shrewd wisdom of chaos. And humanity is caught in the chaotic folly of the impossible.

The serpent addresses Eve, and of course it is these two figures which conduct their infamous conversation. But it is worth noting that all of the words of address, all of the "you" words used by the serpent, are plural. The serpent is addressing Eve and Adam; he is addressing humankind. That Eve in particular is his interlocutor is not stressed in the biblical text. What is stressed instead is the *content* and the *nature* of their conversation, which is to be carefully observed.

What, first, is the nature of their conversation? The serpent poses to Eve a grammatically emphatic question: "did God indeed really say that . . . is that really true?" We immediately recognize a profound change in the nature of every conversation related to God so far recorded in the Bible.

Until now, God has been *present* in the conversation as a Subject. He speaks; he is heard; he is spoken to. God and humankind are in communion, in conversation, with one another. Suddenly this shrewd and subtle creature, the serpent, shifts everything by posing a question, not *to* God, but *about* God; a question lingering in the air as if God were *absent*, as if God were a topic, an item, an *object* for discussion. It is of course an impossible posture, a false discourse from the beginning. The fall begins not in what is said but in the very way in which the conversation is undertaken.

Did God say (notice, not "command")? The subtle and misleading approach continues. A tricky question is posed as if the answer is simple enough, but which in fact has no yes-or-no answer. God's command is quite clear concerning permission to eat of all the trees of the garden, but one. There is no ambiguity. The serpent asks a question that *presupposes* ambiguity in God. Verbal manipulation replaces the clarity of the divine word; did God really say you cannot eat from any of the trees? Eve not only falls into the trap, but adds her own grievous mistake. She answers correctly: God forbade the eating of the fruit of only one tree; the rest are for human enjoyment. All that is true; if only she had rested secure in the divine command. But she adds unneeded and untrue severity to God's clear command: "neither shall you touch it." She has interpreted God's *motive*, beyond his own revealed will; and now the door is open for the snake to press his final point. He not only interprets, he misconstrues, defames, the divine motive. God does not want you to eat it, lest you become divine, just like him! That is the reason for his command; just ignore it, you won't really die! God's command rests on jealousy! Disobedience is freedom!

Eve has already given up all grounds for defense. She is no longer addressing God, but assessing him; and she is assessing him now based on human criteria of meaning and truth. She already shares the same standpoint with the serpent, and therefore has no grounds upon which to resist his final appeal. Besides, the fruit is beautiful; it looks delicious; why not just take it and eat? After all, who can deny the love for wisdom which it offers? She gives to her husband and he eats as well.

The fall is universal to all humanity, according to Scripture; the effects of the fall are indeed cosmological in scope. The entire universe is under the judgment of corruption as a result of this one act of disobedience, so horrendous in its simplicity. But the biblical narrator first shows us one simple truth: the effect it has on the relationship between Eve and Adam, especially respecting their nudity. They were nude; now they *realize* that they are nude. Their eyes are opened, but it is not to their newfound freedom; rather, they see their loss. There is a disruptive breach between the inner and outer self, which is shame. They hide their nudity from themselves and from each other. Shame breaks the solidarity of fallen humankind, and ravages the serenity of the whole self before God. We are alienated from ourselves, and from each other, because we are alienated from God.

What are we then to say of Christian truth in the light of the biblical witness to the fall of humankind? We do not understand our redemption in the light of the fall; rather, we only understand the true reality of the fall in the light of God's redeeming mercy for the whole world in Jesus Christ. God's mercy is infinitely greater than human frailty. We begin with this profound realization. But we do not discount the fact that God overcame human frailty on a *cross*. Christ will say, once again, "take and eat"; but he will become human, lie in a manger, be mocked and crucified, and die, before he will say it to all who partake, even today. We do not understand the costliness of grace by considering the fall; rather, we truly understand the full dimensions of the fall by pondering just for a moment the sheer costliness of grace.

What was our original sin? We—Adam and Eve, and in them all humankind, and therefore us—we wanted to be like God. We were created to be in harmony with God, with ourselves, and with the natural world. We had a blessed *place*, a magnificent and beautiful role, in the divine economy of creation. The world was a garden, and we were there to enjoy and embrace the beauty of that world. Our role was finite; but we were graced, blessed, filled with wonder, in our finitude. We were dependent on God for all things, for the breath of life itself, and the sheer splendor of the natural world. Our trust was to accept our finitude as grace, and to know in the depths of our being that God himself provides all good things. And we abandoned that place, that role, that trust, that dependence on God. Instead of listening to the healing and gracious word of God, and speaking to him, we entered into a conversation about him. We left aside faith in God's living word and grasped the standpoint of human religion—the human conversation about God—which is the standpoint of unbelief. We thought ourselves to be entirely independent of God, coequal partners in a relationship of give-and-take. Surely God is as dependent on us as we are on him? Surely we can fend for ourselves, make our own laws, construct our own norms of life and death, rise up and conquer the natural world that awaits our dominance? We do not want harmony with God, we want a frank discussion of *our* wants and needs. We do not want harmony with creation, we want unlimited access to the goods of the earth based solely on *our* own criteria of human welfare. In short, we not only sinned, we became sinners. The harmony of God, humankind, and creation, was ontologically shattered, because we rejected our dependence on God for all things. And there is no way back to paradise lost; the garden is sealed by a flaming sword (Gen 3:24). Salvation lies forward, never backward. We live only by promise, in hope.

We make a few further points in the light of the fall of humankind, in the light of original sin. We are all sinners, and because of this fact, as Christians, we are realists concerning the way of the world. We are not skeptics; the grace of God overrides the folly of humankind time and again, bringing constant surprise. But nor are we idealists, ready to identify the gospel with the countless programs of human progress, whether on the left or on the right. That does not deny the significance of Christian involvement in, and responsibility for, the welfare of human society. It is simply to state clearly that our involvement and responsibility does not come in the form of embracing a human social or political –ism as God's own word and work in the world. The church learned that lesson—at least some did—in the twentieth century, in the light of the two world wars. Both were fought with the animus of Christian pride, quite certain of its right. Above all, the "German Christians" sided with Hitler, forever staining the notion that the church can find the will of God in a human figure or movement. It was not God, but radical evil, that Hitler offered the German Christians, the German people. Yet, now in the twenty-first century, the same lesson in a different form appears anew. Christians in various nations support populist authoritarian leaders as the will of God for their country. The policies of those leaders contradict at every turn the teaching of Scripture, with racist and anti-immigrant laws in direct contradiction to the biblical mandate. Nevertheless, in the name of "Christian civilization," national Christian communities become the primary political support. But we in the universal church are realists. We recognize the terrible tendency of all humanity— even including, even especially religious humanity—to wrench itself free from dependency on God alone and seek support from another source. Populist authoritarianism—regardless of the country in which it is found— is a lie of the serpent. It is not to be supported by the universal church, but rather to be resisted at all costs, even at the cost of suffering.

The fall of humanity is a fall *into* religion, not a fall *from* religion. Humanity in paradise lives in conversation *with* God; religious humanity after the fall lives in conversation *about* God. The former is single-minded service of the living God; the latter is distorted manipulation of the divine will in the service of human projects and agendas. We are not speaking about the distinction between false religions on the one hand, and a true religion on the other. Rather, *all* religions, including the Christian religion, twist and corrupt the truth of God's word for the sake of entirely human cultural, political, and personal agendas. It happens in two different ways, though both are equally distant from the true reality of faith. On the one hand, there are those, like Eve, who would *add* to the word of God a strict politico-cultural agenda of "traditional values," and in so doing falsify it. There are no traditional values in the Bible; there are only God's commands. And often enough those commands run directly counter to what contemporary society considers a "traditional value." The commandment of God does not validate the way of the world, but turns the way of the world upside down. Only God's command matters; all else is distraction and noise. Indeed, it becomes rather unclear whether such "religious conservatives" arrive at their political agenda from their religion, or perhaps more likely now arrive at their religion from their political agenda. Do they learn how to vote from religion, or, more likely, learn religion from how they vote? Either way, the identification of God's will with a particular politico-cultural agenda is a sign of the fall, and indeed a religious reenactment of it. On the other hand are those who, like the serpent, ask: "Did God really say? Really?" Rather than add to the word of God, the very authority of God's living word is called into question. It is not of course a matter of outright revolt; that would be too obvious. Religious liberalism is not anti-religious but altogether hyper-spiritual. Theology, doctrine, commandments, the content of Scripture as a whole, all are rendered mute, even irrelevant. What matters instead are the *images* the Scriptures provide—among many other sources—for constructing a modern spiritual life. Once again, it seems rather clear that the logic is transparent; religious liberalism does not move from the Bible to its vaunted spirituality, but rather first defines for itself what it means by spirituality and then looks to the Bible for support. The outbreak of self-realizing spirituality is no less a sign of the fall than the ubiquity of traditional values. Both are cultural agendas finding warrants in religion. Both are religious chatter about God, rather than open service to the living reality of God in conversation with him. We cannot return to paradise. If Christian truth is to be found, it can only be in the event of God's gracious promise, given by him alone anew.

Only the grace of the gospel opens our eyes to the full effects of the fall; only in the grace of the cross do we see our sin, and the sins of the world. But see them we do, both public and personal. Our eyes are open when it comes to the frailty of the surrounding world. Human beings are not worms or slugs; but they are vulnerable. They can turn the astonishing gifts of human intellect and creativity into deadly instruments of human depravity and destruction. They can ruthlessly attack innocent people because of religious fanaticism; they can conduct brutal campaigns of ethnic cleansing because of racist arrogance. As Christians, we are free to admire the brilliant accomplishments of human culture. Human beings were made good by God, and even after the fall they have not lost his image. Nevertheless, our enjoyment must always be tempered by the recognition that sin lurks in the heart of us all. That is why we need democratic government to protect human freedom; that is why we need just laws to govern human behavior; that is why, when other measures fail, we must protest, peacefully and nonviolently but actively, to preserve true peace.

It is one thing to recognize the signs of the fall in the world around us; it is quite another, equally important, to recognize them in ourselves. We commonly think that we know ourselves very well. But from the point of view of the Bible, we do not. Genuine self-awareness is a fruit of wisdom that comes only through hard struggle. The fall teaches us that sin is not simply a matter of isolated acts of moral failure. Sin becomes imbedded in our lives. It is manifest in life-patterns that we ourselves can scarcely see. Perhaps you overreact in times of stress; perhaps you waste valuable time and energy worrying about that which you cannot control; perhaps you allow compulsive fear to dictate your action rather than the free service of Christ. We sin because we are sinners; perhaps we catch a glimpse of the sin, but recognizing ourselves as sinners is a hard-won insight. Thoughtful self-awareness is part of the obedience we owe to God. Now, the gospel has nothing to do with self-torment; indeed it frees us from it. But the gospel does include a healthy suspicion of ourselves. We should not be paralyzed by self-doubt, but nor should we fear the steady practice of self-examination. Only then can we greet the risen Christ with lives made whole.

4. God of Grace and Wonder

Genesis 4:1–16

THE STORY OF CAIN and Abel presents us with one of the great dramatic narratives of the Bible. Before we enter directly upon our theological exegesis, a very brief reflection is in order concerning narrative interpretation in the Bible. In the last decades of the twentieth century a school of thought known as "narrative theology" seized upon the narrative elements of the Bible as the key, not only to biblical interpretation, but to Christian witness more generally. And to be sure, every major theologian in the Christian mainstream, beginning with Irenaeus and passing through Augustine and so forth, would certainly affirm that church doctrine as a whole has a narrative cast. God lives in the eternal unity of past, present, and future; the same eternal God works his will in time, moving from creation, to reconciliation, to final redemption in glory. We move from God to God.

But most often far more was meant by narrative theologians in ascribing to narrative the basic element of Christian witness. Not only was the literary category of narrative in the Bible given a certain privilege alongside poetry, didactic, epistle, etc.; but perhaps equally as important, the basic elements of narrative art were given *theological* weight. The literary rhetoric of narrative became a kind of natural theology of the Bible, by which "God" is understood as a character in a story evolving along the lines of plot, character, circumstance, familiar to general narrative art. Who *God* is, can be defined as who "God" is in the narrative world in the Bible.

We ask: is this true? A hundred biblical narratives could be brought forth to test the issue, but one alone will suffice: that of Cain and Abel. We will find that God—that is to say, the living reality of *God*—is quite determined *not* to act according to the universal rules of character, circumstance, and plot, known to the narrative art. Quite the contrary. The living reality of God *overthrows* narrative art even as the story is told. We discover—as we will discover repeatedly in the narratives of God in the Bible—that who "God" is in the story is determined solely by the living reality of *God* himself, and never the reverse.

Adam and Eve, now banished from paradise, have two children. The names—which in the biblical world are more than names, but confer identity—set the early pace for what will become the customs of ancient society, based on primogeniture. The first is named Cain, which in Hebrew means "spear." Eve plays on his name with an explanation: she has produced (the verb in Hebrew sounds like Cain) a man with God's help. We are on familiar ground in ancient narrative. The first son is a gift of God, the primary inheritor not only of wealth but of divine blessing. We can expect great things from this Cain! The second son, by sharp contrast, is given the strange name Abel. No explanation is given by Eve, but none is needed to the ancient Hebrew-speaking reader of the Bible. The word is rich with connotation, especially to anyone familiar with a book like Ecclesiastes. Abel means "fleeting." When the preacher in Ecclesiastes says, again and again, that all life is "vanity," he is using the same word in Hebrew. Surely we are to expect little from this second son; indeed, we are filled with a sense of coming tragedy as he enters what can only be a brief and troubled life, signifying nothing. Abel, we are told, is a herder of sheep, Cain is a keeper of the soil. The nomadic pastoralist and the settled farmer live side by side in the ancient world, and constitute the symbiotic world of ancient economy.

And then God, contrary to all custom and expectation, reverses everything. It happens, after the course of time, that Cain brings a sacrifice to the Lord from the fruits of the earth, while Abel brings an offering from the flock. The Lord accepts the offering of Abel, but not the offering of Cain. Traditional commentators often looked for something in the offerings, or in those who presented them, to account for the divine distinction between the two. Perhaps Abel was more pious? Perhaps his offering was somehow more acceptable, by anticipation of later animal offerings? Perhaps Cain was perfunctory in his approach to God? But there is not the slightest hint in the text of such a distinction. Quite to the contrary; the point is essential that the difference in the way the offerings are received rests solely with the electing love of God. God dwells in the mystery of his gracious wonder: and so he chooses, without explanation, the offering of the *younger* brother, and not the *older* brother. It is, as it is, because God wills it so.

Suddenly the natural order of life is utterly upset by the mysterious grace of God. Cain reacts with distress and depression, as much as anger. He is so upset by the astounding turn of events that you can read his emotion on his face. He is devastated! Why this? But God, with care and patience, steps forward to guide him through the unnecessary personal crisis. "There is no need for such a powerful emotional reaction; there is no reason to be so discouraged and upset. Simply offer a right sacrifice, and you too will be accepted; can you not see that? But if you do not win the battle against your angry distress, be aware; the power of sin is waiting just outside the door of your heart to eclipse and vanquish you. Do well, Cain, and you will be fine." It is friendly concern, not a lightning bolt of divine judgment.

We do not have to wait long to discover how Cain reacts. He invites Abel out into the countryside, away from any possible human inspection and discovery. There he murders his brother. The text records the deed with the simplicity of sheer dismay: we are not told how, we are not given details of the unfolding drama, we are only informed of the awful truth. A man is dead at the hands of his own brother. The deed of course is not beyond divine inspection and discovery, and God comes swiftly upon the scene. He asks Cain, "where is your brother Abel?" The indirectness of the question leaves space for the terrifying confrontation to come. Cain responds with an insulting and belittling play on words. "Am I my 'brother's keeper?'" The word for keeper means a keeper of sheep; do I have to shepherd this shepherd? Yet again, the reader of the Bible knows there is a hidden truth even here, far beyond Cain's awareness; God himself is described as our keeper (Ps 121), our shepherd (Ps 23). Indeed Cain is his brother's keeper, just as God is ours. To love God is to love our neighbor; to care for God is bear responsibility for our brother and sister. To live well before God is to embrace social responsibility. Cain has inadvertently uttered a profound biblical truth, unknown to him, but known to those who know the God who now confronts him.

And confront him he does. The living God reels in horror: "what have you done!" Cain may not admit his terrible deed, but the earth will cry it forth; even the mute earth shows more concern for human life than humanity itself. God then curses Cain with a terrible curse; his way of life as a farmer is over. The earth, hitherto the source of his bounty, will now be his enemy. He can and will settle nowhere upon it; he will be condemned to a life of perpetual solitude and restlessness, alone among society. He is an outcast from all that is living, the natural world and the human world. How does Cain respond to this momentous and terrifying divine encounter? By whining. He who had just taken his own brother's life cannot find it in himself to express any regret, but only complaint. "How can you do this to me? How can I live like this? Even you will no longer know where I am! Wherever I go, everyone will try to kill me! I will have no life worth living at all! It is too much!" While there is truth in what Cain says, we can scarcely summon up much sympathy; after all, Abel has no voice left to complain at all, no voice period. Only his shed blood cries out from the earth.

Now, it is crucial to realize that it is only now that we get to the main point of the great story of Cain and Abel. All that has come before leads up to this astonishing final point. We have already discovered in the story the extent to which God profoundly reverses the way of the world, turning ordinary custom upside down. We have learned that the mystery of God's electing love is measured only in reference to God's own character, not in reference to human quality or concern, or the orders of human social or economic expectation. We are coming to see that God does not act as we expect; indeed that God seems to take rather peculiar delight in overturning human expectation. The conclusion takes this affirmation to its furthest point. God makes the murderer Cain a promise, a promise of *grace*. No reason is given; God is *God*, in wonder and mystery he has mercy upon whom he has mercy. God gives Cain a mark—some sort of bodily tattoo of some kind, we suppose—to make certain that his life is carefully preserved from harm. Cain, who evaded grace, now enjoys it, *despite* himself. Cain will wander in the land of Nod (not so much a specific place on a map, as a region of perpetual restlessness) east of Eden; but he will wander under the constant and loving protection of God almighty, whose love brings constant surprise.

We can only begin our theological reflections upon this classic text with the sober realization that the first murder is committed in the name of religion. And not just any religion; it is committed in the name of the God of the Bible, the true God, the one Lord of all creation. Nor will it be the last such murder: as attested in the Bible itself, and sadly in the long history of religious violence reaching into our own day. The story of Cain and Abel all but reminds us: religious violence is the original paradigm of *all* violence. Such violence is based on the view that "God" fits neatly into "my" narrative of the world. I can bargain with God, I can predict his ways, I can win his approval, I can get God on my side! How? Because I know that my religious action is the true secret to win divine approval. Once I have done what needs to be done; once I have won the divine approval; I can go forth confident that others are left out of the religious equation I have mastered. If they should get in my way, I have every reason, every right, to fight against them, indeed to vanquish them, for God has already shown himself to be on my side. My hand is free to strike and to kill.

Sweeping aside, indeed shattering, this religious calculus of blood, is the true revelation of God's living and mysterious will as attested in Holy Scripture. God does not come to confirm and conform to our preconceptions, even and especially our religious preconceptions; he turns them upside down, reversing every custom, challenging every assumption, bursting through every false and misleading prejudice. God is true; our views must conform to him, not he to us. His electing love is not based on what we think is appropriate socially, culturally, or morally. It is based solely on his gracious purpose, hidden and sovereign and eternal. He is merciful upon whom he is merciful. He loves whom he loves. He is gracious to whom he is gracious. His love bursts through hidebound social conventions, creating a new order of life under his gracious care. He cares for the innocent; but he does not abandon the guilty. Marvelous to relate, his love surrounds innocent and guilty alike, receiving into his care the one, seeking out and protecting the other, never letting go of even the least of his children. The moment we are sure of his plan, we realize he is already out ahead of us, moving the whole world forward to new surprises of mercy and grace. We divide the world up into those inside and those outside; from the moment we pick up the Bible we learn that God loves the insider, yet then marvelous to relate goes in search of the outsider, always free to enact his will according to his one plan of redemption for the *whole* creation. Indeed, Jesus Christ is both insider—God's true Son, better even than Abel; yet also outsider—marked like Cain, only with the nails of the cross; the one true source of God's electing love for all humanity.

Envy divides. We do not have and we therefore despise those who do. We do not have and we therefore must define as beneath us those who have even less than we do. The politics of envy so prevalent in our time does not create these divisions; it only manipulates and uses them. The human heart creates them, and puts them into sordid action when opportunity arises. The result is a society isolated from itself, a veritable epidemic of loneliness. There are of course many causes of the current crisis of loneliness being felt across large segments of global society. The breakdown of village life as a result of the Industrial Revolution; the erosion of forms of community gathering following the two world wars; the social isolation of suburbia; the alienation of race, class, and gender; the rise of social media with its disconnected connectedness; all have contributed to a crescendo of a basic sense of human isolation one from another. Yet if I live in a consumerist world of objects to be possessed, and my fellow human being becomes yet one more object either to be possessed or disowned, sooner or later I will find myself both disowned and disowning. I will find myself alone.

The only remedy is the profound and fundamental realization: I am the keeper of my sister and brother. A life of self-gratification is not a fully human life. Only a life lived in responsibility for the other is truly human, truly *alive*. The Scriptures are fully clear: I cannot know and love God unless I live in basic responsibility for the well-being of my fellow humanity, whether in my own house, across the street, or across the planet. It is a theme set with dramatic clarity in the opening chapters of the Bible in the story of Cain and Abel; it is a theme to which the Bible will return again and again, with ever more nuanced rendering. A form of "Christian religion" that dismisses the "social question" as a waste of time has nothing to do with biblical faith, even if the surrounding cultural climate may conspire to push "religion" into a safe corner of pious irrelevance. We will discover in due course as well from the Bible that a form of religious social activism that dismisses or distorts the centrality of living faith in the gospel is equally without foundation in the Scriptures. But that is a separate question. Here, responsibility to God is linked forever to responsibility for our sister and brother, both upright and sinner, and we are charged to forge that link anew in every new generation.

It is, finally, worth considering the significant arc of the narrative toward the figure of Cain, and its implication for contemporary theological reflection. Traditional Christian exegesis of this passage, following the lead of the New Testament itself, has largely focused on Abel, and that for good reason. Abel is the first martyr, in what will become a long list of martyrs, both in the Bible and of course reaching right up to the present time. Abel kept the faith unto death; and in all circumstances we too are called to do the same. Yet, it is also crucial to hear this passage in the light of its own theological frame, in which the figure of Cain is thrust forward. Have we not all make mistakes in life which we deeply regret? Whether or not we have murdered someone, we have certainly offended God in thought, word, and deed, not once but with a lifetime of foolish choices; we have all failed our sister and brother in need, time and again. Yet God, in his marvelous and incomprehensible mercy, does not abandon us. He puts the mark of his love on us, surrounding us with his protective and ordering grace, making a way forward time and again where none before appeared. If we are marked by grace despite our follies, must we not also extend the same grace to others? If God never gives up on us, can we ever truly give up on a fellow human being? That is the question put to us—and answered for us—by the remarkable story of Cain and Abel.

5. The Covenant of Life

Genesis 9:8–17

GOD SEES THE TERRIBLE corruption of humanity. The entire earth is full of the horror of violence. The background for the divine judgment of the earth is the profound perversion of God's good intention for creation which sweeps over the earth as a result of the fall. Everywhere there is violence; the word in Hebrew means not only physical violence, but every form of abusive speech, harsh and cruel treatment of others, rude inhumanity. God sees the goodness of his creation—human and nonhuman—gone to utter ruin. And he has had enough; he regrets that he ever made humankind, so far have they strayed from the purpose he intended. So, God now destroys the whole human race in a massive flood that covers the earth. Every human being perishes; every bird, every animal, every insect as well. Divine judgment is not a token show of disappointment; it is a decisive act of catastrophic consequence for all humanity, all creation. All life on the planet is annihilated, as the primal chaos held back by God at creation is unleashed upon the world.

But there is one exception. Only one human being truly pleases God: his name is Noah. Noah's entire life unfolds in intimate relation with God despite the corruption of the times. God announces to Noah the coming catastrophe of the flood. Noah builds an ark, and his family is saved from destruction. Inside the ark are pairs of all diverse species of life from the planet, carefully preserved for the future. The floods rise; the waters finally recede; the ark comes to rest. Noah and his family emerge from the ark, making footfall on a new world. All of the animals leave the ark, one species after another. The animals are released in order to abound; life in all its miraculous abundance must begin anew. The old is now gone; there is nothing left living upon earth but these few inhabitants of the ark. What is to happen next?

We learn of a new relationship which God establishes with Noah, indeed with all humanity, indeed with the entire creation. And that is the relation of *covenant*. The word (in Hebrew) is clustered seven times in this short passage. Source, literary, and redaction criticism will see these word-repetitions as evidence of more than one literary tradition lying behind the present form of the text. And that seems likely, though scholarly agreement seems widespread that exact details are difficult to pin down. Nevertheless, the recognition of the prehistory only sharpens the realization that the cluster is left prominent in the final form, with a clear emphatic point: God's new relationship of covenant is the theological endpoint, the true scope, of the story of Noah. And so we are led to consider: what are the features of this biblical covenant, and what does it mean for the future of God's people, indeed for the entire cosmos?

The covenant of God is grounded solely in God's own existence, indeed God's very nature. We will learn more of the nature of God as the biblical story unfolds. We will learn ever greater dimensions of the one covenant of God, culminating in the New Testament affirmation of the cross. But even as we learn, we must not forget the lesson learned here: God surrounds Noah and his family with his merciful love simply because God is *God*. The sheer mystery and sovereignty of his gracious will are self-grounded and self-validated.

Again, we will come to learn in the fullness of time of a human response to the covenant. The call of Abraham lies only chapters away in the canonical shape of Scripture. But here in the first great witness to the divine covenant of grace there is no mention of a human response, or of any response, whatsoever. God acts, and he acts alone, to establish a new relationship with humanity and the world. His grace is utterly prevenient. The initiative is his alone, unconditionally. There can be in no sense whatsoever a concept of human partnership in the covenant as attested in the Bible, or of interdependence between God and his world. God wills a *relationship*; and we will come to learn that that relationship requires a *response*. But we cannot forget as we expand our awareness of the relation between God and his people that it is utterly free grace, based in no sense whatsoever on any human claim or merit.

We learn of the mystery of particularity and universality that will come to pervade the entire biblical witness to the divine covenant of grace. God first gives his covenant to Noah and his family. It is not a general statement, a philosophical proposition, about the divine-human relation; the covenant of God is an *event* of grace. Yet it is crystal clear from our passage that the covenant is not limited to Noah and his family, but through them reaches out to the *whole* of humanity, indeed for all time. The covenant once established is perpetual, and therefore reaches forward in promise to embrace every new generation: not only of God's people, but of *all* people, of all nations of the earth.

We learn, finally, of God's gracious will for good, not only of humanity, but of the entire natural world. God does not establish a covenant with humanity *apart* from creation; God establishes a free and gracious covenant with humanity *within* creation. In the light of the covenant, redemption and creation must be distinguished but cannot be separated.

The covenant, in sum, is entirely sovereign and free promise, pointing toward an eternal future of grace for all creation. Even the rainbow in the clouds serves not so much to reassure humanity of that promise—though of course it does that as well—as to remind *God* of the content of that promise. The beautiful light of the rainbow—out of human reach—is now the divine remembrance of his constant and renewing love, which is the one purpose for all creation. "I will remember my covenant that is between me and you and every living creature of all flesh . . ." (Gen 9:15).

We begin our theological reflection by remembering the classic formulation: the New Testament is concealed in the Old, the Old Testament is revealed in the New. To take the second half of that theological dialectic first: we affirm that Jesus Christ is the one content of the covenant promise of God. Though there are numerous "covenants" in the Bible, beginning with the present text, there is only one content, one covenant of grace, whose subject matter is Jesus Christ crucified and risen. God has one, and only one gracious purpose for the whole cosmos, gathering into one all reality through the cross. It is crucial to pause and consider that there has been, and will be, no mention of a covenant of works in the Bible. From the beginning, the covenant of grace is the true meaning of the entire creation, while the creation is the canvas upon which God paints the rainbow of his covenant love.

But we cannot stop there. We must return to the first half of the theological dialectic, which often enough is left dangling unattended. Jesus Christ is the New, which—though present—is concealed in the Old. We learn from God's word of promise to Noah the full reality of God's one covenant of grace. What do we learn?

We learn that God's covenant love, God's redeeming love for the world, is utterly free and unmerited, grounded solely in his own mysterious will. God loves us because it is his own good pleasure so to do. God wills to establish a relationship with us—a communion of love—because of who he is, not because of our intrinsic worth or religiosity. We will come to know God in the remaining chapters of the Bible as the triune God, an eternal relationship; here in these stories of Noah there is no mention of the Trinity.

But as we reflect, not simply on the witness of the text, but on the reality to which it points, there is no question but that the covenant announced to Noah contains a vital truth for all time, indeed for our time: God loves us because of his gracious mercy alone. We cannot buy that love, whether we are billionaires or destitute. We cannot earn it with our moral deeds, whether we are paragons of upright virtue or fallen and hopeless. To the one, as well as to the other, God extends the bright rainbow light of his grace with only one word of promise. Our only response can be to trust him; to take his word of promise into our hearts and minds, and to live in its light. Faith in the promise of God is the one true life of the covenant of grace.

We learn that the one covenant of grace is universal to all reality. It encompasses the whole creation, including the natural world; a point to which we will return. Here, it needs to be emphatically asserted that the one covenant of grace, according to the story of Noah, encompasses all human-ity. There is no ambiguity in the text whatsoever. We either cut the covenant of Noah off from the one true covenant of God in Jesus Christ, a move thor-oughly rejected by Christian theology and exegesis. Or, we recognize in the light of the covenant to Noah that the one covenant of God in Jesus Christ embraces the whole of humankind. Indeed, the point is affirmed time and again in the Bible; but it is here explicitly affirmed in all its genuine finality. Sadly, the Christian church has time and again fallen into the trap of divid-ing humanity into categories, the one on the inside of God's love, the other on the outside. It is the classic move of all religion; but it is precisely the religious move that is here rejected by God's all-embracing promise of love. The same point will reappear in the covenant to Abraham. Nevertheless, it is here in the story of Noah that we learn for the first time in the unfolding biblical story that God *will not* divide up the world into insider and outsider. Quite the opposite; God rejects and overturns every such human attempt. Only love that is universal is truly love indeed.

The covenant of grace evokes profound reverence for life, all life, all things living. We are all in the same boat. That is true, first of all, of our connection to our fellow human beings. The divine purpose of love *estab-lishes* a connection between every human being on the face of the earth. I am connected to my family, to my neighbor, to my fellow citizen, to every human person on the planet. Notice: *God* himself has already made real that connection by the gift of his covenant grace. I do not make it real by the relationships I may foster; rather, it is the call of the Christian gospel to make that connection *visible* and manifest in the world. It is real; it must be made clear and certain in all times and places. It is gift, glorious gift; but it must be cherished and magnified in the whole world. We must say with crystal clarity: the divine covenant of grace that gathers humanity into one transcends all earthly connection. I am obligated in love to my fellow human being across the street, but also across the border, indeed across the globe. And that is so not because I choose to love (though a human choice is involved) but because God himself has already made that connection even before I realize it myself. Indeed, there is a certain freedom and joy in knowing that every human encounter, no matter how "foreign" it may seem, is *preceded* by the divine covenant of grace that not only makes it possible but renders it effective and lasting.

The same "prevenient" divine connection holds true with the natural world. *We* do not establish our intimate relation with the surrounding creation by our sense of responsibility, a notion born of the same arrogance that has driven the natural world to the edge of catastrophe through sheer human stupidity. Through willful human ignorance and arrogance, we are turning vast swathes of God's beloved world into a wasteland of hunger, plague, heat death, wildfires, dying oceans, unbreathable air, and economic collapse, all in the name of "economic progress"; so much for our glorious sense of human "responsibility." If humankind becomes any more "responsible" for the earth, one shudders to think what might follow; a little humility might be a far better answer. In fact, *God* has already established that connection; we are in the same boat with all his creatures, and not just with one another. It is given to us, once again, to make that connection visible and clear by the humility and care of our actions. Noah once saved all species by gathering them into the ark; we now, it would seem, are doing our best to kill them off by casting them into the dustbin of human neglect and exploitation. God's rainbow love over all human and natural life is no less real and certain; what is at issue is whether we honor God by revering the life he cherishes. The question is of course sadly an open one.

Which brings us to our final point: we cannot give up, we cannot lose heart, there is always hope. The covenant of grace is the divine event of renewal in the earth, ever new and fresh. You may reach a point in your own personal life, or in your family, when all future options seem not only limited but absolutely nonexistent. There seems to be no future at all; even one hour ahead is more than you can imagine, more than you can account for. Time and again you will discover, as God's people have always come to know deeply in their hearts, that God makes a new world appear before your eyes. He opens a door you did not see; he clears a path you did not know was there; he draws you out into a wide-open space and gives you new room for all good things. It is true for the broader pattern of human life on earth. We may perhaps live in dark times, both in the church and the world—times of crisis filled with the same violence of speech, action, and abuse unfolding in the days of Noah. The church may be confused and scattered, uncertain of its message, damaged and faltering in its life and mission. The world may be threatened by falsehood and fear, led by those who have nothing but their own self-interest in mind. Yet, the rainbow of God's promised love is still there. Time and again, the miraculous word of divine promise drives the flood back, opens new doors of renewal and growth, draws forth new sounds of gladness and good cheer. The church not only recovers, it moves forward to fresh dimensions of the witness of faith. The surrounding world not only regains its senses, it reflects even more surely the truth and justice that are the divine will for all society. The covenant of grace creates, and recreates, the new world of God. We learn, day by day, that God's new world is in fact the very world in which we live and breathe.

6. Humanity in Revolt

Genesis 11:1–9

THE STORY OF THE building of the Tower of Babel represents the culmination of the primeval history of humankind, as recounted with imaginative narration in the Bible (Gen 1–11). A narrative which begins in the sheer grandeur of God's finished work of creation on the seventh day, ends in the unfinished ruin of a half-built architectural carcass of human pride and folly. It begins in the divinely intended harmony of God, humanity, and the natural world; it ends in human revolt against God, human disharmony and dispersion, and an entire world now seemingly at the disposal of grotesque human need and want. The story of the Tower of Babel is not told without a heavy lacing of irony, even a certain caustic humor. What happens here is not without elements of the ridiculous and even the absurd. To speak of tragedy is perhaps to go too far; human pride, unbridled and set free to roam at will, ends as always in sheer farce.

We are to imagine, in the faith language of the biblical witness to the early history of humankind, that point in time in which all human beings still speak the same language, and still inhabit one place and one society. We will not find this society on a map; once again, we are speaking of primeval history from the perspective of the confession of faith. Nevertheless, we are speaking of real earth, real human beings, real changes in the human situation before God.

What will human beings do with their linguistic and cultural unity? They are on the move, a migratory people. Humankind, it would seem, is created to be in motion. Yet at one point they stop moving. They find a spot that attracts their desire to locate, their desire to settle and stake a claim. We are still not sure why they settle; indeed, it is clear from the perspective of the narrator that humankind is not sure either.

The confusion continues. A plan stumbles into being, if it can be called a plan. Word just sort of moves around the populace: let us make some bricks. Now, in the ordinary course of events we are well accustomed to drawing up a projected proposal, and then going about the business of finding or constructing the needed elements to bring the proposal into being. Here the order is reversed. They start with the elements: let us make bricks! The narrator is clearly allowing the confusion to surface in our minds, as readers, however momentarily: why on earth are they making bricks? We do not yet know; perhaps more importantly, they clearly do not yet know either. Word is simply going around from one to another: bricks!

So, what to do with all these bricks? Suddenly the story takes on a new intensity. They have elements for a project. Now they must decide on the project itself. They will build a city, and more importantly a massive tower reaching the sky itself. Their plan goes even further and includes a stated *purpose*: they want to be recognized everywhere for their great ability, and indeed they fear that without such a projected skyward tower they will lose their social cohesion. Pride and fear now emerge, and merge, as the twin motives of the new impetus for self-exalted humanity. Pride and fear turn a confused and ill-conceived construction project into a monument to human self-transcendence. This is *our* tower; this is *our* place; *we* are here, and we are not going anywhere; come and admire our new identity if you will.

And so, God does; he accepts their invitation. He "comes down" to look at the city and the tower constructed by proud and fearful humanity. He does not "come down" because he needs to draw near to improve his vision; he comes down because he is so highly exalted in majesty, and the works of humankind are so utterly small and pathetic. The tower reaches to the sky, literally in Hebrew to "the heavens"; yet still God—who made the entire cosmos—in his lofty grandeur must "come down" to catch even a glimpse of this tiny, pitiful pile of brick and mortar, humanity at its finest, humanity at its worst.

God's reaction is immediate and clear. In an instant, he recognizes the consequences of the human quest for self-transcendence. Left to their own devices, pride and fear will impel humankind to ever more confused and distorted efforts, resulting in ever spiraling monuments to human folly and self-destruction. God alone sees the consequences that even a tower built to the heavens can in no way envision. He will now not try to punish humankind for their newfound self-glory, as he did in the flood; rather, he will act to temper their ability to destroy. He protects them from themselves.

Once again, the narrator gently recognizes the irony, if that is quite the right word. Humankind says, come, let us make bricks; humankind says, come, let us build a tower. Now God comes upon the scene, and in the same words (in Hebrew as well) says, come, let us go down and confuse their speech. It is the plural of majesty, not a reference to the Trinity. God now, in a single moment, overturns, overrules, and redirects all the plans and projects of a humanity united by pride and fear.

Where once there was one language, now there are the various languages and dialects of the earth. Where once humanity was located in one place, now humanity is scattered by God across the face of the planet. Where once a tower and a city were being built out of pride and fear to express the greatness and glory of humankind, now a project stands half-built, forgotten in the plains of Shinar, a ruin and a monument only to human pretensions of self-reliance and self-worship.

We have encountered the divine promise of life in the covenant to Noah, a promise that extends not only to his family, but to all humanity, indeed to all creation. How will that promise come to fruition? How will it be visibly manifest? Already one door has been closed, the door of an abstract individualism. We learn early in the prehistory of humankind of two very specific persons; their names are etched in our memory, Cain and Abel. We learn to know the electing love of God which comes even to the outcast, to Cain; but it is not through an abstract individualism that the promise comes. We are created to care for one another; we are keepers of one another. Now we learn a new truth—neither does it come through populist nationalism. It is remarkable that there is not a single name mentioned in the entire story of the Tower of Babel. This is a movement of human self-transcendence arising from the *Volk*, from the new phenomenon of a humanity now finally at long last rooted together in blood and soil. What comes forth from this new moment of human life—it will be repeated countless times in human history, up until our own time—is certainly not the genuine praise and worship of God. If heaven is the true aim of human life in populist nationalism it is the heaven of human imagination, which in the end is always a hell on earth. It is the heaven of racial purity; of national dominance; of caste and class; of segregation and colonialism. The promise of God no more comes through populist nationalism than it does through abstract individualism; that is one great lesson of the Tower of Babel, which history has sadly been forced to relearn time and again. God is no more found in the raging mob than he is in the isolated individual.

The underlying energy of such populist nationalism, then and now, is the perverse dialectic of pride and fear. On the surface there is the language of joy and celebration. We will make a name for ourselves! We control our own future; we work our own will! We will build where others have not built; we will lay down a civilization that will last for the ages, the wonder of the world! We will create marvels of engineering, regardless of their impact upon the earth, simply because we can. If we can do it, we will do it; our will is our own! Our will is our power, and our power is our will! "God" of course is not excluded from such pride, not at all; he is called upon at just the right moment to bless the astounding human endeavor which even he must surely recognize as immortal. Such plans always *include* God. God and *Volk*; *Volk* and God; nothing can stand in our way!

Underlying the celebration, hiding behind the joy, is a paralyzing fear. We are only what we make of ourselves; what if we fail to make anything at all? What if we are forgotten, and therefore cease to exist for all eternity? What if the power of the *Volk* is shown to be limited by forces outside our control, and we ourselves therefore lose our eternal invincibility? Both the pride, and just as certainly the underlying fear, rest upon profound ignorance of one single truth: we live by the gracious and free promise of God alone. Whether as individuals, or as societies, or indeed as the entire human family, God's promise alone is the one certain truth upon which we depend in life and in death. His gracious mercy alone is our future, our name, our glory, our crown, our hiding place, our celebration. The God who enfolds all things, is enfolded by none.

It is often said that the effects of the Tower of Babel are overturned at Pentecost, and while true, the point needs to be carefully delineated. There are religions in which one sacred language carries the message forward among other regions of the world; the new language must be learned if conversion is sought. There are indeed distorted versions of nationalist and populist Christianity in which a particular people's speech is held to be the true sacred speech of the "tradition," and therefore the vehicle of truth for the ages, as for example Latin once erroneously was. Not so in the Bible; not so at Pentecost; not so for the true promise and mission of the gospel. At the Tower of Babel the one language of humanity was diversified into many. At Pentecost the gospel was *not* rendered into one new sacred speech, indeed quite the opposite. The miracle of Pentecost is precisely that those who heard, began to understand the *one* gospel in the *many* languages of the earth. Linguistic unity or the cultural conformity it brings do not spread the word of promise; rather, it is conformity to the one grace of the promise itself, which renews the earth, in all its profound variety, among all nations, all peoples, all tribes, all families of the earth.

Finally, we are given an opportunity here in the opening sequence of biblical narrative to test theologically a metaphor that has gained wide currency in many ecclesiastical circles, which is that of "building" the kingdom of God. It is quite extraordinary that the first such attempt—for that is surely what the Tower of Babel represents—is met with not a single word of divine grace, only divine judgment. The fundamental confusion then is the fundamental confusion now, and always. There is the realization that we can do something—we can make bricks—so why not do *everything*? We have our time, our talents, our treasures; why not build on earth the very realm of God, which after all is promised and willed by God himself? There is certainly plenty of self-righteousness to go around across the religious-political spectrum. The catastrophic assumption of course is that God's kingdom is missing, or incomplete; and therefore it is up to us to bring it into being, to build. Yet the entire message of the Scriptures points in another direction; God's kingdom, God's promise, is *already real* in our midst, already fully complete in every way. God rules, but his rule is hidden, strange, unpredictable, unrecognizable apart from faith. Indeed, at the very moment when humankind would "build" God's kingdom, God himself is acting for the salvation of the world. Not in monumental architecture of human pride and fear; not in the fame and grandeur of human religious arrogance and self-righteousness; not in the purported permanence of national glory, cemented in the glory of a people and its ties to the sacred soil. Instead, God calls a single man to leave his family and home for a faraway country. God's strange, unheard-of, new promise alone works salvation in the midst of the earth.

7. The Promise of God

Genesis 12:1–9

WE COME NOW TO a new narrative sequence in the book of Genesis; we come in fact to a new *time* in the new world of God. Time itself changes. All that has happened before, from creation to the Tower of Babel, is closed off as a section in the book, the prehistory of the world. The redemption of God will come *to* all creation as its setting and goal, but it will not arise *from* creation. Creation is the setting in which God acts; but the new act of God is grounded in his fresh and mysterious will to save, which is indeed the original purpose of creation itself. Creation is the outer realm for God's redeeming love; God's love is the one true inner meaning of all creation.

God calls Abraham. There is no preparation for this extraordinary new turn. It comes as a radically new event, with no explanation, no surrounding circumstances, simply a bolt of lightning streaking across the sky as if from nowhere, yet illumining everything. God speaks to Abraham his command. The same God who spoke, and the world came to be, now speaks to Abraham, and his life is suddenly and radically changed forever. The call of God is always a new creation, calling into existence a new direction in life that comes, as it were, from nothing. We know virtually nothing of this Abraham. He is a Mesopotamian by birth, now already seventy-five years old. We will never learn anything of his youth, his maturity, but only of his older age. God's call defines the meaning of his life—everything else suddenly becomes irrelevant, both to him and to us. God speaks to him; God, the living person, declares his will, to this one human being among all human beings of the earth. The last time we heard God speak was to Noah; now God speaks to this Mesopotamian as one person speaks to another, taking him, as it were, into the confidence of his divine purpose. Yet the cost to Abraham is extraordinary; it will cost him everything.

He must leave everything familiar in his life forever behind. Always the call of God takes us from the familiar to the unfamiliar, from the known to the unknown. God, as it were, starts with the general and moves to the particular; starts with the easier, and moves to the hardest part of all. Abraham must leave his country. Abraham will become a *migrant* for the sake of God, a wanderer on the earth. Civilizations are on the rise; Abraham makes his home in one of the greatest and earliest, in the land between the Tigris and the Euphrates, already an ancient culture from time immemorial. But no more. He must leave the country—its language, customs, food, friendships—he has known for seventy-five years, forever. And he can take none of his extended family with him. The family line that defines his very birthright, his place on this earth, must be left far behind. Last of all, hardest of all, he must leave his personal family, those closest and most precious to him. Yes, the cost is already great, and it will become even more severe.

He is to leave everything behind, God tells Abraham, and go to a country that God will show him. We, as readers, already know Abraham's destination. But he does not. It is a technique the biblical narrator will use often, giving us an outsiders look at the broader picture, even as we see the insider's look from the perspective of this one essential character, Abraham. God tells him to *go*, but not *where* to go. God's word is always clear; but it often leaves the future a mystery. Ahead is a wholly new venture. There is always a risk to faith.

God commands, and he also promises. And if the command is extraordinary, the promise is beyond all measure. The promise comes in a repeated divine refrain: I will, I will, I will, I will. The promise of God to Abraham is grounded solely in God's own electing love, God's mysterious purpose of redeeming grace. There is no precondition in the life of Abraham, no achievement, no merit, no distinction at all. God's love sets its seal on the life of Abraham and makes him who he is; it is true for all who receive the call of divine grace. His promise to Abraham, here and elsewhere, is twofold: land and posterity. Yet the blessing of God, as it were, overreaches his own promise, and fills it with new content. God will bless Abraham in such a way that Abraham himself becomes the means by which all nations, all peoples, of the earth, likewise receive the divine blessing. God's blessing to Abraham makes Abraham the divine means of blessing for the whole creation.

But what of Abraham's obedience to the divine call? It is required; the obedience of faith is essential. God does not work despite Abraham but through him. And yet, there is no lengthy record of the trials and tribulations of Abraham leaving his homeland, his family, his dearest ones behind. There is no record of the inner struggles he must surely have faced. The text records the one thing relevant, the one thing necessary: Abraham goes. Just as the Lord commanded, Abraham leaves everything familiar behind for the new land of promise. He is no longer a participant in an ancient civilized society; he is now a pastoral nomad, wandering the land as a migrant, an alien, among other peoples and cultures. The narrative shows him moving from place to place, wandering the length and breadth of the new land of promise. And then it records three jarring and dissonant facts, which together will determine the course of Abraham's life, and indeed the life of God's people for the future.

First, God makes more clear his promise to Abraham: I will give you this land. Now we know, now *he* knows, *this* is the land God intends for Abraham. But second, the text records, as if to make the sheer contradiction of the promise utterly palpable: the Canaanites live in the land. The land is filled with an alien people, it is not a barren wilderness waiting to be cultivated. The promise of God, therefore, is in direct contradiction to the facts of human experience. Then thirdly, Abraham builds an altar to God there in the new land of promise. It is certainly not much, surrounded as it is by the Canaanite inhabitants. But no matter; God's promise, for Abraham, is already real, despite the contradictions of reason and experience. This altar is the jarring reminder that the land even now is already his, because God has made it so by his word.

The call of God is the utterly surprising, utterly new, utterly fresh entry of God into our lives. It does not enter from within, flowing from our natural impulses and native desires, in a process of inner self-realization; it comes to us from without, from above, directing our lives now according to God's desires, God's will, God's new direction. We live, now, by the guidance of his Spirit, no longer by the fulfillment of our own inner "mindfulness." God's call is personal, yet in addressing us it makes us a new person, giving new shape to all our desires, new focus to all our thoughts, new orientation to all our decisions, new goals to all our steps. We once lived for ourselves; now, we live for him. We once lived according to the natural rhythms of life in society and culture; now, we live according to the new music of divine grace, whose sounds are glorious beyond measure. Once, the fundamental definition of our being was determined by the familiar legacy of family ties and cultural custom; now we are defined by our new relation to God, and to the new role we find ourselves playing in his family of faith throughout all creation.

The call of God always brings God's command into our lives: take up and go. To you it is one command, to me it is another, to yet someone else the command is different yet again. But always the command of God is the concrete word of God, never an abstract, general moral principle. Certainly, God does not command Abraham: do everything in your power to promote family values! Indeed, the command of God forces Abraham to *break* the traditions of family values for the sake of God's word. Those who put a system of human moral values in the place of God's living word of command may certainly think they are doing the right thing in religious duty, but according to Scripture they are evading the concrete word of divine encounter. The living God enters our lives directly from above with the word of direct command, leaving us with the one option of obedience. God's command is never a moral or political program or party system to promote, but a word of obedience to follow. Nor is God's word of command a summons to follow our own inner being to the path of self-realization. To be sure, there is blessing in the service of God: a blessing far beyond any human imagination. The blessing of God is the final and complete fulfillment of all that is human. But the blessing of God does not come from personal self-fulfillment. It comes rather from the service of God, in which *we* become a blessing to others. God's concrete word of command always puts us on a path in which, at the same time, every good blessing from above comes into our lives transforming us from above, and we ourselves are rendered by God a new source of blessing in the world around us.

God's word of command comes into our lives with no human preconditions whatsoever. We are not asked: are you ready for this? Does this make sense to you? Do you feel qualified? Are you completely comfortable with what you are now called to do? Are you getting the full picture? Not at all. Often enough the call of God comes when we are fully convinced that life is going just fine as it is; and suddenly God points us in an entirely new direction, without any preparation or precondition. The need is there, not here, and that is all that matters: take up and go. There are times when we are absolutely certain we know exactly how best to use the gifts and talents we have to serve God to the best of our ability; and God directs us to an entirely new field of endeavor, with wide open spaces of new experience to discover and insights to develop. Why go this direction, and not stay where I am? God does not always explain his purpose, nor does he make mistakes; his purpose is entirely gracious beyond all human capacity to understand, yet for that very reason his command cannot be adequately measured by the resources of our limited reason and experience. Take up and go. Surely, we assume, the command and call of God will always find me where I am, and keep me within the circle of my own needs and abilities, and within the limits of my own zone of comfort. To be sure, God does indeed meet all our needs, in every respect, even needs we ourselves can scarcely name for ourselves. But he does so, not by leaving us within the realm of our own comfortable existence, but by setting us forth on a new adventure of discipleship. Take up and go. Finally, after a life of service to God in the church and world, we can allow ourselves to rest, perhaps to retire from the active life of discipleship. How exactly does that work out for Abraham? He is not called into active service until he reaches the age of seventy-five, beginning at that very moment the astounding story of his new life with God, by which God's infinite blessing comes anew into the world. No, we never retire from discipleship; we never grow too old to serve God. Wherever we are in life, God meets us there ever anew, and puts us on a new path, always both blessed and a blessing to others.

The call and command of God set our lives upon a new path. The promise of God transforms our very being, and indeed transforms the whole creation. The promise of God is the great theme of the book of Genesis. We stress now a crucial point: the promise of God in the book of Genesis always *remains* promise; it is never fulfilled. The entire book of Genesis points to a future that only God can bring about, yet a future that awaits God's definitive enactment. In short, the whole book is framed theologically as an eschatological witness, reaching backward to creation itself, and reaching forward to the various stories of the patriarchs, through the final stories of Joseph and his brothers. The book of Genesis does not point backward but forward. Indeed, according to the witness of Genesis, faith in the divine promise does not *ever* point backward, but always forward. Faith itself can be defined in the book as confidence in the divine assurance despite the evident contradictions of the most basic facts of human experience. The word of divine promise creates new reality; it is not limited to the basic facts of human experience, but rather creates a new experience, a new reality, a new world, beyond all human calculation. The promise of God can only be grasped in faith and hope.

So how are we to grasp the promise of God to Abraham in the context of Christian confession? On the one hand, we read the Bible moving forward from promise to fulfillment. That is, we affirm the truth that Jesus Christ himself is the true fulfillment of God's promise to Abraham, to Isaac, and to Jacob. But on the other hand, we *return* to the book of Genesis in the light of Christ. Even we, even now, in the church of Jesus Christ, are a migrant people, an alien people, with no homeland, always looking forward to the final fulfillment of God's word of promise in glory. Even we now live only by faith, not by sight, just as our forebears did. The wandering life of Abraham is for us direct instruction in the life of faith, always looking forward in hope to the new life to come, never getting too entangled in the things of this world, setting our one true hope on what God in Christ alone can and will do for the life of the whole creation.

And indeed, there is grace in *not* knowing the future. To be sure, hope makes future time present. As children of God, we do not judge our future by the limits of our present; rather, we enjoy our present in confident expectation of the promise of the future. Still, there is grace in only being able to take one step at a time, waiting to discover what lies ahead only when the future comes to unfold before us in the glory of the present moment. God is our past; God is our future; but there is something to be said for the great Christian confession that God is the eternal Now, always greeting us only as we live before him at just this time, in just this place, ready and eager to receive his blessings at just this moment of his unfolding and present mercy. Whatever lies ahead, we *pitch* our tent—not too concerned with building monuments to the future, not paralyzed by fear and anxiety concerning our circumstances—but we *build* our altars of thanksgiving, small tokens even now of gratitude for the God who meets us, and greets us, where we are, yet never leaves us where it finds us. Even now we represent—as if by anticipation—the divine blessing for the whole of humanity. But now we—the living church of God's promise in Jesus Christ—are concealed, hidden in the world, living day by day in the service of the Lord. The journey ahead is filled with the adventure of uncertainty and the unfamiliar; but no matter, for God himself is our kind companion along the way. We are not called to success, or cultural influence—a well-known trap in church history, constantly repeated, and all too evident in the world today. Instead, we are called only to faithful service. To live in such a way—strangers, immigrants, wanderers on the earth—is to share the faith of father Abraham.

8. The Ultimate Question

Genesis 15:1–6

WE HAVE FOLLOWED ABRAHAM has he responds to the call of God and leaves his homeland according to the divine command and promise. We will continue to follow his journey with God through myriad trials. But right now, close to the beginning of his way with God, Abraham confronts the ultimate question of his life, and indeed of every life including our own. The Bible makes very clear that it is the ultimate question of every life, reaching into the very present moment, confronting all peoples, of all places, in all times. For it is the question of faith itself.

The scene of these verses is set with extraordinary drama, yet with equally extraordinary economy of words. It is night, and Abraham—now a nomadic wanderer—is in his tent. He encounters a vision from God, but it is no ordinary encounter; nothing really like it occurs elsewhere in the Pentateuch, and it calls to mind the great prophetic visions of God. It is made crystal clear by the language used throughout this short passage that we are facing something in the life of Abraham that is true, not only for him, but for all God's people, indeed for all humanity. The words used and defined here take on the luster of theological statements that cannot be reversed or set aside. From now on, whatever can be said about faith, about the human relationship to God, must pass through the narrow gate of this short passage.

"After these things" the word of the Lord comes to Abraham. The final form of the text leaves the reference to the past ambiguous; our minds are left free to roam through the journey of Abraham with God thus far. God calls Abraham to leave forever behind everything important in his life: his homeland, the wider connections of his extended relations, even the close affection of his own more immediate family. Abraham arrives in the new land of promise with his wife Sarah and all his worldly possessions, and their life in the new land is hardly easy. Far from it. They are forced by wide-spread famine in Canaan to trek down into Egypt, where God has to rescue them from the wrath of Pharaoh. Abraham is then forced to fight a coali-tion of regional warlords in order to rescue his nephew Lot. It may be the land of promise; but for now, it is a strange and hostile place surrounded by unknown danger at every turn. Abraham lives the life of a pastoral nomad, living in his tent, owning not a single square foot of earth.

God's promise has certainly not meant a life of ease and prosperity for Abraham, so God now come to Abraham with words of staggering assur-ance. Indeed, so great are God's words of hope and blessing that a fresh crisis in the life of Abraham results. God comes in a vision of the night, speaking his word. Night is the time of solitude, the time when sublime yet terrifying trials churn away in the struggling heart. God speaks directly to Abraham with three glorious affirmations. First, do not be afraid. You may think, in your struggles, that I am not here; but in fact, I am always here, always with you, always gracious to you. Second, I am your shield. You may think that your life is utterly exposed to your enemies, and the hostile circumstances you face; but it is not. For I myself am the One who protects you every mo-ment of your existence. And third, your reward shall be very great. You may think my promise appears to be worth little now, but in fact the free gift of my love means more to your future, and to the future of the whole universe, than you can possibly imagine. It is clear that there is no separation here between God and his gifts; God the giver is known in his gifts, while the true meaning of God's gifts is ultimately *God himself* the giver of all good things.

Yet now, suddenly, for the first time in the biblical narrative, we hear Abraham speak to God. His words call us back to the divine promise originally given, of a countless posterity. This promise of God, and the childless circumstances of his life, pitches Abraham into an all-out, bitter crisis. This promise of God means everything to Abraham. It is the very reason he left all behind to come to this strange new world. Yet Abraham can see *no* visible sign whatsoever that God's promise will be fulfilled. He is old; Sarah is old; and they have no children, not one. So, in deepest despair, Abraham complains to God. Notice, he complains, not because he doubts the divine promise of posterity, but because he believes it; faith has its depth of struggles that unbelief can never match. God, how can you speak to me of such a great future to come! What future do I have now! How can you give to me (the phrase is emphatic in Hebrew) any future at all, since I have no children, not one single child! All I have is an adopted servant, Eliezer; is he the great promise you made to me? Is he the one to channel the future of your blessing to all peoples and nations? Where, God, is your promise of the future?

This strange and beautiful nighttime encounter is not over. God once again speaks directly to Abraham. God directly addresses the true source of Abraham's overpowering fear and anxiety. He tells Abraham in plain and simple terms: this man—God will not even pronounce his name, so little does Eliezer figure into God's plan—this man will not inherit your promised future. You will have a child of your own; and this child, *he* (again the phrase is emphatic in Hebrew) will be your heir, the promised future. So far, this nighttime encounter has taken place inside Abraham's nomadic tent. Now God brings him outside under the spectacular radiance of the desert night sky. Look up into the sky, God encourages Abraham, and see the endless galaxies of stars. That is what your future posterity will look like. Now, some commentators stress that in showing Abraham the sky, God is giving him a visual *aid* to faith. The point rather is far different. The sight in the desert of a glorious night sky full of billions upon billions of stars certainly does not make the future promise easier to comprehend. The promise is now clear, graphic, fantastically vivid; but given the present circumstances of Abraham and Sarah, it is for that very reason utterly *impossible*.

There then occurs one of the most stunning verses in the entire book of Genesis, indeed in the entire Old Testament, for that matter in the entire Bible. The phrasing is highly unusual; it comes across almost as a theological confession, a statement of truth, and in fact it will reverberate not only in the New Testament but far beyond in exactly that capacity. "And he [Abraham] believed the Lord; and the Lord reckoned it to him as righteousness." Several aspects of this resounding affirmation require closer examination. The point is not that familiar words are here used in a spectacular way; the point rather is that familiar words now, in the light of this verse, need to become *unfamiliar*, because they are forthrightly redefined in the light of Abraham's nighttime encounter with God.

We begin with the word *faith*. What does it mean to believe? Two familiar answers are at hand in our time. Faith is an inward experience of the divine, ultimate transcendent and therefore inexpressibly nameless. Or, faith is the rational affirmation of true propositions, usually on the basis of adequate evidence, however that is defined. Both these definitions are not only skewed, they are rejected by the biblical witness contained in our passage. Faith has two dimensions, and the two cannot be separated or collapsed into one. First of all, faith is a living encounter with the reality of God. Faith is living trust, absolute trust, in the person of God himself. Faith draws Abraham into personal relationship to the living reality of God; and indeed, the same is henceforth true for all who believe. Yet secondly, faith means to trust in the promise of God as true, even despite the absolute *contradiction* of all evidence. Despite the contrary evidence of all reason and experience, faith affirms the promise of God contained in his word as certain truth. Faith is personal encounter; faith is also affirmation of divine truth. The former leads to the latter; the latter is framed only in the context of the former. Faith is total trust in God, never losing absolute trust in the truth of his word, awaiting his future fulfillment of the promise, despite the ongoing struggles of the present.

There is, secondly, the word *righteous*. For some, the idea of righteousness comprises an ideal of personal holiness, an absolute norm of life lived according to the pattern of personal righteousness. For others righteousness is defined rather in terms of social justice, again defined as an absolute norm of a genuine society lived according to the patterns of just and civil life. Here in this extraordinary verse, we learn that there is no ideal, absolute norm of righteousness, whether personal or social. Righteousness is not an ideal norm, but much rather a *relationship to God*. To be righteous is to be in right relation to God. Righteousness, we learn, is a term of the *covenant* between God and humanity. It will of course include many things, including sacrifice, acts of personal and social obedience, and acts of service. But the crucial point here is resounding and utterly unexpected: *nothing* we do can, or does, put us in right relation to God. No accomplishment of Abraham's, no accomplishment of ours, constitutes our righteousness before God. What has Abraham done? He has believed *God* and his promise; that is all.

And finally, the third term: God *reckons* Abraham's faith as righteous. The term has a legal, forensic sense; yet the biblical statement is not true because of the inherent meaning of righteousness, it is true because God is God. God himself alone determines his relation to Abraham and in him to all humanity. Belief in the promise of God is reckoned by God as putting Abraham in right relation to God. Faith puts him—faith puts us—in right relation to God, because God himself declares it so. We are put in right relation to God by faith in the promise of God alone, not through any form of human accomplishment; that is the revolutionary affirmation of this remarkable passage.

We proceed now from the innermost reality of the subject matter to which the text bears witness in the light of Scripture as a whole, back to the discrete witness of the text in the light of that subject matter. In the light of a holistic reading of the Bible, the Christian church professes: Jesus Christ is the true fulfillment of the promise of God to Abraham. Jesus Christ is the one content of the promise, which comes to all humanity in the gospel of God's redeeming love through the forgiveness of sins. As children of father Abraham, we are not put right with God by acts of personal holiness; we are not put right with God by acts of social justice. We are put right with God alone through faith in Jesus Christ, God's one true gift of redemption for the whole creation. That God's love in Jesus Christ will change our lives forever, that God's love in Jesus Christ will forever put us on the path to social justice, are both true as well. But these are second questions, not to be severed from, but never to be confused with, the primary question: how are we reconciled to God? We are reconciled to God through grace through faith alone apart from all moral striving. Nor is faith itself a work; God himself declares us righteous, "reckons" us righteous, according to his mercy, not according to the "merit" of our faithfulness. Faith, an empty vessel, an outstretched hand, receives the free gift of God offered in the promise, which fills all things with the fullness of divine splendor in love.

Whether we believe in the promise of God is the ultimate question. We all face penultimate questions in life. Every human being faces numerous questions of life, some large, some small. But here we are confronted with the ultimate question. It is not a question any person can evade. One can put it in the back of the mind; one can choose to forget it, or ignore it, but it will not go away. For the question is put to us by the living God himself. How are we—how are you—put in right relation to God? We live in times of moral chaos, and Christians are rightly concerned about the mindless violence of our society and of our world. But you are not put right with God by moral behavior, however stellar. We likewise live in a secular society, and Christians are rightly just as concerned about the widespread indifference to the claims of Christian devotion. But you are not put right with God by spirituality or piety. God comes to you only as gift, as promise. He does not say: here is what I have done for you, now here is what you must do for me. That is not the way of Abraham, that is not the way of the gospel. He says: here is what I have done, and will do, for you. Only believe, and you have it. We hear much talk of moral values; we hear much talk of social justice. But do we hear the one thing necessary: the free gift of God's redeeming love is already yours, believe the good news! Do we hear of faith? If we do, well enough; but if we do not, we are missing everything.

There are two dimensions of faith, for Abraham and for us. We believe God, and we believe the word of God. The act of faith is one; but the dimensions of faith are viewed properly as twofold in nature. First, we believe in God. To speak of the gospel is to speak of personal relationship to the risen Lord Jesus Christ. God himself showers our lives with gifts, some of which we can discern, many of which lie far beyond our awareness. But we are called by the gospel not only to receive the gifts of God with gratitude, but to know and enjoy the Giver in his gifts. The enjoyment of God is at the heart of living faith. He surprises us with his mercy; he daily holds us up in the temptations around us; he comes to us when and where we least expect to find him. We are his, and he is ours; that is the essence of his covenant love. Those who *enjoy* God truly know the heart of the gospel. But second, we affirm the truth of his word. The God of the Bible speaks to us; his promise is clear and certain, and comes to us in the shape of the written Scriptures. It is a false abstraction to say: we do not believe the Bible, we believe God! Those who treasure relationship to God in the most intimate core of their existence are the very ones who search the Scriptures to know his will, to cherish his spoken word, to discover his truth, to trace his wisdom. God is known in his word; the word leads us to know God himself. Without this twofold, dialectical understanding, the full promise of the gospel is sadly missed.

To speak of faith is to speak of an event, indeed to speak of a journey. Abraham here encounters God and believes, but his newfound faith will be sorely tried and tested. Abraham will struggle, not because he *doubts*, but because he *believes*, and will struggle as none after him in the Old Testament do. It is essential to return to our text in the light of the gospel, and recognize ourselves in the mirror of the Old Testament. The advent of Christ does not bring an end to struggle; we too with Abraham face at times the absolutely impossible realities of the world around us. We too hear the promise of God and ask: how can this possibly be? Nor does God endeavor to make it easy or simple; quite the opposite, the promise stretches our reason and experience to the breaking point. Like Abraham, neither can we make sense of God's promise, if we seek to test and assess it by relying upon the canons of human logic. For in his love for the world, and for us, God does the impossible. He brings life from the dead; he engenders a new creation; he makes us, and all things, new. We face a choice in life, not just once but again and again, and the choice poses an either/or. Either we will stand aside, weighing the options of the gospel with the all too comfortable "facts" of our world and our own experience of it. Or, we will walk with God into his future with us, and with the whole creation. We have to choose. Not to make a choice is to stand still, and therefore to move backward into the comfortable past. Faith always moves through struggle to an ever-new affirmation of the gospel.

9. The Grace of the Impossible

Genesis 18:1–15

THE GRACE OF GOD in the Bible shows no interest whatsoever in conforming itself to the canons of human logic and experience. Quite the contrary. Often enough, the event of God's gracious presence overturns all logical expectation. It shatters every previous norm of human experience, turns upside down customs of human society and culture. That is not to say that we can find God in the irrational or the illogical. The point rather is that *we* cannot find God at all. He finds us; and when he finds us, he comes in such overwhelming force that grace sets our lives on a new path, utterly without precedent, utterly unexpected, utterly brilliant beyond all human possibility.

God comes with his impossible grace to Abraham and Sarah. There are no preconditions; grace is grace. However, the form of divine grace is channeled quite clearly through two very human means. The first is the sovereign divine call to human hospitality for the stranger. Grace sets the stranger before us, and calls us to extend welcome. The second is the unexpected promise of the future in the form of a blessed child. Grace calls us to a new hope that exceeds every human possibility. Hospitality and hope become the new forms of human life called into being by the living and active promise of God.

We are summoned by the biblical narrator into the vivid and intimate world of Abraham and Sarah, only to discover that their world, through the gracious power of God, opens out directly onto our own. We are told by the narrator straightaway: the Lord appears to Abraham where he is pitching his tent by the terebinth trees of Mamre. It is a technique with which we will become increasingly familiar in the Bible: the narrator gives us information, as readers, that is not available—or at least not yet clear—to the characters in the account. *We* know that the Lord appears to Abraham; but from Abraham's perspective, at least initially, the encounter is far more ordinary. The setting is

54

immediately conveyed with vivid familiarity. Abraham is sitting in the shade of the entrance of his tent, under cover from the heat of the noonday sun. We see the scene now from Abraham's perspective. Suddenly, he spies three figures, three strangers, appearing as if from nowhere. It is a strange, even startling, time of day for travelers to pass by; ordinarily, the heat of the day is the time for rest, not the time for movement. No matter, Abraham immediately displays an extraordinary measure of the great call of God to human hospitality. He does not know these three men, but that does not matter at all. They are here, now, at his tent, and they are no doubt hungry and thirsty from travel in the heat. Abraham does not hesitate; he does not wait for *them* to make their needs known. He does not even make a normal human approach; he *runs* to meet them and *bows down* in his greeting. Abraham in every respect takes the initiative in extending hospitality to these three strangers. He shows every honor and respect, and no reluctance or aversion. Again, the text is quite clear: Abraham does *not* know what we know, that somehow this encounter is divine. He only knows that God requires *every* offer of human hospitality to be both generous and humane.

We are now privileged to witness an intimate yet ordinary moment of human interaction in the life of father Abraham. This is his life; this is how he acts; this is the way he treats strangers. He does not ask if they need something; he *invites* them, even *implores* them, to share the hospitality of his possessions. Please stop now and take some rest from your weary journey; please take a little water for your thirst, and remove the dust from your feet; please rest just a bit in the wonderful shade of this terebinth tree; I can bring you just a crust of bread, and then you can be back on your way. Abraham actually promises very little, only a momentary respite. He is not here to impress with words, but to provide, and provide he does, far in excess of what he has offered. Once again, the scene is a miniature life lesson in hospitality without any restrictions. Abraham knows nothing of these three men, not even their names, yet suddenly the entire household of Abraham goes into action at his direction once they agree—rather brusquely in fact— to stay for a bit. He promised a little crust of bread; instead, he invites his wife Sarah to bake a massive (three *seahs*!) and fresh batch of breadcakes, from choice flour (the same used for meal offerings to God). Be quick! A calf is selected and prepared from the herd, for a nomad an epic and regal feast! Curds and milk are provided (our yogurt), again the stuff of nomadic delight. When all is ready, Abraham does not sit down and enjoy the feast with his guests. Rather, Abraham himself serves the meal to his guests, and stands aside, until they have finished eating, attendant upon them. He had offered little with his words; he provided in extraordinary abundance in his deeds, in the form of comfort, rest, nourishment, strength for the journey. That is the true nature of openhearted hospitality.

As the mysterious encounter between Abraham (and eventually Sarah) and these three figures unfolds, the veil is lifted. Nevertheless, the mystery remains. It becomes clear to *Abraham* that in conversing with these three men Abraham is in fact conversing with God. God is God in heaven; God is God also now encountering Abraham right here, right now, as he extends hospitality to these three figures. Until now he has been entirely unsuspecting; suddenly he realizes he is conversing with God himself. Now, it is crucial to understand: the biblical narrator never clarifies the means by which God speaks through these three figures. Does he speak through all three, or just one of the three? Or is God himself yet another character alongside the three? The text is silent. God is able both to be himself one way in heaven, and yet to be another way on earth, without compromising his singular activity and reality. Divine mystery in the Bible, even when its truth is disclosed, remains forever a mystery.

God has reached into Abraham's life through the grace of hospitality; God now surrounds Abraham and Sarah's life with the future grace of promise. The men ask Abraham where his wife Sarah is. Whatever is about to happen involves both Abraham and Sarah together. She has in fact been listening in on these strange events just inside the entryway to the tent, and Abraham says as much to the three strangers. When it is now clear that both Abraham and Sarah are listening attentively, one of the three announces the divine promise: it is now time for Sarah to conceive, and to have a son. The promise is not general but specific; not just in the unknown future, but in this coming season, a son will be born to this couple. As readers of the book of Genesis we are already well aware of the advanced age of both Abraham and Sarah. But just to make sure we understand the utter futility, the utter absurdity, of this promise, the narrator reminds us: in fact, *both* of them—not just one or the other—are much too old to have children, and in fact Sarah *long* ago ceased menstruating. The promise, in other words, is in direct contradiction to every known fact of human reason and experience, both that of Abraham and Sarah, and that of our own, readers of today and every day. This is a promise that defies logic. It cannot and will not happen. Indeed, it is so utterly ridiculous to suppose that Sarah can have a child at this point in her life that she cannot help but laugh, tucked away inside the entrance to the tent, scarcely able to conceal her astonishment at the absurdity of it all. I am an old woman; my husband is an old man; and now I am supposed to have a baby? Ha! Ha! It is laughter at the ridiculous and the ludicrous; but it is at the same time laughter that expresses the sheer failure to believe the sovereign power of God's promised word. For God's word is the object of her laughter.

Only now does the text say what the reader has known from the beginning: God the Lord is speaking to Abraham. Again, we are never told the how, whether it is one of the three men, all three, or a separate divine epiphany. We are simply told; God now speaks to Abraham, and chides him for the laughter of Sarah. Did Sarah just laugh at the promised word of God, the Lord asks? But his point is not to cast judgment; his point is to shed light. God's promised word creates a new reality where none existed before; that is what Sarah fails to consider. God's promise is not limited to the ingredients of the past, or of the present, or even of the future; God's promised word creates a new future as if from nothing. Indeed, we are only now at the central focus of the entire passage: "is anything too wonderful for the Lord?"

The promise of God does not in any sense whatsoever owe it to human persons—even those chosen by the electing love of God—to conform to human expectations, or canons of human logic and experience. God is *God*; he accomplishes his promise because of who he is, and brings it forth through the unlimited resources of his creative love. The promise is then repeated, as if to make it quite clear and certain: now is the time for Abraham and Sarah to conceive a son, and in due season next year the son will be born. Sarah realizes only now that her laughter has not only been found out, but that she is in danger of offending the Lord himself. Rather than learning from her mistake, she responds with fear. She does what fearful humanity always does when first confronted with our follies; she denies what she did. I did not laugh! The guest does not let her off the hook, but nor does he censure and blame her. With simple and dignified firmness, he responds: yes, you did laugh.

The strange new world of the Bible turns human life upside down. We would question God; but in the biblical world, it is God who breaks into our lives and questions us. We turn to God when it is convenient for our timetable, but God encounters us according to his own time, which is the true fulfillment of all time, and is indeed our best time. We look to God to complete our plans and agendas in life; God shows us his totally new and different way, his plan, his purpose, his intention for our life. *Faith* discovers that the strange new world of God in the Bible is in fact the true world all around us, the world in which we live, and in living with God, flourish.

God meets us by veiling himself in that which is his opposite. He who possesses all power does not meet us in power but in weakness. God rules and overrules all things, yet he does not meet us in centers of influence but in the crossroads of ordinary life, where none but he himself is witness. As we read the Old Testament in the light of the New, this truth is fully expressed of course in the incarnation of God in Jesus Christ, who has nowhere to lay his head, who died powerless on the cross at the hands of sinners, who is nonetheless fully divine even as he is fully human. But it equally important to return to the Old Testament, in order fully to understand the true majesty of the New in light of the Old, especially the brilliant narratives of the Bible.

God is present in heaven above; yet clearly in the witness of the Old Testament, God is in some absolute sense present in this different reality here on earth in the manifold reality of human existence. We should not point to this passage and say: Christ is one of the three men! That is the wrong conclusion, that is bad theological exegesis. Nevertheless, in light of the subject matter to which this passage, the entire Old Testament, and indeed the entire Bible, point, we both can and must say: Christ himself is present among us in the sheer mystery of everyday life. The mystery of his presence is never a formula we can solve, and then move on to something else. The mystery of his presence is real, yet it always remains a sheer surprise, a miracle of love, coming into our lives from above, utterly without preparation or warning. He is the naked we are called to clothe; the hungry we are called to feed; the lonely we are summoned to visit; the hurting we are eager to comfort; the imprisoned we are longing to serve. Christ himself meets us among the weak and the vulnerable we are called to serve. The living faith of the gospel is always eager to respond to the ordinary call of Christ in daily life.

Certainly, at the top of the list is the welcome of strangers. We will meet the claim of the stranger upon our obedience to God again and again in the Bible. Here we meet it in the paradigmatic example of Abraham. Care for the stranger is not only a fundamental element of true worship of God, true discipleship of Jesus Christ. It is in fact a central element of the very nature of our created humanity. To be fully human is to be fully open-hearted, open-minded, open-handed, in response to the stranger we meet along the way. We are here in the presence of a basic, sacred obligation before the living reality of the risen Lord. To ignore the plight of the stranger is to ignore Christ. To welcome the stranger is to welcome Christ. Our hospitality cannot be grudging but rather must be eager; must not be limited but overflowing. We dare not hold anything back, but must instead go well beyond the expected norms of human custom.

Of course, it is no secret that we live in a time in which the migration of humankind is growing, and will perhaps continue to grow as never before. Refugees sadly must flee their homelands broken by war, looking for a new country. Migrants lose the opportunities afforded by the land from time immemorial due to climate change cause by sheer human stupidity, and must look elsewhere for the means to feed their families. Nationalism and ethnic identity close ranks, and squeeze out the claims of humankind upon ordinary kindness. Sheer human brutality against the stranger is often enough the obvious result, with the weakest of the weak—immigrant children—the hardest hit. In the community of faith in Jesus Christ we must insist: there is a *universal right to hospitality*. We know the truth of that fact straight from the clear word of God. Yet we proclaim that right, not just as a limited right of one religious community, but as a basic human right shared by all human beings in every culture and society. It is a civil right never to be broken by the church, and never again to be forgotten or neglected by the world at large.

God's promise is an *event* of God's time, which encompasses past, present, and future, in the unfolding moment of God's eternal purpose. At best, we try to measure the future by the ingredients of the present and the past. Even human imagination, however inspiring, cannot escape fundamentally the limits of human experience, projected outward onto the canvas of human consciousness. Yet God's promise is not based on human experience, but rather shapes and defines it. God's promise is based solely on his own sovereign purpose, which draws together the unlimited scope of his rule over all reality into one moment of time. God's promise is not a logical proposition to be parsed into its constituent elements; God's promise is *God himself*, binding his own inmost reality to a future which only he himself designs according to the beauty of his love for us, indeed for you. God is not only Lord of all reality; through his promise he is Lord of your life, both ready and willing to sustain and enrich every aspect of your existence through his fresh entry into the world.

You will never reach the end of the road; for God's promise will always show you a new direction to take, even if it is for now hidden from your eyes. You will never run out of resources to live out the abundance of your life, no matter how depleted those resources may at times become; for God himself is the ultimate resource upon which you depend, and his promised love is secure beyond all human calculation. You will never encounter any obstacle that finally and forever calls your life project to a halt; for God's own promise is your project, forever unfolding your future in unexpected ways, drawing your life forward far beyond your own limited plans, far exceeding your hitherto limited discoveries. God's promise is never a static substance, which once given is now possessed. Nothing of God is ever *possessed* by humanity. Rather, God's promise is always sheer *gift*, and as gift comes ever anew into your life, ever afresh from above, setting you on your feet and drawing you forward to a new future you could never truly imagine. You can count on his promise; you can rely on it with your very life, your entire existence.

For it is grounded, not in your need, but in God's gracious purpose, which fulfills human life far beyond our needs and wants, giving us a satisfaction known only in God. God's purpose remains hidden in the mystery of his sovereign freedom. God's purpose for your life remains his own. You cannot manipulate it; you cannot evaluate it according to human criteria of success of failure. You can only receive it in the humility of faith.

"Is anything too wonderful for God?" We are of course not invited by this extraordinary confession to speculate concerning what God can do, but rather concerning what God *will* do. God can do whatever he wills; the realization to ponder is that the scope of God's will, God's gracious purpose, is all-embracing. Perhaps we are willing to concede, in faith, that God's purpose embraces the whole creation, the whole cosmos; but it astounds us to realize that his purpose embraces a single child. The wonder of God is often sought in "the divine," which is the immense, the unlimited, the timeless, the abstract, the transcendent. Yet God's unlimited and transcendent purpose—such is his true wonder—is often enough found in the small, the confined, the ordinary, the fleeting, the immanent. He is here; right here, where we live, and breathe, and have our being. He is in our thoughts, guiding us by his word around the noise of our time to a new and better wisdom. He is in our feelings, culling out the toxic emotions that steal away our humanity, and filling us with new sources of enlivening joy. He is in our bodies, willing our health despite our frailty, upholding our strength despite our weakness, standing us on our feet ready again for the new day. When we feel cut off from the future; he is our future, and in him we are ultimately secure.

God's love never becomes routine, it is always new. God's gracious will never ceases to be an amazing surprise. The moment we discover something new about the reality of God, at that very moment we realize that God has already discovered us. At the same time that we grow in the knowledge of God's splendor, we recognize that it is we who are fully known by God. God makes no effort whatsoever to conform his way to our expectation. On the contrary, the biblical God takes delight in overturning human expectation. We seek a direct God, but God is always concealed and never obvious, always working behind the scenes where we easily overlook the traces of his love. We look for God to conform to our timetable; but God works according to his own plan, established before we were born, indeed established before the universe itself came into being. There is nothing so wonderful that he cannot and will not do it for our sake. That is the good news of the gospel.

10. Dialogue with God

Genesis 18:22–33

WE ENCOUNTER IN THIS passage one of the great moments in the Bible of anguished conversation between faithful humanity and the living God. There are of course many prayers in the Bible, all of them highly instructive for living faith. But here, we find not simply a prayer *to* God, as important as that is, but a conversation, a dialogue, *with* God. Indeed, all true prayer is dialogue with God, for God himself speaks to us in his word. Abraham approaches God with almost infinite humility, even submission. Yet at the same time he expresses an unlimited and expansive humanity. It is clear that the two horizons—his devotion to God and his love for humankind as a whole—are not unconnected, and it is precisely this passage that lays bare the luminous relation.

The dialogue itself will be our main focus, but the setting in all its manifold dimensions is crucial. There is first of all the *geographical* setting. The three mysterious strangers have come to meet Abraham at Hebron, by the terebinths of Mamre, and it is now clear that in meeting them, he is meeting God. The passage we are considering never unravels the basic mystery of God's *incognito*; God is in heaven above, yet God is somehow connected to the appearance of these three mysterious strangers. He is not the three; he is not one of the three; yet is not apart from the three. God is there in ineffable glory; and yet somehow is now right here, conversing with Abraham. After renewing the promise concerning a son, the three figures set out east of Hebron for the city of Sodom. We are given the narrative geography in chapter 13. Hebron is situated on the heights above, Sodom is located in the plains of the Jordan River, clearly visible below. As God and Abraham will converse about Sodom and its human inhabitants, the entire city is clearly visible off in the distance. This is not an abstract theological discussion.

There is secondly the setting in the *relationship* between God and Abraham. Of his sheer mercy and grace alone God has called Abraham, and extended to him the extraordinary promise that through him, and his posterity, the blessing of God will come to all families, all peoples, all nations of the earth. The promise of a child to Abraham has just been renewed; now the extension of that promise to the whole of humanity comes directly into play. Moreover, God uses astounding words of familiarity concerning Abraham. I have "known" him; he is my familiar, my friend. How can I now conceal from the one I call my friend what I am about to do? There is no sense that God has compromised his sovereignty in befriending Abraham. Quite the contrary, he has exercised it, in precisely this way.

There is, thirdly, the *social-political* context. God has received, concerning the cities of Sodom and Gomorrah, an "outcry." This is a word with definite connotation in the biblical witness. The people of Israel will make an "outcry" to God in their bondage in Egypt. Widows, orphans, immigrants, the poor and dispossessed, make an "outcry" to God when their basic human rights have been utterly stolen away. When an outcry from humanity reaches God's presence it signifies a total collapse of basic human decency so pervasive that no other remedy is possible. Where there is injustice, exploitation, manipulation, indifference to suffering of others, such a cry goes up to God.

There is, finally, the *pedagogical* context. It is the role of Abraham—indeed the role of God's people—to teach and to live the meaning of justice and human right. One generation must teach the next generation just what it means to live in the light of God's basic care for human well-being. An outrage has reached God from these cities in the plain; God has come down to examine the case. And now he has involved Abraham. The question now becomes: will Abraham turn away indifferent, or will he himself become involved in the well-being of this pagan population, who are, after all, total strangers? God, as it were, presents the case, then awaits Abraham's questions. God is approachable, as the friend of Abraham. And suddenly there occurs one of the great dialogues in the Bible between God and his beloved friend, as the city in the valley down below continues life as normal, utterly unaware of the life-or-death drama unfolding concerning its fate on the heights above.

Having set the larger context, the narrator now switches to the perspective of Abraham, as he enters into this extraordinary dialogue with God. Again, two points need to be made or we will miss entirely the grand sweep of the biblical depiction. The first concerns the *scope* of Abraham's concern. Abraham, we know, has family down in the city of Sodom, and it is natural to assume that they constitute his primary concern; after all, isn't the Bible all about family values? But, of course the Bible, here as elsewhere, is silent about what we consider our most pious religious and moral values. The Bible depicts humanity from the point of view of *God's perspective* on us, not our perspective on God, however rigorously moral. No, Abraham is not primarily concerned about Lot (Abraham's nephew) and his family, which are unmentioned. But nor is he concerned about saving the righteous, while at the same time damning the wicked. Abraham is not trying to convince God that some should be saved, while others judged. That is simply not the point of the dialogue, and those who construe it that way badly miss Abraham's true concern. Nor is there any mention of repentance; this is not about leaving open the possibility of repentance for the evil majority as long as possible. Rather, the scope of Abraham's concern is made crystal clear: he is concerned about the divine salvation of the city of Sodom *as a whole*. Indeed, as the dialogue unfolds, it becomes clear that Sodom is in some ways a kind of cypher, a parable, for humanity as a whole; how does it stand between God and humankind? That is the scope of Abraham's ultimate concern.

And secondly, we need to focus on one crucial question of Abraham's: shall not the Judge of all the earth do what is just? In traditional exegesis of this passage, an appeal was often made to an abstract standard of moral justice to which both God and Abraham are in some sense morally beholden. We now know that exegesis is faulty; it is not based on the Hebrew text. Since the latter part of the nineteenth century, it has become quite clear, through careful study of Hebrew usage, that God's "justice" unfolds only in God's covenant love; that is, justice in the Bible is not an abstract norm, but a relational term, by which God himself freely involves himself for the good of humankind. Only now do we catch the full import of Abraham's question, and why it is so crucial just now. The promise of the birth of his son is still in his ears. That promise is the basis of the covenant, which embraces Abraham and his family, but through him all family, peoples, and nations of the earth. So God has told Abraham, from the very beginning. It is that promise that is now at issue as they glance at Sodom on the plains below. Do they too not stand in some sense *inside*, rather than *outside*, your covenant love, Abraham is asking God. The gracious promise of God is the unspoken presupposition for this profound dialogue.

And so we come to the central issue. It is not just a numbers game. Abraham is not haggling with God as he moves from fifty righteous in the city ultimately down to the barest minimum of just ten. Abraham is rather probing the mystery of God's very purpose. Does God ultimately have *two* purposes for the world—grace and judgment—or just *one*, grace alone? Are grace and judgment in a kind of coequal balance in the divine estimate, or is judgment ordered to grace in such a way that God always sees mercy toward the righteous—no matter how few—as infinitely more important than judgment of the many—no matter how numerous? That is the real question. The answer comes only in stages: fifty, forty-five, forty, thirty, twenty, ten. Abraham is not just learning of God's mercy, but is in some sense drawn in by God himself to actively petition for it. And so Abraham learns: the God of the promise is a God who forgives, above all.

We are called by the freely given promise of God to live in intimate dialogue with the living God. We clearly do not earn this invitation; it is grounded in the eternal divine purpose of love. We do not suddenly stand before God as equals—even here, in dialogue with the living Lord of all creation, we are dust and ashes. Nevertheless, the invitation is real, precisely because it is not grounded in us, but comes as a free gift of grace. Jesus said: "I do not call you servants any longer, because the servant does not know what the master is doing; but I have called you friends . . ." (John 15:15). We have already watched in the book of Genesis as the almighty God has created the heavens and the earth, has sent forth the peoples and nations of the earth to populate the world, has summoned Abraham with his special electing love from among all those surrounding nations. And now, suddenly, a new dimension of biblical faith appears.

God and Abraham, Abraham and God, engage in what can only be called a dialogue, a conversation, a real encounter that goes back and forth from one to the other. Discipleship means to live daily in that encounter with God. There is boldness, even audacity, in authentic faith. God may rule all things in sovereign glory, but God is not a tyrant, nor does faith mean bitter resignation in the face of life's difficulties. God is a friend who draws near; the one true Friend, who always stands waiting to listen, to understand, to respond. True faith means speaking with God openly and honestly about the joys, the concerns, the anguish, the give-and-take struggle of our daily lives. We enter into dialogue with God in company with the faithful of all times and places in worship; we also encounter God in the individual privacy of the heart, which alone knows its own deepest joys and sorrows. God is always waiting; that is the freely given promise of the gospel.

We learn from the beautiful humanity of Abraham the difference between piety and authentic faith. Piety—including sadly Christian piety—always divides up the world into "us" against "them." There are, over here, people we are concerned about, our people; and there are, over there, people we can safely leave aside, their people. True faith, founded on the freely given promise of God, overturns the false pieties of this world, and transforms our very humanity. Abraham has already learned that the promise of God extends to all nations and peoples. Faith recognizes that

God's gracious will knows no limits, no bounds, no territorial framework. There is, as the old hymn puts it, a wideness in God's mercy. And with that wideness comes a new expansiveness in the very core of our humanity. A threat to anyone is a threat to all. We not only feel empathy for the plight of those who cry out in the distress of marginalization, or oppression, or threat; we recognize no limits whatsoever to the range of our empathy as followers of a risen and exalted Lord.

He has called us into friendship with himself. At the very same time, he calls us into friendship with every human being on the face of the earth. Piety is always eager to call down divine judgment upon those deemed unworthy of his blessing; always ready to divide up the world into the righteous and the unrighteous. Faith sees the *whole world* differently. If every human being on the face of the earth is my friend, then I can never give up on my fellow humanity. I can never draw a line in the sand and say: God's compassion begins there, but it ends right here. Because we are invited into friendship with God, we are sent out in friendship toward the whole of humankind.

What is the relation between God's will to save and God's desire to punish? Does God have two purposes for the world, judgment and mercy, balanced as it were in perfect equipoise? We certainly learn an astounding truth as we contemplate Abraham's anguished encounter with God: the divine mercy infinitely outweighs the divine desire for judgment. Even just a handful of righteous is enough to save the entire population! God is not willing to divide up humanity into two camps, and upon one camp execute his wrath while upon the other execute his grace. Rather, in the end, God has one purpose for the whole of humanity, which is forgiveness. The theme will certainly be fully expanded in the remainder of the Old Testament: "I will not execute my fierce anger . . . for I am God and no mortal, the Holy One in your midst, and I will not come in wrath" (Hos 11:9). Yet in the end, the relation between divine mercy and wrath will only be fully manifest on the cross. Wrath and mercy are not two divine purposes at all; rather, on the cross, God's judgment is poured out in such a way as to destroy sin, to bear it away, and so to enact love triumphant. There is no Easter without the cross; but here we are reminded that the way of the cross does indeed lead to Easter. As for Sodom, while it will be destroyed shortly after this remarkable prayer, it will also eventually be restored to divine favor: "I will restore their fortunes, the fortunes of Sodom and her daughters . . ." (Ezek 16:53). God's wrath against human injustice is real, but in the end, his wrath is the instrument, the means, of redemptive love for all, a love beyond all human imagination.

We are led by the text of Scripture to meditate as well on the flexibility of God's living will. God's will is not impersonal fate; God is a living God, whose rule over all reality is without obstruction or restriction, yet whose guidance of the creation is ordered toward the timing of his own sovereign decision. He wills, and he acts; often he delays his action in patience toward his creatures, giving every possible chance for repentance. The integrity of God's purpose is not compromised but confirmed by his patience. The sovereign God—without in any way subjecting his sovereignty to conditionality—interacts with the flow of human life. God is not a lifeless principle of causality, though he is the ultimate Cause of all things. God is a living Lord, who speaks, and even dares to listen. Our times are in his hands.

11. The Trial of Faith

Genesis 22:1–19

BY WIDE CONSENT, ANCIENT and modern, Jewish and Christian, the story of the sacrifice of Isaac is considered the highest reach of narrative art in the Pentateuch. Yet it is narrative in service of a theological purpose, and quite literally everything depends upon discerning the theological framework of the story. It is not about the legality or morality of child sacrifice; nor about trauma; nor about the transformation of primitive sacrifice into ethical consciousness. All of these concerns are written onto the text, not learned from it; and sadly, such extraneous issues blunt the brilliant lesson that is indeed here to be learned. The lesson is not easy, then or now, but it lends itself to wide-ranging imaginative application in all dimensions of daily life and struggle.

The passage opens with a brief indication of the theological scope of the unfolding drama: "After these things, God put Abraham to the test." What are these things? Abraham's entire life with God has been consumed with one great issue, which is the *promise*. God calls Abraham to leave his past forever behind, and promises him not only a posterity, but that through him all nations of the earth will be blessed. But at first, such a promise appears null and void, since Abraham and Sarah are old, and Sarah can no longer have children. First Abraham suggests to God that one of his household servants should count as his heir, but God tells him that only one of his own children shall be the heir to the promise. Then, a solution is sought through Ishmael, born by Abraham through Sarah's maid Hagar, but God makes it fully clear that neither is Ishmael the child of promise, though he too will receive a blessing. Finally, at long last, Isaac is born to Sarah and Abraham in the midst of old age—is anything impossible with God?—and God explicitly states that Isaac himself is indeed the bearer of the divine promise, the one through whom God will extend the blessing, not only to

67

Abraham and his family, but through him to all nations and peoples of the earth, throughout an endless future.

Then comes the stunning statement: God puts Abraham to the test. The syntax in Hebrew emphasizes the word *God*. We might wish to psychologize the story of the sacrifice of Isaac, but the text itself insists upon being read theologically, even theocentrically. God himself sets this event in motion. But the theological framework also employs a technique we are now accustomed to in biblical narrative art. There is a twofold viewpoint quickly introduced at the outset. The reader—we—are told that God is only testing Abraham. What follows is in the manner of a trial of *faith*, not a trial in *fact*. But Abraham does not know this. *We* know more than Abraham, which gives us some relief from the pressure he feels; yet we can scarcely avoid the mounting tension, for we cannot for a moment yet see how God can possibly resolve the trial he himself has set in motion.

For with the promise of an heir firmly fixed in mind, we now hear the terrifying divine command. God calls to Abraham, and Abraham responds with eager readiness to follow the divine instruction: here I am. And then come the words that sound through the millennia with the same exact terror as if spoken into the present moment: "Take your son, your favored son, Isaac, whom you love, and go to the land of Moriah, and offer him there as a burnt offering on one of the heights that I will point out to you." In Hebrew the progression follows increasing levels of intimacy and therefore tension: your son, your favored son, the one whom you love, Isaac. It is the first use of the word *love* in the entire Bible. Clearly as the story unfolds the beauty of love between a parent and a child is both present in the background and excruciating. But in the end, the foreground points in a different direction.

Isaac is not just, here, a beloved son, though he is that; he is the *heir* of the divine promise, long awaited by Sarah and Abraham, and much celebrated at long last. Isaac is the divinely promised future not only of Abraham and his family, but through him of the *entire creation*. And now God is commanding Abraham to slay his son Isaac, this son. The *command* of God is in direct contradiction to the *promise* of God. There can be no human resolution to the unspeakable self-contradiction. God alone can and must resolve what once again appears to be a human impossibility.

The journey of Abraham and Isaac to the place where he must sacrifice his son is told with unbearable detail. They arise early in the morning; Abraham is ready to obey God, despite whatever questions and doubts must surely be raging in his mind and heart, all silently passed over by the text. He is even careful in his preparations, making sure to take wood for the sacrifice, not yet knowing their exact destination and therefore the availability of fuel for the sacrifice. Two servants accompany them, but at the right moment they will be left behind, inappropriate and irrelevant witnesses to a lonely drama between a man, his son, and God Almighty. It takes three days—three agonizing, unending days—to get from base camp in Beersheba to the place where God directs them. This is no ordinary test of faith, here now, gone and forgotten soon enough; this is a test in which eternal torment suddenly invades time itself and will not soon be shaken free.

When they arrive at the place, the servants are left behind, while Abraham and Isaac proceed on ahead. Isaac is now presumably a young man, not yet fully mature, but no longer a mere child. Twice the text repeats in somber yet somehow tender refrain: "the two of them walk on together." The image is indelible. The older man carries the dangerous implements, the fire and the knife; the younger son carries the wood, safe for now, yet the very wood upon which he will presumably be sacrificed. Isaac is old enough to realize that something is amiss, and so he asks his father, in intimate language, why they are not bringing an animal to sacrifice. Abraham responds, with the same tone of intimacy, that God himself will provide a suitable animal. Despite the tension of the scene, a father and a son, a son and a father, are still sharing an extraordinary adventure, if that is what it can be called. The innocent child suspects nothing; the agonized father expresses nothing. And Abraham, in answering his son, speaks the truth—God *will* provide—but it is a truth of which Abraham is as yet himself completely unaware. Three long days have brought them to this point. Once again, the pace of the story slows down even further, until we are allowed—compelled—to watch every individual action without flinching. The narrator knows the value of significant detail.

The emotional qualities of the ordeal of what follows are never directly named. Rather, the narration slows down even further to the point of describing briefly individual motions, one by one. One movement after another, we are led from terror to terror. Abraham and Isaac arrive at the place designated by God. Abraham builds an altar for sacrifice from the wood which Isaac—the one to be sacrificed—has carried. Abraham binds his son—his favored son, whom he loves, his son Isaac—and lays him on top of the wood of the altar. Abraham reaches for the knife, and is poised to slay the sacrifice now on the altar. Why does the narrator not name the emotions directly, for surely we all feel them? Recall from the beginning; we have been told that this is only a trial, a test of Abraham's faith. We know from the beginning of the story what Abraham does not: that God is not going to carry through the command to sacrifice Isaac. But by narrating the details without commenting on the emotion, the narrator creates, as it were, space in us, the reader, to feel the power of what Abraham felt, despite our twofold perspective. We forget what we know; and we too, with Abraham, are thrust into a moment of utter contradiction between God's command and God's promise, a contradiction that defies any human solution.

God himself, and God alone, can resolve the struggle of faith. An angel cries from heaven—there is no time for the angel to appear on earth, the usual mode of angelic presence in the Bible—and forbids Abraham from harming the boy. God himself is now openly speaking, in what is clearly the climax of the entire story. Abraham, it is now fully demonstrated, "fears God," by which is meant not an emotional reaction but an authentic response of obedience to the divine command. What God has commanded, Abraham has carried out—or at least prepared to until stopped by God himself. When the command of God seems directly to threaten the promise, Abraham is nevertheless ready to obey God's command. Abraham trusts that God alone will resolve the contradiction, in faithfulness to his word of promise, despite every appearance to the contrary. A ram suddenly and surprisingly appears caught in a thicket, and Abraham now offers it as the sacrifice in the place of Isaac. He names the place "God sees"; but it is transposed into the passive verbal form by posterity: here in this place "God is seen." The full promise of God to Abraham, originally set out in chapter 12, is now repeated to Abraham as we have come full circle through the many trials of his life to this final test. Abraham, Isaac, and the servants return back home to Beersheba.

The promise of God's free grace in the gospel of Jesus Christ is real, and it comes to all. But it always remains promise; always remains free; always remains gracious. The free promise of God can never under any circumstances be converted into a demand, or an expectation, or a claim upon God. How does this happen? It happens for example when Christianity becomes a cultural or national phenomenon, a religious cause. Of course God loves us; of course God is on our side, we are all Christians here in our nation! It happens whenever the gospel of promise is converted into a so-called "Christian worldview." I am a conservative, therefore of course I am a Christian! I am a Christian, therefore of course I am a conservative! I am a conservative, therefore of course I am loved by God! I am an adherent of Western Judeo-Christian values, therefore of course God showers me with the blessings of his promised love!

All such claims upon God are false claims. The gospel is not an ethno-nationalist realm, not a worldview, not a legal-traditional set of moral values. Indeed, the free promise of God forces us—as it did Abraham—to *abandon* forever every claim and tie of nation, family, worldview, moral system, and culture, and binds us directly to the free grace of the living and gracious Lord. Jesus Christ himself is the living promise of God. He will not be compromised by human stratagems of self-righteousness. He comes to us as promise; he remains with us only as promise; he calls us, finally, to himself, as the one great promise of life, which makes us whole and keeps us forever.

The God of promise is the God who provides, the God who sees. Once again, we can set upon God no restrictions, no human conceptions of success or failure, no limits of interpretation. God provides according to his own timetable, often enough coming when we least expect him. He provides not only in large ways, but more commonly in the smallest ways, easily missed, yet once understood, the very best of all. He does not only provide at the beginning of our journey, when we are still full and eager; he waits until we are tired and hungry, overwhelmed and overcome, and then he comes: not as we expect him to come but suddenly and without any preparation at all. Every possible way in front us of may well be closed off; and then suddenly a new way will appear, as if from nowhere. Every hope in our hearts will be extinguished; and then suddenly, new joy will flourish, and new possibility arise in astonishment. But we must take even one step further. God not only appears to us, he makes himself manifest. That is, he opens our hearts and minds to the living reality of his love. He gives, and opens our eyes to the gift, and indeed to the Giver. In his light we see light; in his love we see love. In his grace we find grace for the journey, and never again look back.

The trial of faith comes to the whole church; the trial of faith comes to the individual Christian. While it may strike suddenly and then disappear, just as often we are called to a steady endurance of the harsh realities of inner conflict and outer turmoil. Reason and experience may tell us: God must have completely forgotten all about us, or worse, God has turned against us and become our enemy. For all of us baptized into the name of God, there are times when God's promise of new life seems directly contradicted by the command we must obey. We are all tempted by the terrible thought at such times: what will I do if God has simply turned against me? We look around at the perplexing circumstances of our lives, and we measure God by the limits of our perplexity. If my life is filled with so many problems, surely that is direct evidence that God has simply decided to hate me outright. Yet the impossibly new world of God in the Bible turns our way of thinking upside down. It is *especially* in times of trial that we are forced to make a choice: am I going to define God, or am I going to allow God to define himself, and therefore to define me? And am I going to tell God what he thinks, or am I going to listen to what God says? The God who defines himself, the God who speaks for himself, is certainly not a God who hates you; his love for you is eternal and unchanging. Yet he calls you to new life through radical obedience. That is the first response in times of struggle: to obey the command of God.

But we cannot obey unless we trust; we cannot trust unless we obey. Absolute trust in God in times of trial and struggle is the sure way of Christian discipleship. Here, and here alone, you learn that the word of God's promise is the highest truth of your existence. Everything else—even what is most dear in your life—is secondary; God's promise alone is primary. God's word of promise gathers up your past in his love, surrounds your present in his mercy, and guarantees your eternal future in his unlimited kindness. How do you know his promise is true? If you measure it by the empirical evidence around you, you can never reach a conclusion. One day you may be convinced, but another day you may lose all hope. The only answer is absolute trust in God's living word, a trust that clings to his faithfulness in every hardship and temptation of life. God is always with you; God is always for you; God will always see you through. Put your trust in him.

God sees; God provides; God makes his pleasant blessing manifest, even now, in our world and in your life. His ways are endlessly rich, challenging and enriching human imagination. The God of Abraham is the same God who now governs our world, who now rules over his church, who now lives in the depths of your being. He manifested himself then by a single ram hidden in the bushes. He manifests himself now, often in ways we scarcely notice unless we are attentive to his extraordinary blessings. He still sees every intimate detail of your life, he still knows every dimension of your everyday existence even better—far better—than you know it yourself. He does not always come when, and where, and how you expect him. But he is always faithful to his promise, whether he comes early or late, visibly and openly or almost imperceptibly, through extraordinary means or in the most ordinary rhythms of daily existence. He provides for every need in abundance, in some ways you may know very well, in other ways you may never fully know or comprehend. He makes himself known in your life, with a love than cannot fail. In trial, there is grace. In every loss, there is gain. In death, there is new life, for God is with us.

12. In Death, Life

Genesis 23

ON THE SURFACE, NOTHING could be more different from the literary shape of Genesis 22, the sacrifice of Isaac, than Genesis 23, the purchase by Abraham of the cave and field of Machpelah from Ephron the Hittite. The one is perhaps the most dramatic narrative in the entire Old Testament, told with consummate narrative skill; the other is by contrast a seemingly mundane, at times almost comical, rendition of an ancient ceremony of sale of land. The one follows Abraham and Isaac as they are finally alone together; the other follows Abraham from private grief over the death of his beloved wife Sarah into the very public world of the Canaanites, and even goes out of the way to stress the public quality of the rather elaborate proceedings. The one portrays God setting the story into motion, and intervening at just the right excruciating moment to bring it to its climax; in the other, God does not even appear at all, leaving one to wonder what if anything this story has to do with the theology of Genesis.

In fact, the story in Genesis 23 has *everything* to do with the theology of the book, and indeed with the entire Pentateuch; and it is expertly paired by the canonical editors in the final form with the story of Genesis 22. Recall how the sacrifice of Isaac ends, with God repeating to Abraham the promise, the very same promise that called him from his original homeland to a new land, the land of Canaan. The promise is filled to overflowing with blessing, which indeed will ultimately encompass all nations and families of the earth. The promise will go through Abraham's son Isaac, who is reaffirmed in chapter 22 as the one inheritor of the promised blessing of God. But one other element of the original promise is stressed: "your descendants shall seize the gates of their foes" (Gen 22:17). God has, all along, promised to Abraham, not only posterity, but also the land of Canaan, as far as his eye can see, in every direction. Yet until now, Abraham does not own a single square foot, a single square inch, of land. So, the question cries out for an answer: what about the promise of *land*?

The question does not reach a point of crisis until the death of one of the first generation, in fact Sarah. She lives to the good old age of one hundred twenty-seven years. The text records that she dies in the area near the terebinths of Mamre where Abraham and Sarah have long pitched their tent as pastoral nomads. One day it will be called Hebron, the text relates, a major center of religious and civic life for the people of Israel. But for now, it is simply nomad country among the Canaanites. We are not allowed into the inner life of Abraham as he mourns the death of his life partner in the high adventure of faith. That he mourns her loss is self-evident, but nothing more is said. Rather, what comes quickly to the forefront is the crucial question: what will be done with her earthly remains, her body? Until now, the issue of the land of promise has always been in the background; now it is suddenly front and center. A burial means a grave; a gravesite means land, at least at the very minimum. Suddenly the reality of the promise is no longer a "theological" question merely but the most practical material issue facing Abraham. He is a foreigner without land; where can he bury his wife? He knows exactly what he wants, and how to get it; the story that follows records the public transaction by which ownership of a small piece of land legally passes from Canaanite possession to the possession of Abraham.

What now follows in the narrative appears on the surface to be an elaborate, stylized record of an ancient real estate transaction. What is in fact occurring is far more consequential; a *cultural transaction*. Possession of property in Canaan brings with it *citizenship*. Until now, Abraham (and Sarah) have wandered the land as nomads, not possessing a foot of earth; they are therefore immigrants, in fact and in ancient law. But the moment Abraham acquires property, he becomes a citizen, by right. He must therefore cross a major threshold. In order to become a citizen of Canaan, he must be approved by all the citizens in the surrounding city; so he approaches the citizen body and announces his intentions. He reminds them of a fact they well know: he is until now nothing but a "resident alien," possessing no property and therefore no rights among them. But he wants a small piece of land to bury his dead wife. Does he have their permission?

They respond—the gathered citizen body—by calling Abraham a "mighty prince." On the one hand, they are not going to let him off easy. A mighty prince, as opposed to a mere resident alien, can surely afford to pay handsomely for a plot of earth; the art of the sale is not new to the modern world. But the reader of course sees the double meaning; in God's eyes, and in our eyes, Abraham, as God's elect, is indeed exactly that: a mighty prince among God's children. At any rate, Abraham has crossed the first hurdle.

The gathered community has agreed to the sale of a piece of property, and therefore citizenship in the land. It is a major step.

Now the question becomes: *which* piece of property? Abraham of course enters into these negotiations knowing full well the exact plot of earth he is hoping to acquire. He names the place: a cave belonging to one Ephron son of Zophar, the cave of Machpelah. He invites the gathered citizenry to summon Ephron for further discussions. Once again, we are witnessing the elaborate and rather humorous ritual of ancient buying and purchasing of land. (Doubtless future generations will dig up real estate purchases from our contemporary era, and have their own interesting commentary to make.) Ephron has been in the audience all along, and now steps forward for the *second* hurdle: actually closing a deal on a specific piece of land where Abraham may bury his beloved Sarah.

Abraham wants the cave of Machpelah because it is at the edge of a field, and thus has ease of access. For his purposes he obviously only needs the cave, a common type of burial site in ancient times. But he needs it badly, and right away; and Ephron is a local, while Abraham has only just crossed the threshold into respectable Canaanite acceptance. In short, Ephron can do with Abraham as he please, and both he and Abraham know it. Ephron therefore in grand style offers to "give" Abraham the cave *and* the field in which it is located. Three points. First, the word for give, sell, and buy is actually the same word in Hebrew, used seven times in this short transaction passage. The shades of ambiguity are built into the very language of subtle transaction. Second, recall that Abraham only asked for the cave. He is now under no illusion. If he wants to buy the cave, he will have to buy the entire field. In short, he is being stiffed. And third, by offering to give him the place of burial, Ephron is trying to keep Abraham's status as a foreigner, a resident alien, intact, one last time. Without a land purchase Abraham cannot possibly keep the cave where he buries his wife. He will forever be at the mercy of its true owner, Ephron, who will of course take it back at his whim. No land, no citizenship.

The negotiations now take on the details of a final purchase. Abraham has no choice. He must buy the cave and the field. He knows it, Ephron knows it, everyone there knows it. So he makes the offer: I will pay for both, set your price. Ephron nonchalantly tosses out a figure as if it is the last thing on his mind: four hundred shekels silver. It is an outrageous rip-off! Again, everyone there knows it. But what can Abraham do? Until he buys the land, he is not even a citizen. So he carefully weighs out the silver—there were no coins yet in human history—and the passage concludes with a summary amounting to a deed of sale. This field, and this cave (even the trees in the field are mentioned, a common feature of ancient Near Eastern contracts of sale) have legally passed from the possession of Ephron the Hittite into the possession of Abraham. And there he buries Sarah his wife, in the cave of Machpelah, his cave. One day Abraham too will be buried in that same cave, as will Isaac and Rebekah, and Jacob and Leah.

The promise of God to Abraham is not finally fulfilled; but here there is a foretaste. In death, they inherit the promise, no longer resident aliens but citizens, children of the promised land. In death, there is new life.

The God of the promise is always a God of new beginnings in your life. To be human is to live in hope; to be fully alive is to trust in God's expected promise. To celebrate life with wholehearted enjoyment comes from deep-felt confidence in God's gracious rule over all reality. Life does not always go according to well-laid plans. It will certainly take many twists and turns we do not expect. Nevertheless, from our faith in the promise of God we derive courage to be, for God is the author of all new beginnings. The God we serve makes all things new in your life. The promise of God is present and powerful in your everyday existence. The God of infinite and unlimited resources uses the fulness of his blessing to shape your life for good. Suddenly they are there: a fresh start, a new perspective, hope reborn, insights gained, fresh blessings received; and you become aware that God's promise is at work. Cherish every new beginning in your life, for God himself has put them there for your ultimate fulfillment.

The kingdom of God grows from small beginnings, not large. For Abraham, a small cave, at the edge of field, is the first step. Yet one day, God will give to his people Israel the entire land of promise in which that cave and field are located. We measure time by the limits of our experience. But God measures time by the eternal wisdom of his unlimited vision, which gathers past, present, and future into a single moment. We measure time by the brief span we are permitted to live on this earth; but in God eyes, a thousand years are but a single day. To trust in God's promise means to leave in God's hands the proper timing of his gifts. He acts in his own good time, and in his own mysterious way. He performs wonders in your life that are easily overlooked. Yet the eye of faith sees these wonders for what they really are: fresh beginnings of his constant love. The promise of God is easily overlooked. Abraham found his entire future confirmed in a little cave, which an ancient GPS could scarcely locate. There are times when God works in thunder and lightning, but just as often he comes in a silent whisper, supplying our needs, granting our desires, fulfilling our dreams. Never overlook the simple gifts of God's loving kindness, which make you whole.

A small cave will one day give way to the full scope of the promised land. God is Lord of the future. Abraham cannot see the future directly, or he would not have hope. But he lives now, acts now, in light of the future.

Hope is never passive in the present, but always active. It may not be able to accomplish everything; but it will never rest easy with accomplishing nothing at all. Hope always finds something to do. Above all, authentic faith always looks forward, never backward. We cannot measure God's future by what we know of the past. Good days have come and gone for us all, but God ever and again creates a new future that is yet to be. God directs our path whose end we cannot now see. We know only that God himself awaits us in the journey ahead, and that is enough—infinitely more than enough—to keep us going, one step at a time. God constantly creates anew fresh possibilities in your life, where none existed before, all according to his eternal design. God shows you new truths that you have never before understood, perhaps even never truly considered. God teaches you fresh lessons that transform and renew your comprehension of his will. God grants you new blessings that point forward to yet more blessings to come. Authentic faith looks forward to the future; for Jesus Christ the risen and exalted Lord is the future toward which you daily strive. In him, the *new time* of God's eternal kingdom has already dawned and your future is already in his hands. Act in the present for the sake of the future, for God himself will surely accomplish his purpose in your life.

We learn from Abraham the fundamental *tension* of the life of faith, a tension that is not removed by the fulfillment of the promise in the gospel of Jesus Christ but rather fully embraced. On the one hand, Abraham is fully at home in the world of human affairs. We can only marvel in deep admiration at the character of Abraham. He is an immigrant in a foreign land, legally a resident alien without any rights whatsoever. Yet he conducts himself with a quiet grace and dignity that shines through every word, every gesture. He understands the rules of civil life and embraces them. He does not treat his neighbors with contempt, even when he knows he is being cheated. He takes the high road, and treats all alike with the same dignified humanity. He comes to own property; he finds himself a full citizen; he is now a member of the civil life of the community. Surely, on the one hand, as children of our father Abraham, we too must share responsibility for a new society in which civil life is shared by all. We too must honor our neighbor, whether they are our fellow citizens, strangers in our midst, or foreigners living across the face of the planet. Honor everyone, declares the gospel.

Yet on the other hand, Abraham and his near descendants only come fully into possession of their inheritance when they die. He owns only a grave, and a field surrounding that grave. The great first generation of faith must pass away in order to inherit their place in the land of promise. And so it is with us. As long as we are in this world, we are all immigrants. As long as we are in this world, we are all resident aliens, like our father

Abraham, like the Lord whom we serve, who had nowhere to lay his head. The moment we find our fundamental orientation of life in the things of this world, this age, we are lost. The moment our highest priorities become oriented around what we own, the values and morals of this world, the traditions of this present age, the goods of human culture and society, including its political agendas, we have lost the gospel. We do have an inheritance, greater than can be imagined. It is revealed in a cave, a tomb, an empty tomb. Only in death do we find life.

13. God Rules, and Overrules

Genesis 25:19–24

AND SO WE COME in due course to the stories of the family of Isaac, as noted by the familiar formula of the book of Genesis: "These are the generations of . . ." We are suddenly made aware of the passing of time, not by the changing dates on a calendar, but by the immemorial rhythm of the movement of time through the experience of one generation to the next. A family is still the same; yet a new generation arises, with new challenges to confront, new opportunities to pursue. Families do not unfold through time; rather, time unfolds through the changing experience of family. The biblical narrative makes no attempt whatsoever to situate the story of Isaac and his family with reference to the cultural, religious, political, and social forces that no doubt surround it. The focus is entirely elsewhere, and without that focus, we will lose our way. It is, according to the divine word to Abraham and Sarah, through Isaac, that the *promise* of God will now go forth into the future. The promise of God is now more than ever the focus; for we first here confront the question of how God's living promise will move from one generation to the next. How does God's overpowering promise of grace to Abraham and Sarah suddenly now became real in the life of Isaac and his descendants?

We will quickly learn that there is no set formula. The divine promise is sure and certain, yet that certainty is by no means translated into a human life without ambiguity. Quite the opposite. Isaac's son Jacob will inherit the promise, and we now begin the unfolding series of his life stories, beginning with his birth and only finally ending with his death. Jacob's life, from the very beginning, will appear haphazard, at times even chaotic. Old Testament narrative refuses to make life clean and neat, refuses to eliminate the ambivalence that is inherent in human frailty. It tells the stories of human life realistically, and despite the vast cultural distance

79

to be overcome we immediately recognize the frailty of our own world, indeed our own lives. Surrounding the whole of Jacob's life, even from before his birth, is the sign of God's promise; yet at no stage of Jacob's life is God's purpose fully clear to Jacob himself. Yet somehow, every single stage of life points forward to God's ultimate plan. God's purpose in Jacob's life controls everything, as we are told from the beginning. Yet God's action is full of profound mystery, and leaves room for amazing surprises to the very end. Indeed, so it is with each of us.

We enter the lives of Isaac and Rebekah, and we sadly confront a familiar problem. They have tried, and failed, to have children. Instantly we are of course reminded of Abraham and Sarah, but the same problem will recur in the Bible. The fact is, God's blessings (of every kind) seldom come into the world, into our lives, without struggle. We are given by the narrative the perspectives both of Isaac and Rebekah in turn. Isaac is now forty years old. It is long past time for him to start a family, according to his contemporary expectation. He prays to God, pleads before God, in hopes of a child. His prayer will be answered, and doubly so. Rebekah will conceive twins. When God answers prayer, he often gives even more than we ask, or even imagine. Yet Isaac must wait twenty years for the answer. He is sixty when the twins, Esau and Jacob, are finally born. God's blessings are fulsome, but they come only when he is ready.

Yet it is the perspective of Rebekah upon which the narrator focuses most sharply. The pregnancy is a difficult one. She too turns to God in prayer, yet hers is a fragment of despair, best translated by the King James Version: "If it be so, why am I thus?" What is the point of it all, if the pain is so unbearable? God answers her prayer of despondency with a brief, poetic declaration, which serves as a preface to the entire cycle of stories of Esau and Jacob. Your two sons will be nothing less than two nations, God tells Rebekah. Yet against the ordering of nature, the older will serve the younger. The mystery of God's overruling love is communicated to Rebekah alone, and her subsequent actions will confirm her implicit understanding. The first child is born ruddy and covered in hair. He is named Esau, a synonym of Seir (the country that will one day call him their ancestor), which sounds like the Hebrew word for hair. The brother comes out grabbing his heel, and is called Jacob, which sounds like the word for "heel." Esau from the beginning is some kind of hairy creature of the wild from *Grimms' Fairy Tales*. Jacob is a born grasper, always overreaching, always trying to climb into someone else's shoes. God's promise is real, but it does not cancel out the real particularities of human personality and their inherent moral ambiguity.

The narrative now quickly moves from the birth of Esau and Jacob to their adult lives, focusing on an episode pregnant with the future. Biblical narrative, as we have seen, is not modern history; it ignores calendar-time, and completely neglects those features of human life and society that interest the modern historian. Neither is biblical narrative biography. The biographer will look for developmental information that the narratives of the Bible pass over in sovereign silence, in total disinterest. Did the youth of Esau and Jacob affect the way they eventually worked out the trauma of their relationship as adults? The Bible is simply uninterested in the question. The focus, rather, is exclusively upon the unfolding of life under the promise of God. Biblical narrative is a witness of faith from beginning to end, and can rightly be understood according to its own inner logic only in relation to the promise to which it points.

Still, the promise of God does not depress or erase human individuality—far from it. The narrator takes pains to illustrate the growing differences in personality and lifestyle between Esau and Jacob, with quick strokes that define two fundamentally different ways of life. Esau is a hunter, a person of the field. His is a solitary life of danger and death, a life always tinged by violence, always alone on the hunt, eager for the kill. He eats only when he kills, otherwise he goes hungry; so, the possibility of death by starvation is his constant companion. He has no time or interest for the settled world of human culture or companionship. There is of course a clear edge to this brief biblical depiction of violent individualism, but it is not really accentuated.

Jacob by contrast is a shepherd. He lives the settled world of the tent, coordinating his life and activity with his fellows. He is not self-dependent; he is rather a member of a community of mutual respect and tolerance, which must get along, and thrive together or not at all. Jacob is a respectable participant in social life, and understands the moral obligations which bind person to person. Complicating this profound difference in personality and way of life is parental intervention. (Is it not always so, we may well wonder?) Isaac sides with Esau. The narrator is not shy about holding his shallow reason in suspicion; Isaac can (literally) taste the wild game in his mouth. Esau serves good meat! What a son! Our explanations are often abstract, philosophical; our real motives are commonly enough visceral, basic. Rebekah sides with Jacob. No reason is given, but we are reminded earlier in the narrative of her extended family in Mesopotamia. She too is well versed in the social arts of give and take. Perhaps she sees similar skills in her second son, the tent-dweller.

These differences between the two boys finally come into open conflict, and the issue at the heart of it all—though it remains in the background for the time being—is of course the divine promise. Yet it is important not to psychologize the episode, as much traditional exegesis does. We have already witnessed how the narratives of the Bible often operate on two different levels, in which the reader has more, and better, information than the participants. That is certainly here the case. *We* know that the promise is at stake as the brief episode before us unfolds. For Esau and Jacob, it is murky, ambiguous, and highly questionable.

Esau lives by what he kills; Jacob prudently stores his resources, and can live plentifully in times good and bad. Suddenly one day Esau bursts into Jacob's tent literally starving to death. He speaks abruptly, rudely, boorishly; give me some of that red stuff you are cooking so that I can gulp it down (the verb is the same used for animals feeding)! Once again, the narrator has a little fun at Esau's expense; his ancestors will call his country Edom, which sounds like the word for "red."

Jacob is ready with a portentous response: fine, but first you must sell me your birthright (the rights and privileges as head of family which come from being born first). Esau again responds less than thoughtfully, but with rather brutal realism; if I am going to die anyway, who cares about a birthright! Take it! Jacob insists that he swear, making it legal, and Esau does so. Jacob gives him what he is cooking; only now do we learn that it is lentil stew, hardly the kind of fare Esau is used to. In several quick verbs the text describes Esau's abrupt manner: he eats, he drinks, he rises, he leaves. Who cares about anything else if I am dying of hunger? A final comment by the narrator however makes clear that standing over this episode is a decisive transition: this is how Esau spurned his own birthright. We are led to remember God's original decision even before the two infants were born. God's sovereign will intersects human life from above; even when the *participants* can scarcely see the implications, we are given by the narrator to see that in the sight of *God* a momentous change has even now been set in motion.

We must think dialectically if we are to understand the profound biblical witness concerning human encounter with God. On the one hand, when the Bible talks about human beings, it tells stories, it narrates human action through space and time. Who we are is deeply affected by the variety of people we meet along the way, and the changing circumstances we face, both good and ill. Our families shape our very existence. Our personalities, so very mysterious in their origin and development, move us in certain directions. We do not so much experience life through time; time itself is shaped through our experience. The Bible never once suggests that life is meaningless; but it does insist that meaning cannot simply be read off the surface of life according to a pious formula. The meaning of life—every human life—takes time to mature and grow. Every experience we encounter adds to the total effect. Every new stage of life effects our own special way of being a human being. Psychological and sociological understandings of human personality and experience can be valuable in shaping insight. But the fact is, the biblical word cautions us to take the hard but fruitful journey of lived experience with a kind of basic admiration and validation. We are who we become; we become who we are. Every human life has a story to tell.

Yet, we must at the same time move to the second moment in the dialectic, equally important, indeed in the end far more basic and fundamental. God alone is the origin of your life. God alone is the goal of your life. God alone is the true measure of all your days. At no point in your life is God's purpose fully manifested to you; and yet at *every* point in your life, God's purpose is fully clear to him, and fully at work in your midst. Long before you were born, God set his seal of love upon you. His love for you did not begin with your birth; his promise of grace did not begin as you grew up in life.

His grace was already real for you life before you were born. He named the family into which you entered. Indeed, before God made the universe, God knew you by name, and called you as his own. God's love in the Bible is electing love. He chooses to love us, not because of who we are, but because of who he is. His love is not based on anything you have done, not based on your merit or moral achievement; it is based on grace alone, sheer divine merciful favor. For that very reason you can without fail count on his love. No matter what circumstances your life brings, God's love for you is forever secure, forever assured. God's love for you was already there at the beginning of your life, and it will be there long after your life on this earth comes to an end. His love for you is eternal.

Is there no intersection between the human and divine sides of the dialectic? Indeed, there is, of the most intimate sort. The promise of God is a miraculous *event* in which God enters directly into the real life—the messy details of ordinary existence—of flesh and blood human persons. God's living promise does not hover above human well-being in a realm of ideas cut off from lived human experience. Not at all. Yet just here we must enter a note of caution. Even from a literary point of view, we must remember that we are watching Jacob's life unfold from a twofold perspective; that is, we as readers are given information about God's embrace of his future that Jacob himself does not—or does not yet—have. We must learn to see human life, as it were, looking *down* from the divine promise, where the future is certain, but also *under* the divine promise, where even the next day or the next moment seems up for grabs. God always does what he does for a purpose, and that purpose is without fail full of grace and wonder. But he does not always share that purpose with us. God's action in our lives is often indirect, where we cannot see him; God's presence is often hidden, far beyond our awareness. God's purpose is always the one, true, ultimate guide of all reality, including my reality; but it is often filled with great surprise. God does the unexpected, overturning ordinary custom. God works behind the scenes, where we least expect to find him. Good plans fall apart, only to be replaced by an even greater plan; circumstances spin out of our control, only for us to discover that an entirely new direction lay up ahead. One stage of life comes to an end, yet life is not over, for a new season of life quickly springs up. Never underestimate the capacity of God to astonish.

We ask one final question as we enter the cycle of Jacob stories. Does God's free and gracious promise work in spite of human personality, or through it? The answer of course is "yes." On the one hand, the narrative is hardly shy in portraying Jacob as an eager social climber, working as hard as he can (from the moment of birth!) to get ahead of his slightly older brother. Jacob is no saint. Yet on the other hand, he persists. He never quits. He will, as we shall see, never relent in his single-minded pursuit of the divine blessing, regardless of the means chosen. The text leaves us to consider: there is something to be said for tenacity. Where Esau so flippantly *throws away* literally everything for a moment's relief, Jacob *risks* everything, time and again, and will not relent. God's enduring promise will find its echo in sheer human perseverance.

14. Wrestling with God

Genesis 32:23–33

FROM THE MOMENT HE is born—indeed, from before his birth—the life story of Jacob unfolds along a twofold trajectory.

On the one hand, there is the personality of Jacob, guiding the unfolding journey of his life. As is his name, so is he: the "Supplanter," the grabber, the grasper, in short the cheater. Jacob is a born mischief-maker, always fighting a perceived enemy, trying to step into someone else's shoes. The first such enemy is his own brother Esau. He cruelly tricks his brother into selling the family birthright, a preface to the saga of his entire life story. Then, with the guiding hand of his mother Rebekah, he cleverly outmaneuvers his brother Esau into receiving from their father Isaac the patriarchal blessing. Despite Isaac's clear preference for his firstborn son Esau, the old blind man is outwitted by his younger son in a way that can only be described as morally offensive. Yet the blessing is given to Jacob, and once given is conferred and received as an objective reality. Nothing can be done to alter what has already been settled once and for all. The bitter cry of Esau—what about me, bless me too, Father!—surely evokes our sympathy at the human cost of Jacob's manipulation. And yet it is crucial to realize that the focus of the story, however brilliant in its depiction of Esau's anguish, lies elsewhere.

Jacob's second "enemy" is his own distant relative Laban. Because of the murderous anger of Esau, Jacob is forced to flee his homeland; indeed he will never see his cherished mother Rebekah alive again. He is instructed by Isaac to find a wife among the same clan from which Rebekah came, and Jacob sets off on a lonely journey across the vast spaces of the ancient Near Eastern world. He encounters, and falls in love with, Rachel, the younger daughter of Laban, and contracts with Laban to serve him for seven years in order to marry her. But the trickster is tricked; he finds himself married to Leah instead on his wedding night, and must serve another seven years

to have Rachel as well. In the end, Leah and Rachel, and their maids Zil-
pah and Bilhah, will bear twelve sons to Jacob, the ancestors of the twelve
tribes of Israel. Once again, Jacob finds a way through manipulation and
cunning to increase his wealth, this time at Laban's expense, though Laban
is hardly innocent. Now with a large family and numerous possessions,
Jacob is becoming, like Abraham and Isaac his father before him, a true
patriarch. Yet he lacks one thing: he lives in a foreign land, a refugee. Only
if he comes home to the land of promise can he fully inherit the blessing he
once wrested from his brother.

Yet the second truth about Jacob's life—ruling it, guiding it, overruling it in turn—is the active presence and intervention of the divine promise.
Even before Esau and Jacob are born, God tells Rebekah their mother that
the younger, Jacob, will rule over the older. The entire moral and social order
of life is already overturned by God's active will, even before the children
are born. The blessing of Isaac comes to Jacob, not just as a case of mistaken
identity, but as an objective reality that alters forever Jacob's status before God
and humankind: "May God give you of the dew of heaven . . . Let peoples
serve you, and nations bow down before you" (Gen 27:27–29).

And then, suddenly, as Jacob is fleeing east alone for his life from
the wrath of Esau, as the sun is setting in the desert, God himself for the
first time encounters him directly, and repeats the miraculous promise of
blessing already given to Abraham and Isaac. In a dream Jacob hears: "I
am the Lord, the God of Abraham your father, and the God of Isaac; the
land on which you lie I will give to you and to your offspring; and your
offspring shall be like the dust of the earth . . ." (Gen 28:13–14). It is the
same promise given to Abraham before him; that God will bless not only
Jacob, but through him all the families of the earth; and that God's freely
given promise will guide and direct his way always, never relenting until Jacob has in the end fully inherited the blessing, and returned to the
land of promise. There is no attempt to adjust the divine gift to the human
machinations of Jacob that preceded it; as sheer gift, the promise comes
into his life freely from above, by grace alone apart from all moral striving
or achievement, indeed despite all moral failure.

And yet, neither does the narrative attempt to explain the fundamental
contradiction between the abundance of the promise and the sheer fragility
of Jacob's circumstances. The text only records that Jacob responded with
astonished affirmation, and went on his lone journey. God speaks directly to
Jacob a third time in the land of his distant family origin, as Laban's bullying
becomes outright enmity: "Return to the land of your ancestors and to your
kindred, and I will be with you" (Gen 31:3). It is time to go back home, this
time as a wealthy man with flocks, possessions, and a large family. He has

fought his enemies, Esau and Laban, and triumphed. Only now will he realize that his true adversary all along is indeed his only true Helper.

It is an extraordinary night, this final night in the land of his distant ancestors, as Jacob ushers his family and all his possessions across the final physical barrier separating him from his brother Esau: the river Jabbok. The night crossing could only have been both difficult and dangerous, both for the large family and the large flock, and would have taken its toll on the patriarch Jacob. They all make it across, but he crosses back over one last time, perhaps to make certain that nothing and no one has been inadvertently left behind. He will spend his last night in the distant land of his ancestors alone, now returning *to* the land of promise, just as he once spent his first night alone, fleeing *from* the land of promise. Then he met God in a beautiful and glorious dream, just as the sun was setting; now he will meet God in a very different way, hardly beautiful, but in its own way no less glorious, just as the sun is about to rise.

A man comes and wrestles with him; God comes and wrestles with him. We know from the narrative that it is a man; we know from the narrative that it is clearly God. As elsewhere in the stories of the Bible, God often comes incognito, no less himself for being at the same time other than himself. God is free to be himself now this way, now that way; now glorious in vision, now hidden in the figure of a man wrestling along the riverbank, yet the very same God. And with stunning and profound mystery, the narrator states simply: Jacob is not losing the wrestling match! So his opponent merely touches the hip of Jacob, and it is thrown out of joint; he is too injured to continue the match.

Yet *still* Jacob clings to his opponent, who demands to be released as the sun is about to rise. It is not mere stubborn tenacity on Jacob's part (or not only that); he wants something that only his opponent can give. He wants his blessing, God's blessing, the blessing that only his divine opponent can give. He refuses to let him—God—go until God blesses him; such is the simple but overpowering statement of the narrator. Jacob now understands: he has not been wrestling all his life with figures such as Esau and Laban; he has been wrestling with God! And now he is here with God by the banks of the river Jabbok; he clings to one hope, one desire, one ultimate goal only, that God himself will surround his life with his ultimate goodness. The divine figure asks him his name, and he tells him, "Jacob." We recall that in asking his name, he is asking for the essence of his very character, which is to supplant, to cheat, to strive. The figure—clearly now God—gives him a new name, Israel, and explains that this patriarch has throughout his life striven with both God and human beings, and has won. He has prevailed— we think of Esau and Laban; but also—against God!

Yet as soon as we are shocked by the statement, we are given greater context for its understanding. Jacob—now Israel—in turn asks for *God's* name, and God refuses to give it. God will give the blessing, will even be overtaken by the victory of Jacob; but at the very same time, he in sovereign freedom will remain true to himself, utterly free from human grasping, human striving, human definition. Jacob knows that he has seen God, face-to-face, and so names the place accordingly. Yet as the sun rises, Jacob limps away, wounded and bruised from the struggle. He is at the same time both blessed and broken; he does at the same time inherit the divine blessing he so desperately desires and yet fails to capture the sovereign God in his clutches. He sees God face-to-face and lives; yet he will for the rest of his life bear the scars of his vision.

The God of the Bible is not an idea, or a principle, or a metaphysical or theological proposition; nor is God a symbol of underlying human experience. God is a living reality who encounters us in the lived reality of the here and now. God is not a convenient idea, subject to human political and moral manipulation. God is not a projection of human aspiration, however noble. God is an utterly free, living reality, whose identity is primary, and whose sovereign existence radically precedes every human response. He encounters us, not in the convenience of our own cherished ideals, but as an event which breaks into our lives from above, totally unprepared.

He does not come when we are strong, but often enough when we are at our weakest moments. He does not enter our lives when we are most sure of ourselves, but when we are most exposed, most vulnerable, most alone in his world. The event of his love does not exclude all other loves, but it certainly puts them all into proper perspective; it is with God alone that we have to do, if we are truly to learn to be human, truly to learn how to love, truly to live the blessed life on this earth. When he meets us, he takes away every human security, that he alone might be our gracious refuge. He finds us alone, that he might establish us again, surrounded among a vast host of his people. When one danger is behind us and another danger is in front of us, full of fear and anxiety, he enters our lives, the only One whom we must truly fear, therefore the only One who can relieve all lesser fears and chase away all our anxieties forever, giving us his blessed peace. God encounters us in weakness, that his grace might be sufficient in all things.

He comes in both freedom and love. In his love, he meets us where we are. We do not need to labor to find him; he finds us, and enters our lives so unmistakably that we cannot escape his grasp. He will not let us go. He knows us better than we know ourselves, and therefore holds us close to himself even when we would walk away. He does not overpower us with his love, but gently guides and blesses us along the way. He gives us nothing less than himself, which is infinitely greater than all reality. Jacob watches his family, his flocks, his possessions cross the river; only when he meets *God* face-to-face does he truly find the blessing he seeks. God in love blesses us; but in every blessing his presence is the gift. Yet in giving himself to us in loving encounter, God does not give himself away. In freedom, God always remains true to himself. He surrounds us with his blessing, but he himself will not be enclosed by human pious causes. He embraces us fully with his unconditional love; yet God alone remains the true measure of all good, and he never surrenders his sovereign good into the wasteland of human moral abstractions. He makes himself fully known to us, in every way; yet he does not disclose the ultimate purpose of his will, which even for his children yet remains a mystery, for which we wait in hope, day by day. God is free to love us because he is God; God loves us only in freedom, because he shares his divinity with no one. God *alone* is God.

And so we come to the struggle with God which is the reality of our lives. The living God is primary; the human response is secondary; and therein lies our lifelong wrestling with God. There is of course no struggle, no wrestling, where we can conveniently fit God into our pious human schemes, our pious human projects, our personal agendas. There is no struggle, but nor is there any growth in faith, any expansion of insight. It is just here that the living God enters our lives from above, and turns our religious world upside down. *He* seizes our thoughts and hearts, that we might know him rightly, and worship him truly. We wrestle with God, because *God* himself first comes into our lives to wrestle with us, to wrest away from us the illusion of control that we falsely maintain over ourselves, our world, and even over God.

His goal is not to defeat or destroy us, but to teach us the true knowledge of himself, and his way in the world. The will of God is that we learn to know and love him as he is, and thereby to receive the greatest joy in human life. We come before him, not as we pretend to be before others, but as we are in truth, sinners in need of grace. Even in our exposure to him we resist him; yet even in our resistance to him, he will not let us go, and that is his mercy to us, that is his genuine blessing. Yet come we must, for we desire God, only God, in all our folly and self-deception, in all our life struggles and worries. We would be with God, and God alone, for he himself has graciously come to us, to abide with us.

Encounter with God always brings a cost. In the Bible, every human life has multiple dimensions from which it can be viewed; here it is the physical dimension of life that is thrust forward. Jacob limps away. God is in our head, and in our hearts; he is, according to the Scriptures, also in our bodies, and as we long for him and follow him, we all bear the marks of his service. Most of the great battles of faith in some way or another involve the human body. We are not immaterial spirits living inside of a machine; we are whole creatures, and the struggle of faith often includes the physical ailments and limitations of life. Temptation strikes when we are tired and frustrated after a long day, often in solitude. The hard work of discipleship brings fatigue and exhaustion.

The desire to know God fully, and to do his will, costs us everything, and for many that includes weathering the loss of physical comfort. We cannot turn away from God, for that is to lose everything. The paradox is, just as the cost of discipleship can bring physical hardship, so the Lord of our lives is the only true comfort and hope. We come from him in difficult struggle, only to return to him in renewed joy. God himself makes us weak, that he alone might give us new strength, for his strength is made perfect only in our weakness. We are all wounded in spiritual struggles; we all come to recognize with humility our utter dependence on God for all things; yet precisely in our lowest moments we are upheld by sheer exultation.

Wrestling with God means change, radical transformation of our very existence. It is not we who make God in our image, much as we try. Quite the contrary, it is we who learn to know God as he is, and in knowing him are shaped by him into the image of Christ. Indeed, the marks we bear in our bodies, are they not the marks of Christ? God is a living reality who claims our entire being for himself. Authentic encounter with the living God forever changes who we are. Faith is not a form of identity crisis. We do not struggle to find who we are, and come up with "God" as an answer to our quest. There is certainly in the Bible the constant quest to understand ourselves in the light of God. But the crisis does not come from us at all; it comes *from God*, who wrestles with us until we learn to know him as he is. What does knowledge *not* bring? It brings the beauty of truth; the joy of discovery; the sheer delight of human relationship to the living reality of God. For we discover a God who loves us more than we can possibly conceive, who wants for our lives more abundance than we can possibly imagine, who makes us new, not once, but each day. When does the struggle of faith with God end? Only with the breaking of the day, God's new Day, when all will be made clear and certain.

15. A Shattered Dream

Genesis 37:12–36

GOD'S PROMISE HAS COME to Abraham, to Isaac, and to Jacob. A major transition now occurs in chapter 37, using the familiar formula that structures the book of Genesis theologically: "Jacob settled in the land where his father had lived as an alien, the land of Canaan. This is the story of the family of Jacob." Jacob too remains an immigrant nomad, just as his ancestor Abraham and his father Isaac. The remainder of the book of Genesis will focus on the figure of Joseph in a tightly knit and brilliantly portrayed story, different in kind from the complex of individual narratives which make up the life histories of Abraham, Isaac, and Jacob. But there is more than narrative style that characterizes the break. Joseph is nowhere in the Bible considered one of the patriarchs of Israel, despite his importance in the book of Genesis. He has a prominent role, a vital role, in preserving the people of God who inherit the promise of God; but he is himself not the one who inherits the promise.

Indeed, the opening verse gives us our clue. We are instructed by the narrator that we are now turning to family of *Jacob*, not just to Joseph. Though most of the remaining material focuses on the Joseph story, there are two vital exceptions. On the one hand, Jacob *himself* will return to the story at the end of Joseph's travail in Egypt, where Jacob will pronounce the family blessing upon all twelve sons, the future tribes of Israel. The future belongs not just to Joseph but to the whole people of God. Perhaps more importantly, on the other hand, the Joseph story itself is interrupted by a brief narrative concerning *Judah*, as we will see. In fact, it is not through Joseph, but through Judah—despite his disobedience—that the promise of redemption is to come. So, these are indeed family matters, of Jacob's clan, though the story of Joseph in brilliant splendor is certainly at the center.

We meet Joseph in the story at an exact age, seventeen years old, not yet a full-grown man, no longer a child. As we would say today, he is still a teen-ager, not yet old enough for direct responsibility, yet at least able to help out his father. In fact, an inexperienced and self-absorbed youth, Joseph makes one mistake after another. Above all his immaturity is shown by his utter lack of *foresight*; he cannot envision what he cannot see. He will grow, and mature, and indeed gain profound wisdom as the biblical story of his life unfolds. But it is important to be clear-eyed at the beginning, as traditional commentators often are not: Joseph is a spoiled and immature imp.

The first mistake he makes is to tell tales on his older brothers. They are the ones who do all the work as keepers of the flock. Joseph is just there as a "helper." But like helpers from time immemorial Joseph takes it upon himself to report what he considers the bad behavior of his older brothers. Who likes an informer, especially an informer who does not share in the labor? Who can put up with a tattletale?

The second mistake is made by Jacob. He gives to Joseph—and to Jo-seph alone among the brothers—a very special coat. It is a luxurious coat, made for pleasure not for work, with long sleeves and long sweeping lines to the ground. The brothers are not stupid; they see the preferential treatment given to Joseph. He is obviously the favorite of their father, the very same one who tells tales but does not labor by their side. The text is frank; they hate him for it. They cannot utter a peaceful word to him; literally there can be no "shalom" between them.

Then Joseph makes his own remaining mistakes. He dreams a dream to the effect that he will rule over his brothers, makes the dream public, and their hatred multiplies. He dreams a second dream, filled with brazen pre-tensions of grandeur, which includes the servitude of even Jacob. The sheer self-important conceit of the dream startles even the boy's doting father, yet the narrator makes clear that the dream lingers long in Jacob's haunted imagination. Jealousy and hatred have now reached a fevered pitch among the brothers; *four* times the word *hatred* is used in these brief opening verses. This is not a happy situation. We ask: are these dreams from God? The bibli-cal witness certainly makes clear that they are, especially in what unfolds. We ask: are these dreams from the heart and mind of an arrogant young man? We can again only answer yes, as the biblical witness portrays the immature youth who stands so clearly before us. God continues to appear concealed in mystery, indirectly, shaping human life unaware.

And so, we come to the real beginning of Joseph's story with an im-possible mission that he cannot possibly fulfill, a life seemingly doomed to failure from the outset by his own loving father, however unknowingly. The remaining sons of Jacob—Joseph's brothers—are in the fields pasturing the flocks near Shechem. Jacob calls his son Joseph and gives him instructions to visit Shechem to see how things are going, and Joseph professes his ready willingness to carry out his father's wishes. Joseph's reply is couched in the language of obedience: "here am I." The language is of course highly ambivalent. Joseph is ready to serve his father; he is, without knowing it, ready to serve the purpose of God, which will take him to a place neither he nor his father can possibly anticipate. Jacob compounds the irony by his choice of words. He tells Joseph to see to the welfare (shalom) of his brothers and the well-being (shalom) of the flocks. We have already learned that the brothers of Joseph cannot and will not regard him with shalom; why on earth would Jacob send him on a mission of shalom into what is clearly a hostile climate filled with nothing but foreboding? The text is silent, brooding, menacing. This cannot end well.

The young Joseph wanders off from Hebron in the direction of Shechem. It would be the last time he would see his father's house. We again catch a glimpse of the sheltered naivete of this young man, which will of course so quickly and so violently change in such a very short time. He is found by a stranger simply wandering around in the fields, not sure of where his brothers are, not sure of where the flocks are, clearly not sure even of where *he* is. He is reduced to asking this stranger where his family and flocks are located, and the unnamed person knows better than Joseph himself how to find them, so unprepared is he for the simplest of human responsibilities; this same young man who will one day be given the greatest and gravest of human responsibilities—but that is far over the horizon. As Joseph follows the detailed instructions of the nameless man, the viewpoint of the narrator shifts to the perspective of the brothers. Naivete gives way to hatred, which now finds it opportunity to strike, and to strike with utterly lethal intent.

Unlike Joseph, who sees nothing, the brothers see him coming from a distance, and prepare for his arrival. The text is blunt and unambiguous; they conspire to kill him. The narrator records the heated conversation, which must be carefully observed. Their hatred focuses on the fact of the dreams of this hated dreamer. What is at issue? Joseph, they believe, has been empowered from above to dream, and his dreams have the power to shape the future. The only way to kill the dream is to kill the man, and so be free of his arrogant pretensions of lordship—and of course the potential future involved. The ironies of course abound; by thinking to kill the dreamer and his dreams, they bring them to fulfillment, yet not to their hurt, but to their ultimate salvation. But that is still concealed in the mystery of God's purpose hidden behind human events.

Their plan, at first, is simple. Grab him, kill him, throw his body in a deep pit to rot away. We can tell our father, so they think, that he has been killed by a wild animal, and so be free of his dreams at last. Our future will be our own. Reuben (the oldest) at least shows some humanity. He tries to persuade them simply to throw him into the pit alive, where he will die of hunger and thirst. He apparently has some vague hidden plan in mind to pull him out of the hole later, and save Joseph's life from the brothers' fury. The brothers agree to Reuben's plan, and when Joseph arrives, they strip off the hated luxury coat, and throw him alive into the pit, which at the time is empty of water. He will die soon enough, is the point. And then, the text records with evident and brutal realism, they sit down to eat a meal, obviously unconcerned and even oblivious to the screams of their brother from the pit, empty of food and dry.

It so happens that, at the precise moment of their meal, a caravan of nomadic spice traders passes by on the immemorial route going down to Egypt. Another brother steps forward, this time Judah. He argues for yet another variant of the plan; let us *sell* Joseph as a slave to these traders. We must take his coat and dip it in the blood of a sheep, in order to prove to our father Jacob that he is dead. And so it happens. When Reuben returns from some brief errand and sees what has happened he is utterly undone, for he intended to save Joseph for their father. But no matter, the plan is carried out, and they bring the bloodied robe to Jacob, who immediately assumes the obvious; Joseph has been mauled and killed by wild animals in the harsh countryside. The brothers not only need to convince their father Jacob for psychological reasons that Joseph is dead; there are legal reasons involved. Jacob is, as it were, the coroner; his pronunciation of Joseph's death is legally binding. The brothers are guiltless, at least in legal terms. Jacob is inconsolable with grief, a grief he will carry to his grave, he tells his family.

Meanwhile, the spice traders sell Joseph as a slave in Egypt to a highly placed official in the service of Pharaoh. There, the young man without foresight will learn to make plans for the whole world; the pampered youth will face prison and near death, only to find himself exalted to highest honor; the favorite of his father Jacob will become the favorite of the king of all Egypt. But what of his family? What of the hate of his brothers? What of his father Jacob? And above all, what of the *promise of God*?

The word of God's promise does not hover above the real world in which we live. Quite the opposite; it enters directly into the messy reality of daily life. Life can be exalted and uplifting, but often enough it is surrounded with pettiness, sordid human folly, mundane jealousies of every kind and sort. We may meet the most exquisite human courage along the way, but we also sadly enough will find plenty of callous insensitivity, egotism, and yes, sheer hatred among humankind. We see hatred in the world around us, and that is bad enough; yet we are fully aware that every family has its own problems, no matter how successfully those problems may be concealed from the world. Life is complicated. The word of God's promise does not leave us, abandoned, to our own fate, not at all. But neither does it say: you must get your house in order first, or I will not come to be with you, will not come to make my dwelling in your home and in your life. God's promise—which is the living reality of Jesus Christ himself—comes to meet us where we are, not to leave us in our folly and misery, but to transform our existence in every respect. But he does not wait for us. He comes to us, even before we are aware he is there. He enters our lives even beyond our ways of knowing his presence. And he changes everything.

Nor does the gospel come and work only through our perfections. For the fact is that we have none. We all have good qualities, no doubt; but all are captive to the inward pull of the human self that asserts itself over against God and the human world around us. We are all lords of our own little kingdoms. Yet God is merciful; God is slow to anger, abounding in steadfast loving-kindness. He works through even our imperfections to make good his perfect will for our lives. He chastens our arrogant pride until it becomes fruitful self-confidence. He molds our dreams of glory until they serve his purpose of genuine discipleship. He shatters our high aspirations until they reach even higher to the throne of his grace alone.

We learn from the story of Joseph the unlimited power of God's transforming grace to change human life under his care. People change. Over time, people grow, and mature. Their perspectives on themselves are deepened; their openness and compassion for others are widened; their natural abilities are seasoned. People change, and as a result their relationships to others are changed as well. Now, the Bible is realistically aware of the limits of human change; the fact is that some people will never get past the blind spots that hold them back. Nevertheless, the Bible presents human beings as capable of even profound transformation. And it is in such transformation that human discipleship unfolds. One thing is certain: we are all changing, for better or for worse. We cannot simply stand still in life. We are either moving forward toward the call of God, or we are moving backward, away from his merciful love. We are either growing up in life or dwindling down. The idea of standing still in human moral existence is an illusion. If our goal in life is simply to remain where we are, we will lose even what we have. Jesus said: "To those who have more will be given; but from those who have nothing even what they have will be taken away." Real change requires hard work, but it is worth the effort.

Real change brings openness to the world around us. We are all tempted to believe that the universe necessarily conforms to our limited experience. We are all tempted to live as if the world revolves around us. We shine the light of our experience on the world around us, and are not surprised to discover that we see exactly what we expect to see. Christian discipleship changes the way we *see* the world. Our lives become a mirror of what is truly there. We see the reality of other people as if for the first time. We notice lives very different from our own. Truly to see other people for who they are is an extraordinary gift.

We cannot see if we judge. Judgment of other people comes all too easily. We measure other people by the standards of ideal humanity in our own minds. If others do not conform to those standards, then they must surely be lacking. Yet who are we to form a standard of ideal humanity? And who are we to apply that standard in measurement to others? The gospel dissolves the measurement of other human beings. Measurement is replaced by sympathy. We begin to imagine what it must be like to live as other people do. The gaps that separate their experience from ours are no longer a threat; now they are perceived as invitation to discovery. Now we are no longer ready to judge; now instead we are ready to understand, and to leave all judgment in the hands of God. Withhold judgment for the sake of clarity, and a new world will open up before your eyes.

To live is to change; but where does authentic change come from? To grow is to gain sympathy for others, but how are we to discover the lives that are truly there, often right in front of us? We grow most in times of struggle and suffering. No one wants to suffer, but God uses suffering to make changes in our lives. In times of loss, we discover what truly matters most in this world. In moments of grief, we are awakened to the infinite worth of love for others. In periods of adversity, we are challenged to excel. It is when we are removed from the security of our comfort zones that genuine and lasting change becomes a reality. We can no longer lean on what is easy and familiar; instead, we must look for new resources we never knew were there. The sheer shock of the new opens our eyes to what has been there all along. The gospel invades our comfort zones, and sets us on the adventure of discipleship.

16. Courage

Genesis 38

THE STORY OF TAMAR and Judah is most often treated as an inexplicable interruption in the otherwise seamless web of the Joseph story. And certainly, in the final shape of the book of Genesis, the story is quite clearly inserted just after the beginning of the Joseph story, where it dramatically breaks the narrative flow. While some modern commentators have tried to fold the story into the larger Joseph cycle through various verbal resonances, the effort has been misplaced at best. The fact is, the story of Tamar does interject itself decisively into the narrative continuity of the Joseph story; the question is not whether, but why?

Traditional commentaries have little if anything to say about the larger questions concerning the theological significance of the chapter, and are largely concerned with condemning the morality of Tamar, and saving the morality of Judah, which in fact runs against the moral grain of the text itself. Tamar, as we will see, is clearly set forth as the model of faithful Israel, even though she is a Canaanite; while Judah is most certainly condemned for his faithlessness, even though he is the son of the patriarch, Jacob. Still, the chapter is not a tale in morality, though the ethical dimensions are clearly near the surface.

We will return to the broader question of the significance of the chapter after we have recounted the story. However, to anticipate: we must keep always in front of our mind in reading the book of Genesis the profound significance of the *promise* of God. It is the promise of God—here not of land, but of future posterity—which is at stake in this chapter, and which provides the life-and-death quality to the unfolding drama, so important as to temporarily cut right through the larger story of Joseph. We now rehearse the basic shape of the story.

Judah has moved away from the rest of his family, the sons of Jacob, and is now married to a Canaanite woman. She bears him three sons, named Er, Onan, and Shelah. His firstborn, Er, takes a Canaanite wife named Tamar. For reasons unspecified, Er is "displeasing to the Lord" and God takes his life. According to immemorial custom (the so-called law of levirate marriage), it is now the duty of the second brother to impregnate the widow, Tamar, so that she can raise a son as the posterity of Er, the firstborn of Judah. Onan refuses to fulfill that duty—he will in fact be giving Tamar a son who will disinherit his current exalted status as the oldest living male—so God takes his life as well. Now only Shelah is left among the three sons. Judah lamely promises Tamar that someday Shelah will do the duty of providing an heir, but the text tells us what we have already guessed: Judah has no intention of fulfilling his vow to Tamar, custom be hanged.

Finally, Judah's own wife dies. After the ritual period of mourning is over, Judah and his close friend Hirah travel up to Timnah where the sheep are being sheered, always a time of joy and revelry. Tamar finds out, and acts quickly. She takes off the garb of a widow that she has been wearing all this time, and puts on the garb of a prostitute, including the veil. She positions herself on the road to Timnah, where Judah and Hirah are sure to pass. The narrator reminds us of her motive; she is fully aware that Shelah is being withheld by Judah, and now has no recourse to fulfill her obligation to perpetuate the lineage of Er, the firstborn of Judah.

Judah does in fact see her; does in fact assume that she is a prostitute, and makes arrangements with her for a tryst, having no idea that it is Tamar, his daughter-in-law. He promises her a young sheep in payment, but when he cannot provide it immediately, she asks for certain crucial pledges: his seal and his staff, both personal identifying markers in antiquity. The tryst consummated, she conceives, and returns home to resume her widow's garb. Later, Judah sends his friend—Judah is too embarrassed to go himself—to retrieve his precious personal items, and deliver the promised sheep. But the prostitute—actually Tamar—is nowhere to be found. Fearful of being exposed for their naivete, they simply let the matter drop.

Three months later, the pregnant Tamar begins to show, and Judah is informed. His righteous indignation knows no bounds; in fury he announces a punishment far more severe than usual. She is to be burned, not stoned, for her outrageous immorality! Within inches of her death, making no public protest whatsoever, Tamar with profound courage delivers simply and straightforwardly a discreet but decisive moral prodding of Judah. She sends the seal and the staff, and sends word that she is pregnant by the man to whom these belong. They can only belong to one man, and it is Judah. Yet she does not expose him to public ridicule, as he did her. She simply reminds him of the duty that was his all along—to make certain that his own eldest son should have an heir. She, Tamar, has acted faithfully in fulfilling that obligation, despite Judah's repeated denials of her rightful claim. And in the end, he admits she is absolutely in the right all along.

She gives birth to twin boys, Perez and Zerah. *Perez* thus becomes the one to inherit the legacy of the firstborn. Tamar was right all along.

Few now return to the question: why is the story of Judah and Tamar inserted so abruptly into the unfolding cycle of the story of Joseph? Yet the question is essential, even vital to the biblical story. Recall that we are following in this section of Genesis the family history of Jacob, not of Joseph; and Judah is one of the twelve sons of Jacob. But why this son, and the strange encounter with his daughter-in-law? To answer the question, we must first remember that the theological framework for the story of the family of Jacob is the *promise* to the patriarchs of both land and posterity; here the promise of future *posterity* is at issue. But in what sense? We must look backward into the patriarchal narratives, and forward to the final appearance of Jacob in the book of Genesis, to find our answer.

First, looking backward, we find two astounding texts, both involved in the divine promise. After God changes the name of Abram to Abraham, he makes the promise of future posterity even more explicit: "I will make you exceedingly fruitful; and I will make nations of you, and kings shall come from you" (Gen 17:6). God's gracious promise to Abraham includes not only the nations of the earth, but the *rulers* of those nations. Then, Jacob himself receives a new name, and the same promise of regal posterity: God tells him, "Your name is Jacob; no longer shall you be called Jacob, but Israel shall be your name . . . a nation and a company of nations shall come from you, and kings shall spring from you" (Gen 35:10–11). The promise of God reaches forward toward a new dimension of *royal* lineage.

Second, looking forward, as the dying Jacob gathers his sons around him for the final blessing before his death, only *Judah* receives the unexpected promise: "The scepter shall not depart from Judah, nor the ruler's staff from between his feet, until tribute comes to him, and the obedience of the peoples is his" (Gen 49:10). More than just a promise of future royalty, it is through the line of Judah that God's redemptive blessing will come upon Israel, and through Israel upon the whole world. Of course, as readers of the canon of Scripture, we know that ten generations later, King David will be born in the family of Judah, the direct ancestor of Judah and Tamar, through their son Perez.

In the community of faith in Jesus Christ that treasures the whole Bible, we can only look one step further into the future of the divine promise. Jesus Christ, the Son of God and Son of Man, the Savior of the world, is born the son of David. And so in the genealogy of the Gospel of Matthew, Tamar and Judah—the very story we have just recounted—have their rightful place: "Jacob the father of Judah and his brothers, and Judah the father of Perez and Zerah by Tamar . . ." (Matt 1:3). Tamar becomes the first of four women in the genealogy of Jesus, all in some sense "outsiders," just as Mary is treated as an outsider because of the mystery of her pregnancy, just as Jesus himself will become the one true outsider in the Bible whose love encircles all the world. The story of Joseph is rightly considered a masterpiece of biblical faith; yet the enigmatic, brief story of Tamar and Judah that briefly interrupts it points to the unshakable hope of the future under the divine promise, God's promised rule through his coming King.

Affirming the promise of God is not about perfect or even ideal conditions of human existence. The living promise of God, rather, enters directly into the messy imperfections of the world all around us. Sometimes the circumstances of life leave us only one way forward. It is not an easy way, but a difficult one; it is not a choice we would make, but indeed a burden we must carry. The promise of God enters a world filled with shame and guilt; a world overflowing with human passions, parental anxiety, love both requited and unrequited, honor and dishonor, all churning up in the entangled labyrinth that is human relationship. The divine promise does not wait until we have made things right in order to enter lives; just the opposite. The divine promise enters the real circumstances of our lives, exactly where we are, and with often unimagined results, makes a new path forward. The promise of God always carries one message: there is a goal for your life. The risen Lord Jesus Christ is himself the one true goal of your life, and indeed of all human life, indeed of the entire cosmos. That goal does not suddenly make your life perfect. But it does make your true direction clear, and does set the oftentimes painful and difficult setbacks of life in their proper perspective. Follow the goal of God's promise wherever it leads, and you will never lose your way.

True courage is a rare gift. It is of course easy enough to stand with the moral crowd in opposition to the immoral and make one's voice heard. We are reassured that we are in the right, that God is on our side, that all is right with the world. But what happens when the opposite is the case; when we are called by the gospel to stand against the moral crowd, and are condemned by them as immoral? Often the voice of human moral custom says: no, it must be done this way! You cannot do it any other way; for this alone is right! True courage recognizes that there is a higher authority than human moral custom, and that is God's word. When God's word speaks, let the whole world of human moral custom be turned upside down. For the sake of God's word, let all the clamor of human moral voices fall silent.

Jesus Christ alone is God's gracious word of promise to humanity, and true courage will listen to his voice alone.

Courage seizes upon the word of God's promise in Jesus Christ, and embraces it with head held high. True courage follows the way of God's freely given promise to the end, where new blessing always awaits. It does not take courage to stand with the moral majority, even though the morality of the majority contradicts the will of God. It takes courage to stand under and with the will of God *against* the moral majority, knowing that in the end a life well-pleasing to God is infinitely worth living, even if it means standing under the sign of rejection by the pious crowd. Do not lose your focus on the one thing that truly matters, which is to do God's revealed will.

An essential dimension of courage is tenacity, indeed dogged resilience. The Bible is not filled with stories of success. In fact, it is filled with stories of failure. Abraham dies without inheriting the land of promise, apart from a grave in which to bury his family. Moses dies on the edge of the promised land, forbidden by God himself to cross the river Jordan. King David loses the throne to his son Absalom, and comes within an inch of losing his life, but for the bravery and shrewdness of his supporters. Good King Josiah leads the great reform of the kingdom in accordance with the law of God, then suddenly dies in battle on the plains of Megiddo, all hopes of reform utterly dashed to the ground. The prophets, one by one, proclaim the truth of God's living will, and pay for it with struggles unending, and ultimate rejection. Jesus enters the world the Son of God and savior of all humankind, and is nailed to the cross.

In all these cases, what stands out is not the success of the narrated character, but the resilience and tenacity in the face of unspeakable opposition. And yet, hovering over all these accounts is the living promise of God, which gathers them into the redemptive purpose of divine love for the whole world. So it is with Tamar; so it is with us. We cannot always know the meaning of our struggles. But we can know that the answer is always to see them through, to never yield to the temptation of walking away. Ours rather is to find a way to move forward, knowing that God himself is the living future in front of us. If one way seems closed off, then we try another way. If one obstacle is too large to remove, then we simply find another path forward, around the obstacle. If for a time we are stopped in our tracks, then we take a breath, gather our courage, and strive forward once again, surrounded by the great company of all those who have gone before us, who are with us now, and who will come after us.

We are reminded by the story of Tamar that true courage often speaks in a female voice. Women face burdens of life that men do not face, it is that simple. Women face those burdens with a dignity and persistence that men are not always called upon to manifest, if ever. It is not so because it should be so; it is so despite the fact that there is no reason it should be so. Women and men should share the burden and joys of life in equal measure, should be called upon to manifest the courage of faith in like circumstances. But they do not; and as long as they do not, we owe a special debt of gratitude to women of courage everywhere for showing us the way forward through trials of life. Indeed, as the genealogy of Jesus makes perfectly clear, it is often enough women, those considered "outsiders," those stigmatized for one reason or another, who end up receiving the call of God and the promise of God. God does not follow the order of this world; God turns the order of this world upside down, making a Canaanite woman, Tamar, the very model of faithfulness pointing forward to the birth of the Messiah. This story of Tamar—while often neglected—belongs among the most widely read and proclaimed in the Bible.

17. A Time to Heal

Genesis 50:15–21

WE ENCOUNTER IN THIS short passage yet another of the most astounding accounts of the entire Bible, that of the final encounter of Joseph and his brothers after the death of their father Jacob. In some respects, it certainly brings the story of Joseph to a fitting conclusion. The cycle began with Joseph telling his dream to his brothers, and now ends with the brothers coming to him for a final reckoning, just as the dream predicted. Even more, in many ways it brings the great theological theme of the book of Genesis to its final formulation. God's living promise never hovers above the gritty details of everyday life, but enters directly into the lived reality of ordinary human existence, even at its worst. And now, God's promise brings new life to a family, indeed God's own chosen family, through whom all the families of the earth are blessed.

We pick up the story. Joseph is sold into slavery in Egypt, but ends up in the house of a high Egyptian official. He is not only a blessed person; through him, through Joseph, blessing comes to every life he touches. He grows, not only in responsibility but in moral stature, and not only in moral stature but in intellectual grasp of the way of the world. He first proves himself by resisting temptation in a position of trust in the house of Potiphar. The reader quickly grasps: there is something about this person Joseph that is genuinely decent, truly humane in a way that every human being can admire. He is tested further while in prison. There he proves himself gifted with a crucial ability: foresight. It is the foresight of Joseph that finally brings him into the presence of Pharaoh, where he offers not only the interpretation of Pharaoh's dream but invaluable counsel concerning plans for the coming years of plenty and need. Joseph is elevated to the status of Pharaoh's chief counselor.

The plenty comes, and then the famine, which spreads into the land of Canaan as well. And suddenly Jacob and his family are brought back into the story of Joseph, or perhaps we should say that Joseph in Egypt is brought back into the story of Jacob and his family. After much delay, the brothers are finally sent into Egypt by the aging patriarch to buy grain. Joseph designs a series of tests to see whether the brothers have changed after all these years. It is quite clear from Joseph's reaction—he cannot contain his deep emotion—that he himself is the one who has changed most. At first, the brothers do not recognize him; but finally, he makes himself known to them, and with absolute astonishment they promise to bring Jacob their father to Egypt.

Jacob and Joseph finally meet again after so many years, a father who thought he had lost his beloved son forever, a son who thought he would never see his father again, a scene moving beyond words as they embrace weeping without restraint, deep emotional scars healed in a single convulsive encounter of released pain and joy. Jacob is presented with great solemnity to Pharaoh.

Jacob lives to give the final blessing to his sons, including Joseph, and the sons of Joseph, Ephraim and Manasseh. On his death bed, Joseph one last time embraces his father Jacob, and kisses his face. Joseph, the brothers, and a distinguished retinue of Egyptians accompany the body of Jacob back into the land of Canaan, where he is buried in the tomb with Abraham and Isaac, in the very cave Abraham purchased in Mamre from Ephron the Hittite in the field of Machpelah, the one plot of earth now owned in the land of promise by the people of promise.

It is when Joseph and his brothers return to Egypt that our passage occurs; for a life-or-death question remains hanging in the air. The brothers decide to force the issue, for their very future depends upon the outcome.

Jacob the father is dead, and the situation of the brothers in relation to Joseph finally comes home to them. Without the authority of their father to fall back on, they are at the mercy of this brother whom they once sold into slavery, shortly after deciding to kill him and then changing their minds. No higher human authority now stands between them and Joseph; and they are, as things now stand in Egypt, entirely at his mercy. He can have his way with them. They are obviously afraid that years and years of bitter revenge will now come down on their heads at the very moment of Jacob's passing from this earth. Has not Joseph been lying in wait for this exact moment all these years? We hear of course their fear in their words, but also their guilt. No amount of time can erase the horrific deed they visited upon their brother, and they know it. Worse still, they are fully aware that he knows it too. Two short scenes develop in which the brothers try their best to alleviate the bristling tension in the air.

In the first instance, they dare not approach their brother Joseph directly. To do so would of course put them immediately within his power before they have sounded out his intentions. So, they send an intermediary with a message. The message is put into the mouth of their father Jacob. Commentators are divided over the question of whether the reference to Jacob is a bold lie, or in fact a reference to an actual supplication passed on from Jacob the father to Joseph the son through his brothers. But the resolution matters little. The substance of the message is commensurate with the wishes of Jacob, as the brothers know full well, and more importantly as Joseph does also. The message is simple. Jacob—so the message relates—asks Joseph to forgive the guilt of the brothers who have acted so treacherously toward him. The basis for forgiveness is crucial. It is not based on mutual family obligations, but on "the God of your father." It is shared relation to God, not familial or tribal allegiance, which grounds genuine human reconciliation. Joseph's response is eloquent without words; he instantly dissolves into tears. Years of lost opportunity for love are gathered up into the renewed prospect for new life with his family.

The brothers see the tears of Joseph, and take enough courage to approach him a second time, in this case directly. The scene is dramatic, and of course calls to mind the opening dream of the Joseph stories. For the brothers fall down in obeisance before Joseph, and offer themselves as his slaves. Clearly the end of the Joseph story is reaching back to the beginning, just as the beginning is in some sense fulfilled in the end. Yet the answer of Joseph to the offer of his brothers redefines the true meaning of the dream in God's own purpose.

First of all, Joseph immediately clarifies for his brothers their mutual relationship to God. He tells them not to be afraid; for he is no substitute for God. What does this mean? It would be cold comfort for the brothers if his answer simply means: do not worry, I am not going to judge you, I will leave that up to God! And indeed, that is not his point at all. His point rather is a profound theological meditation, which in many ways summarizes the whole book of Genesis.

God has in fact *already* made his gracious purpose quite clear, in using Joseph to save the family of Jacob. God's promise has already worked itself out in human life in ways that no one, including Joseph himself, could possibly have anticipated or understood going forward. God has rescued his people through the marvelous events that have unfolded; so, who am I, Joseph, to undo the work that God has already done to save, by standing over you in human judgment? That is his point. Even the evil plans of humankind are part of the outworking of the good and gracious purpose of God—for those very people! God's intent rules and overrules human intent, far beyond human awareness, for human good.

And second of all, Joseph makes his relationship to his brothers and their families crystal clear. I am here to sustain you, to help you, to provide for you and your children. The word "I" here in Hebrew is emphatic; Joseph is not just uttering pious platitudes, but committing himself in kindness to their welfare. Their very future has now been secured by the one whom they once sought to slay; such is the mysterious way of God in human life.

The living promise of God alone brings the power of forgiveness into human life, restoring what was lost, reconciling what was estranged. It is essential to recognize that already in the first book of the Bible, the Christian Old Testament, the word of forgiveness is not based on ties of family, or tribe, or nation, but upon the claim of God. Jesus will of course make this same point crystal clear in the Sermon on the Mount: "You have heard that it was said, 'You shall love your neighbors, and hate your enemy.' But I say unto you, Love your enemies . . ." (Matt 5:43–48). The divine word of promise brings a claim of forgiveness directly into human life, a claim which extends well beyond the boundaries of ordinary human custom to embrace the entire human family, especially our enemies.

We live in a world in which "god" functions to seal the bonds of family, tribe, and nation. Such a "god" is called on whenever there is friction: to settle disputes, to overturn insults, to smooth out rough relations. Yet the reach of this "god" stops, always, at the border, and is therefore no god at all. The God of the Bible alone is *God*. Whether outside the familiar boundaries of human experience, or inside the most intimate connections of human family and friendship, only the living promise of God grounds true and lasting forgiveness, bringing genuine reconciliation among persons. Only the promise of God is powerful enough to bring together what human beings have torn apart, creating true unity where only discord has reigned until now.

Authentic reconciliation heals human life. It is difficult to describe directly. The narrative in Genesis is content simply to describe the figure of Joseph melting into tears as he hears the appeal for peace by his brothers. Anger and hatred eat away at the human soul. By sharp contrast, peace and good will change the very existence of those who know what it means to let go of the grudges of the past. There are of course those who cannot and will not let go, and grudges slowly but surely eat up all that is left of their humanity. Grudges harbored in anger over time are a corrosive acid to the well-being of human life under the gracious mercy and blessing of God. Reconciliation and forgiveness, on the other hand, not only change the relationship between us and the other based on our relationship to God; we ourselves are changed, from the inside out. Anger released into the air forever is a balm to the human heart, knowing that we too have made our fair share of terrible mistakes in life. Grudges let go are freedom to the human spirit, knowing that we too have been on the receiving end of the merciful kindness of others, a kindness that we certainly did not and do not deserve. Reconciliation brings healing; healing brings reconciliation; such is the power of God's promise to forever change our way into the future in fellowship with him.

The living promise of God encompasses the profound paradox of divine grace. On the one hand, God is actively at work in the most intimate details of your life. He is there in your relationships to your family, both in times of struggle and in times of fulfillment. He is there in your intellectual growth, putting you in the exact situations you need to grow in life, far beyond human calculation. He is there in your physical growth, surrounding you with nourishment even in the hardest times, keeping your life even in times of famine. He is there in the depths of your emotional life, working over time for your well-being, providing for your emotional health the right resources at the right time. The God of the Bible does not in any sense whatsoever hover above the real world in which we live; for our world is his world, his world—the world he made and called good for our sake—is our world. He is not God of a part of us, but the whole of us, the whole person, whom he fashioned in his image. Nowhere in the Bible than in the extended story of Joseph and his brothers is it made more clear that the living reality of God is fully involved in our lives, just as our lives in every respect are fully involved with him. That is one side of the paradox.

Yet the other side is equally important. God works in mysterious ways far beyond human understanding, indeed far beyond human awareness. It is not simply that we cannot fully comprehend the way God works; it is, even more, that much of the time we have not the vaguest idea that God himself is in fact all around us at work for his good pleasure in our lives. Indeed, there are times when, looking backward, we realize how his purpose has granted our every prayer. But looking forward, and looking around in the present, we do not see. We walk by faith, not by sight. The challenge of the paradox of grace is to put our trust in him. It is not to force the issue, somehow contriving circumstances in which God must either show himself and therefore prove himself God, or be proven false; God will not be tested. Nor is it to conclude that, unless we see his work, his work is not real, as if our perception is the true measure of reality. Far from it. Time itself is God's servant for our good; but that means that we must live in patient trust in the ultimate triumph of God's good will. We live by the promise: he will never leave us or forsake us. Those who know that promise in the deepest dimensions of their being will rest easy.

Finally, the God of Genesis, the God of the Bible, who is Lord of all, is a God of new beginnings in human life. It is easy to become trapped in the past; trapped in old grudges that fester with each passing day; trapped in old mistakes that plague and shame us; trapped in old regrets that forever seem to hover in the back of the mind. The God of the promise cleanses the core of our lives with fresh new life. The mistakes of the past are gone, forgiven and forgotten by the only One who matters, which is God himself. The regrets of the past belong only in the past; for Christ the risen Lord draws you always forward, never backward. As you have been forgiven, it is required of you as a disciple of Christ to forgive others. Only forgiveness of others makes us whole again. The gospel requires us to risk change, especially where change is hardest to come by. Harboring a grudge is a form of bondage; forgiveness alone set us free to a new humanity. Take that risk for the sake of Christ.

Your life too is a carefully woven story. The most important dimension of your life story is your relationship to God. He has been there from the beginning; he will always be there. He has been with you through every triumph and disappointment, every failure and success, every pain and joy. But above all, he has been there, working his good purpose for your life at all times, and in all ways, often enough far beyond your awareness. Then too, your life unfolds in our relationships to family and friends, and to the world around you. You learn, you grow, you mature, from every encounter with those you love. Above all, the story of Joseph reminds you: your story is still being written, and God himself is the author. No matter what circumstances you face, the promise of the gospel remains firm: God works all things together for your good. Trust in him!

II. Exodus

1. Anatomy of Oppression

Exodus 1:8–22

THE BOOK OF EXODUS opens with an astounding depiction of the anatomy of oppression, as God's people Israel are brutally and cruelly enslaved by the Egyptian Pharaoh, and the Egyptian people. Before turning to our analysis of this historic shift from welcome to enslavement, and the reasons for it, it is essential briefly to notice the opening verses of the book that set the theological context for the entire narrative to follow.

There is a brief recapitulation of the names and number of people who come down into Egypt during the days of the founding generation, during the days of Jacob and Joseph. Jacob himself comes down after the miracle of seeing his son alive, whom he thought was dead. Joseph has lived most of his adult life in Egypt, where he has become a powerful and deeply respected member of the royal entourage, second indeed only to Pharaoh himself. The other eleven sons of Jacob come down, and each bring their wives and children with them, and all their possessions, immigrants to a new land during a time of famine and regional displacement. The total number of people is carefully repeated from the closing verses of the book of Genesis; seventy come down into Egypt, a family, not a people. Egypt is for them a haven, a place to survive the hardship of the times under the patronage of the royal household thanks to the boundless respect for Joseph and his contribution to the salvation of the Egyptian people.

So far, we are still on familiar ground from the previous book in the canon. But the text then makes a clear change. Three points are stressed. First, Joseph and the entire founding generation pass away in the manner of all flesh. Whatever else is soon to take place, a new historical epoch in the history of God with Israel is about to unfold. The change does not just happen in time; time itself changes. Second, the text stresses that the children of Israel flourish as never before. What was once only seventy now becomes a countless multitude. A *family* becomes a *people*. We see before our eyes the transition from the "age of the patriarchs" in the traditional rubric to the new time of God's people Israel. Yet third, and profoundly important, the text stresses the divine blessing under which this new people live. The verbs pile up one upon the other: the Israelites are fertile and prolific, they multiply very greatly and increase, they fill the land everywhere.

It is this last point that can be easily overlooked. For these are words of divine *promise*. More specifically, these are words of God's promise both to Abraham, and even before him, to Adam. Whatever this new time in Egypt will hold forth for the people of God—as yet it remains a mystery— it will unfold under the selfsame promise of God to Abraham that guided the founding generation of old, indeed the selfsame promise of God since the very creation of the world. God's abundant promise resides at the be- ginning of the book of Exodus to guide both the people, and the reader, through all that follows. We leave the patriarchs behind; but the promise of God to the patriarchs, to Abraham, Isaac, and Jacob, is precisely what carries us forward.

The shift in historical epoch is then quickly told from the side of the *Egyptians* in words redolent with dread of the future: a new king arises who does not know Joseph. A new absolute ruler steps forth who is ignorant of history, and therefore ignorant of the just relations history demands. He is a king for whom might is always right, and he immediately sets to work on his deadly task. Now the biblical writer continues to use the familiar cadences of poetic faith narrative already familiar to us from the book of Genesis. Major shifts in economic, social, political, and moral consequence are told in such a way that modern historians have virtually no access to these consequences; yet these shifts are no mere "story," no mere "narrated world," but are filled with the flesh-and-blood human suffering still all too familiar in our world today. Indeed, the dynamic used by Pharaoh to set about oppressing the people of Israel is as old, and as new, as the story of brutal injustice always and everywhere. You can read about it in tomorrow's newspaper.

The oppression begins with a familiar tactic. The people of Israel are migrants, long-welcome guests in the land of Egypt. The Pharaoh immedi- ately establishes a different relation; they are now deemed foreigners, "them" as opposed to "us." Keep in mind that their only "crime" has been to flour- ish under the divine blessing—on that point the biblical text is quite clear. They moreover celebrate a historic lineage of great aid to the welfare of the Egyptian people through the figure of Joseph. All that is now swept aside, for no reason at all, beyond the immemorial cruelty of human stupidity—which Pharaoh of course calls "shrewdness." They are treated now with contempt for no other reason than baseless fear, fear of the "other." Every accusation

launched against them moreover is hypothetical. They "might" become trai-
tors in the event of war; there is no evidence to suggest this, and no reason
whatsoever to suspect it. Ignorant fear, based on sheer prejudice, leading in
turn to violent enslavement, is a potent dynamic in the long history of human
depravity. Just relations between two peoples now gives way to one people,
the majority, seeking to gain profit from the oppressed labors of the other
people, the minority, not because it is right, but because it is possible.

Thus, even now as the book opens from these two different vantage
points, the promise of God and the brutality of Pharaoh, a contest is unleashed between two forces: the cruelty of unrestrained human power and
the kind mercy of God. Time will tell in the book of Exodus which is more
powerful.

The cold calculus of oppression unfolds in three stages, each more
brutal and bloody than the previous. The first, simply but ominously told,
is the enslavement of the people of Israel by the Egyptians, who form them
into forced labor gangs. Cruel taskmasters are put over them and they are
forced to provide labor for Pharaoh's pet building projects. Their existence
is made bitter through harsh labor in the fields, as their labor is forced to
serve not their own interests but that of the Egyptians, enforced through
ruthless violence. Bodies are broken; life is embittered; work is enslavement, not gift. Yet the effort fails; God's promised blessing continues its
work among the people despite Egyptian bondage, and the people of Israel
flourish. Not only does the first attempt fail; now the people of Egypt dread
the Israelites. There was nothing to fear; now the Egyptians are slaves to
their fears that result from their own ignorance.

The second attempt leaps from slavery to outright murder. Pharaoh
first of all secretly seeks to enlist the aid of two Hebrew midwives, Shiphrah
and Puah, in destroying the new generation of male Israelite children.
Those who welcome life into the world are now tasked to snuff it out. Female babies are to be allowed to live, presumably for the service they might
render to the Egyptians; but male children of the Israelites are to be killed
at birth. The midwives practice civil disobedience. They fear God, not Pharaoh. They recognize that God's law is right, and therefore Pharaoh's edict
to them is wrong, and quietly refuse to carry out his command. When confronted with the fact that young boys are still coming to birth and living,
the midwives concoct a story to Pharaoh to cover their obedience to God.
The text makes no comment on their fable to Pharaoh, but most certainly
commends their obedience to God. God blesses their own families and
households for the obedience they have rendered.

The final and third stage is the most terrifying of all, an open and direct pogrom of total annihilation. Pharaoh commands the entire people of

Egypt to murder all male Hebrew children by casting them, helpless, into the Nile. Baseless fear has become the utterly barbarous murder of a whole people. Cruelty and rage now define the character of Egypt, guided by the crass power of a fearful and hateful king.

God's gracious and merciful promise is eternal and abiding. It does not come and go with the changing circumstances of human life, for it is not grounded in human nature or experience. God's promise is not altered or adjusted according to current mode or fashion, as if human need requires an ever-changing definition of the divine commitment of love. No, God's promise is defined solely by his own gracious purpose. God's loving mercy extends to embrace humanity solely based upon his own will to establish a relationship of communion with his creation, a relationship grounded in the mystery of love which is God himself.

God's constant love for humankind does not change; will not change; cannot change, simply because God is God, and he commits his very identity to the purpose he has established and continues to establish. Is his purpose always clear? No, it is not; we walk by faith, not by sight. Is his purpose always manifest in the details of human existence in front of our eyes, whether in the life of the individual, the gathered community of the church, or the way of life in the world? No, it is not. God's purpose always remains his own. God's love is always real, even when we struggle to see it in our own lives and in the world around us. But we can and must never let go of this truth: God has one eternal purpose for your life, for my life, and for the entire creation, and that is his abiding love. On that truth you can wager your entire existence.

Yet while we must affirm the eternal purpose of God as constant and unchanging, we must at the same time recognize, on the basis of Scripture, the changing history of God with the world. Times change, not despite God's rule, but because of it. God is not caught by surprise when one generation passes away and a new generation arises. God is not suddenly forced on the defensive when things we thought we could count on suddenly disappear, and new challenges arise in their place. God's purpose is eternal and real, but always as an event, never as a static proposition, a lifeless principle.

God has a real history with the world, with the church, and with your life, simply because God is a *living* God. He is at the same time sovereign and eternal, high above the heavens and the earth; and yet near to every human life, directly entering into the changing fortunes of human life and welfare. Change does not contradict his purpose, but completes it, just as change does not thwart our humanity but fulfills it. Those who would assign to God the defense of a changeless order of church or society do not know the God of the Bible; for no sooner do we come to understand his purpose with one generation than *God himself* alters the landscape of human affairs and all is new.

And there will be some changes, to be sure, which at least at the first seem at best painful, at worst disastrous. The pain is real; the struggles to understand the disaster are struggles of faith, not doubt. Seasons of struggle come to every faithful servant of Christ, often to the church at large, and at the worst of times even come to the whole world. At such times maybe the best we can do is simply not give up, not lose hope, not forget that we are not alone in our struggles, but are joined to all who have endured and, in the end, triumphed through the healing presence of God's kindness.

The narrative of Exodus sets up from the very beginning a contest, as it were, between the gracious plan of God and the murderous plot of Pharaoh, King of Egypt. From a human point of view, all the power is in Pharaoh's hands, and it is essential that we who know the outcome of the story not abandon that sense of human frailty as it unfolds. We too live in the tension between earthly powers who arrogate to themselves the dictum that might makes right, on the one hand, and the overpowering might of God which at times seems hidden and distant. We too struggle to know the meaning of our time.

Yet even so, Pharaoh is but the first in a long line of tyrants even in the Bible, from the Assyrian, Babylonian, Hellenistic, and Roman autocrats who oppress the poor and helpless; and the line hardly ends with the biblical world. Indeed, we are instructed by Scripture itself to recognize the figure of the tyrant not only in history, but in our own time. Where is the much-vaunted progress of civilization? The tyrants of the twentieth century have scarcely passed from the stage before the new tyranny of the twenty-first settles in, now even in areas where democracy once ruled. Sadly, when the gospel goes forth into a world, suffering is usually there to greet it. Where the proclamation of Christ alone as Lord and King of all is rightly made, there often arises a tyrant who is wise in his own eyes.

The way of tyranny is the same, then and now. Establish an "imagined community" by creating a false boundary between "them" and "us." There need be no truth whatsoever to the boundaries established; there only needs to be a sense of threat that "those people" over there are going to do away with "our" rights and privileges over here. Once that boundary is created, the "other" can be treated as less than human, as cattle. They can be pushed into labor they do not desire. They can be expelled from societies to which they rightly belong. They can be hunted down and murdered by mobs of an-gry people who by so doing supposedly establish their own basic identity as "solid citizens." Mistreatment of the other within society in the form of vio-lence and prejudice, or on the borders of society in the form of xenophobia and anti-immigrant hatred, is clearly as old as the oldest narratives in the Bible. Yet it is as new as this morning's news story. Children were murdered then; and they are viciously and senselessly murdered now. The hysterical insanity of fanaticism was alive then, and it is certainly abroad now across the face of the earth.

Then, and now, God works in contrary ways. The One who is most powerful works his will through the powerless, the despised, the other, the outcast. The One who overthrows the rulers of the earth, and sets at naught the plans of monarchs and nations, guides the world through the actions of the frail, often the few, certainly the neglected and the unheralded. Then two ordinary midwifes outwitted the plans of Pharaoh, absolute ruler of Egypt. Even now, ordinary Christians living in the service of God—no matter the cost, no matter the ways in which their actions run counter to the dominant ways of surrounding culture and society—are the instruments through which God works his mysterious will in the world. The beginnings of God's redemptive will are always tiny, never impressive, and rarely successful, indeed humanly impossible. Yet God uses just such frail beginnings to transform the whole creation.

2. Drawn from the Nile

Exodus 2:1–10

OLD TESTAMENT NARRATIVE SHOWS a remarkable flexibility in moving swiftly back and forth between two very different angles of perspective. We have already, in the book of Exodus, witnessed the *macrocosmic* scale of profound political and social turmoil, ending in the outright enslavement of one people—the Israelites—by another—the Egyptians. The tale is told with economy in three unfolding stages of terror, with the final stage resulting in the mass murder of Israelite infant boys by the Egyptian people. We now encounter the second angle of perspective, the *microcosm* of daily, ordinary human life. We wonder: how can ordinary human life even persist against the backdrop of such widespread terror and fanaticism? The narrative does not answer the question directly, or theoretically. Simply by shifting the scale from the macrocosm down to the microcosm, the narrator points out: life does somehow go on. Even here, even now, God finds a way. But it will not be easy.

Two people meet, fall in love, and are married. We are not yet even told their names (we will only find out as the story unfolds). The point is quite clear: this is commonplace life at its most basic level. They are both Levites. In the course of time the woman becomes pregnant, and has a son. Again, in the world of the Bible nothing could be more normal, even against the backdrop of the grotesquely abnormal reality of oppression.

Yet suddenly the two worlds—the macrocosm and the microcosm— collide, for of course they are the same world, life in bondage down in Egypt. A male Israelite child is a threat to Pharaoh, or so he conceives in his poisoned imagination. He has already ordered all such children to be thrown mercilessly into the Nile River, there to drown. So, what is this new couple to do with their infant child? The text records with fine detail the loving sigh of a new parent: oh, he is such a beautiful boy! For three months they keep the child hidden, but then can do so no longer.

The mother does not so much conceive a *plan* as a desperate attempt to stave off the inevitable. She constructs a small floating basket, complete with a sealed top, with minute care. She makes certain that it is fully waterproof. She places her son in the small basket—the word used in Hebrew is ark, like Noah's ark, used only here and in the story of Noah in the entire Old Testament—and places the floating basket, with the child inside, just alongside the bank of the Nile among the reeds, where the flowing waters will not topple or engulf it. Again, it is not so much a plan as an act of sheer desperation.

Two new characters now enter this microcosm, from profoundly very different worlds, yet both of whom arouse our admiration. The first is the daughter of the two Levites. She carefully stations herself where she can actively observe without being observed; she is obviously highly resourceful as the unfolding story quickly confirms, a quick-thinking youngster. The child may be floating in the Nile but it is not really abandoned; the basket is just there, with her waiting to see what will happen. The idea is left unexpressed: what else can we do?

Now the second character enters, this one from the world of the macrocosm, in fact none less than Pharaoh's own daughter. She comes to this very spot along the Nile with her attendants to bathe. Again, it is a very ordinary scene, yet it will have astounding consequences, both for Pharaoh and the Egyptians, and of course for the people of Israel. She sees the floating basket, and sends a maid to retrieve it. She opens the sealed top, and there inside is a child, crying. She instantly understands what has happened. A Hebrew child has been left to its fate. Yet she is also drawn to the child by a basic human reaction of care and concern. A child is a child, and a hurting child needs help.

Suddenly the sister reenters the picture, as she sees the astounding picture unfolding before her. Thinking on her feet, she ventures a brilliant proposal: shall I go find a Hebrew woman to nurse the child for you? Notice how the question is phrased, as if her primary interest is in helping the woman out of her sudden conundrum of what to do with this newly discovered infant. In a different world and time, we could imagine a youth straight off the back-alley streets of a Dickens novel, filled with pluck and brio. Pharaoh's daughter is glad to have such an opportune offer, and the mother of the child is summoned. A fee is arranged—a fee! The mother now not only has her child back, safe and in the clear, but is paid wages by Pharaoh's own household to raise him.

When the child grows to young adulthood, he is brought back to Pharaoh's daughter, who gives him his name. The boy is not only rescued but adopted into the household of the Egyptian King. The murderous plan of Pharaoh is miraculously overturned twice; the boy is saved, and is saved by Pharaoh's own daughter! This child is Moses, drawn out of the Nile, adopted son of Pharaoh's daughter, with a future yet unknown, under God's sovereign and mysterious purpose yet to be revealed.

We also need to recognize that the birth story of Moses shimmers just beneath the surface of another biblical text, and that is the infancy narrative of Christ, especially as attested in the Gospel of Matthew. The typology is clear and significant. Once again, a paranoid and fanatical tyrant—Herod the King, this time—acts against fantasies of his own imagination to create death and destruction. He enlists the help of unwitting accomplices, the three magi, who just like the two Hebrew midwives outsmart him in the end. Yet the fury of Herod is unleashed against the innocent children who perish at his command. The infant Jesus is saved only at the last possible second by flight down into Egypt, where he stays safe until it is time to return. When he finally comes back to the promised land, he is now openly declared the Son of God, as one who has fully identified with the suffering of God's chosen people. The connection between the two stories is never made explicit, but the typological relation is fully clear. The question is certainly relevant: what is the effect of reading both passages together in the light of the one Scripture of the church?

On the one hand, the Old Testament is only revealed in the New. Moses is a type of Christ, but Christ is the one true substance of faith itself. Clearly the figure of Moses is profoundly important not only in the Old Testament but also in the New. Yet something happens with the birth of Christ that has not happened before. Eternity enters time. God himself enters the world in the birth of this child, without being any less God. In this birth, the final event of God's redemptive love for the whole world is now fully present, as the adoring magi come to realize when they offer their gifts of gold, frankincense, and myrrh. All faith looks forward to Christ, who is now the final end of time itself, present in the world. In this one birth event, all the divine promise of the past, the present, and the future are gathered into one eternal moment of pure gift. That is one side of the church's dialectical relation to a twofold Scripture of Old and New Testaments. Moses points forward to Christ, yet in Christ something far greater than Moses is here.

But we must not stop here, though often enough exegesis limits itself to only the first side of the dialectic. Rather, we must now remember that the New Testament is already concealed in the Old. We must remember to read the story of the birth of Jesus in the light of the Exodus account of the child

Moses. And what are we to conclude? Despite the finality of God's decisive intervention in Christ for the salvation for the world, real persecution, real oppression, real political and social disruption, continue to exist, and the church is not removed from any of these maladies of the world. The church has its hope fixed on Christ, but it continues to live in the world where autocrats rule, and misrule, and kill, and even destroy whole generations of children. The church is not immune to the suffering of the world. We share in the grief that cries out for lost generations.

There are tranquil times; there are troubling times; there are disastrous times; yet through them all, ordinary life persists. The daily life of Christian discipleship is the primary arena of Christian service to the living Lord throughout time. That is not for one moment to suggest that the church is immune to the struggles of the world, far from it. The church not only participates in both the joyous triumphs as well as the miserable failures of the world, but if anything feels them even more deeply. Yet the fact remains, we are not defined by the triumphs and failures of the world, however momentous, but by the daily call to discipleship. Love of neighbor, care for family and friends, practical concern for the needs of the weak and the vulnerable, worship of God and prayer in his name, these are the microcosm of daily life that in fact encompasses the macrocosm of world occurrence, rather than the reverse. The ordinary daily life of the Christian is a small sign, set up in the flow of world events: even now, God's mysterious and loving rule is more powerful, and more real, than all resistance, and therefore we will live our everyday lives fully confident in his ultimate purpose, which indeed surrounds the entire cosmos and all that it contains.

Still, the fact remains that the macrocosm of the world will inevitably yield times of great stress, even including outright tyranny. The Egyptians, the Assyrians, the Babylonians, the Hellenistic monarchs, the Romans, parade across the pages of biblical narrative in all their regal finery, only to be defeated by the hidden and mysterious purpose of God, which overturns every human stratagem. Nor does tyranny cease with the Bible of course; it continues up to the present moment, and we who are instructed by the biblical word can only understand tyranny now in the light of the message of Scripture.

Two responses to tyranny are contained in our passage today. On the one hand, there is the response of brilliant creativity, as typified by the older sister of the infant Moses. She knows when to act, and when to refrain from acting; when to watch, and when to step forth into the limelight. She risks everything by appearing before the daughter of Pharaoh, yet does so with such utter lack of self-concern that even the daughter of a tyrant is moved to empathy. There are times when we are tempted to think that only brute force can win against autocratic rule, but we are wrong. Sometimes the best weapon is thought, imagination, careful planning, and in the end unyielding courage. Sometimes a little pluck can slay a monster.

And then there is the reaction of the daughter of Pharaoh, who, despite knowing that the infant she is rescuing is proscribed by her own father, not only rescues him but adopts him into Pharaoh's own family! We are always tempted to believe that all people are determined by the "side" they are on; you are either on one side or the other, and everything about you can be fully predicted by which it is. But is that necessarily the case? Are we not guilty of treating people as instances of a statistical norm rather than living, breathing, human persons when we make such judgments? It is one thing to judge *positions* as wrong; but it is quite another to hold in contempt the *people* who hold them. People pass in and out of foolish sets of ideas all the time.

Have our own ideas, our own actions, always been perfectly pure throughout life? Of course not; then why should we hold up perfect purity as a standard of judgment over others? It is essential to give every human person the benefit of the doubt, room to change and to grow, just as God has in his mercy given us time to repent and to change. People constantly surprise us when we see the mystery of God at work in their lives. That does not mean being naïve to the intransigence of systemic violence. Pharaoh is still Pharaoh, Egyptian society is still Egyptian society, as the unfolding narrative in Exodus will amply demonstrate. But withholding judgment for the sake of giving people time to learn and to grow is not only required of us as disciples of Jesus Christ; we may find ourselves with allies we never expected if only we show a little extra patience.

We are of course reminded by the struggle of the people of Israel in Egypt that the people of God are never without times of difficulty and danger. The church alive is the church in struggle, and has always been so. The church asleep is a church at peace with the world; but the church which is true to its mission in word and deed will always be a threat to centers of power and influence. The church that covers itself with signs of glory and majesty, will only lose its very identity, so that the gospel will struggle again to find hearers and followers in the world. The church which, by contrast, opposes the hideous bloodshed of autocrats and tyrants, only to feel their wrath, and may of necessity go underground, or even be prepared to die for the mission of the gospel; that is the church which is worthy of the name. And the most astonishing thing of all is the risk—the eternal risk—that God himself undertakes by choosing to identify not only the message of his mercy, but his very identity with those who are so exposed to the violent whims of power. God once risked everything—his eternal promise—on a baby floating in a basket in the waters of the Nile; God once risked the very nature of his eternal being on a child in flight from Herod's wrathful and murderous vengeance. That same God even now risks the truth of his merciful love in solidarity with those who love him above everything the world offers, and who stand by the faith of the gospel against the allures of political, social, personal, and economic power. The risk of faith is tempered by our firm confidence that God himself stands with us and by us precisely when we are most exposed.

Precisely here we—you and I—are instructed by the paradox of grace. There are times when you cannot even be for yourself, so limited have your personal resources become. It is precisely in such times that *God* is most for you, most certainly around, behind, and ahead of you, surrounding you with his undying love. Even when you would forsake yourself, he will not forsake you. There are times when you find yourself in the weakest moment of your life, without resources to face the struggle of the day. It is precisely in such moments of weakness you are most strong, because God himself is now the only true strength by which you live, and his strength is made perfect in your weakness.

You will at times in your life find yourself utterly alone, not just lonely but isolated from the company of support upon which you once thought you could count. God himself is most present in your life when you are most alone, floating helplessly down the river in a basket, with no one watching over you but him. He is sufficient for all your needs. You will at times come to believe that you are utterly without resources in life; yet precisely then you will discover that God works far beyond your awareness, indeed far beyond your imagination, for your good. To be sure, the life of faith is a life of struggle. But Christ himself is the goal of that struggle; he is the joy that even now gathers us all into his blessed love. Even now, surprises surely await.

3. The Flight of Moses

Exodus 2:11–25

ONCE AGAIN, THE BIBLICAL narrator proceeds with a style of poetic depiction that is fully appropriate to the witness of faith. Every extraneous fact, every stray piece of information, is left unremarked, unnoticed, unrecorded. All that matters is the witness to God's deliverance of the people of Israel that is the subject of the book. The style clearly defies every mode of modern history, whether that of the critical reconstructionist, or the conservative apologist. Suddenly we are told of Moses as a young man, without any attempt to describe the years between his infancy and his coming of age and entrance onto the world stage. What about the influence of his upbringing in the Egyptian court? Sheer silence; we are not even given the name of the Egyptian Pharaoh in whose household Moses is raised, so little does it matter to the perspective of the biblical witness. If we are to understand what follows—and of course the word from God that comes to us from this astounding book—we must follow the special mode of narration set forth by the biblical writer, despite the doubtless legitimate historical concerns on both the left and the right that are bypassed with sovereign neglect. Three episodes are quickly recorded in this section of the narrative.

It so happens after Moses has grown up that a new point of time enters his life. He comes to share not only *concern* for his people, Israel, but to take up an active *identification* for their well-being. He wants to know more; he finds himself in sympathy with their plight; he begins to understand the burdens under which they are laboring, and to empathize with the suffering those burdens cause. And so, Moses makes a conscious, intentional decision, resulting in a life-changing alteration in the direction of his existence. He leaves the luxury of the palace in which he has been raised, and goes out to see, for himself, the sufferings of his own people. The grammar of the Hebrew makes it clear how purposeful his act is. He *chooses* to identity with

123

his sisters and brothers. It is not just a *discovery* of his own identity, but a willing *participation* in their oppression as his own. He sees the burdens under which they groan, and protests the injustice of their condition.

His resolve is quickly tested. He sees an Egyptian—presumably one of the dreaded taskmasters—beating an Israelite. Not just "an Israelite" in the abstract, but now for Moses a fellow Israelite. What was before a matter of empathy has suddenly become an intensely practical matter of action. What to do? The text makes it clear that the coming act of Moses is not ventured in a moment of passionate release. He looks around, this way and that. The violence he is about to commit is carefully designed to be secretive. He sees no one around, and feels safe to do what he feels is right. He kills the Egyptian, strikes him to the ground, dead. He buries him quickly in the desert sand. The various clauses in Hebrew are told with stark rapidity: turns, looks, strikes, hides. The act of Moses, once unleashed, is swift and decisive. Nevertheless, as he is immediately to discover, the consequences will be enormous and costly, far beyond the act itself.

The narrator comments on a surprising development; another fight breaks out, and is witnessed by Moses, but this time it is between two Israelites! Where before he could solve the problem by killing the hated Egyptian, now he feels he must mediate between coequal sides in a dispute. He is not here interested in solving a tribal dispute between offending parties; he is clearly trying to evoke a restoration of justice. What wrong has been committed and how can it be made right? But the effort is immediately rejected. The Hebrew who is in the wrong, defiant and mocking, refers to the Egyptian whom Moses has killed. Are you going to kill one of us too? Moses immediately realizes that the slaying of the Egyptian was not in fact kept secret; that indeed if an ordinary Israelite knows, then surely Pharaoh knows as well, and it is only a matter of time before Moses himself will be captured and killed. He had gone out among the people to learn, and even to deliver; instead, he now must flee from Egypt itself, running for his life. The very people whom he would deliver mock his assumed authority and mission, and drive him indirectly into ignominious political exile.

The second episode unfolds, once again, using the poetic narrative techniques so particular to the biblical witness of faith. All unimportant details are left out, no matter how important they may seem to modern readers. Moses has murdered an officer of the Egyptian king, and is now fleeing for his life into the wilderness of Midian. It is desert country, filled with nomads and emptiness. The one break in the bleak and isolated existence of the desert is the *well*, the life-source of water for humankind and animals, and the center of social gathering and mutual personal intercourse. The text says simply: Moses sits down beside a well. We can well imagine his fatigue, his thirst, his anxiety and dread, his utter perplexity about what has just happened in Egypt. How could I have misjudged the situation so badly? How could matters have gone so wrong so quickly? But we can only imagine, for the text itself is silent. Instead of the inner turmoil of Moses, the text records a new chapter in his life that begins with the arrival of seven daughters of a Midianite priest named Jethro.

Moses knows nothing of this priest or his daughters. But he observes a scene that not only unfolds before his tired eyes, but has happened now time and again. The women do all the work of drawing all the water out of the well to give drink to their thirsty flocks; then the male shepherds callously and brutally drive the women off after the real work is done, and lead their own flocks to the drawn troughs of water. This one time, however, the shepherds get a surprise. Moses rises to the defense of the seven daughters of Jethro, clearly ready to fight for their right to water their own flocks at the all-important well where they have themselves done the work, and his defense wins the day. He not only defends their right; he proceeds to water their flocks for them. What is this? An Egyptian defending a group of desert bedouins to the water rights at a Midianite well? Once again, we are clearly witnessing a concept of justice that transcends any boundaries of nation, or religion, or tribe.

The daughters return to their father Jethro. Not unlike a modern novelist, the biblical writer does not simply summarize information, but rather draws out the necessary details in echoes from conversations. The father, Jethro (he is here called by another name, Reuel), is accustomed to his daughters taking much longer, given the customary violence of the shepherds and their nefarious tactics. Yet here they are back already, mission completed; how is it that you are back so soon?

They give a brief description of the action that they can themselves still scarcely comprehend: an Egyptian—an Egyptian!—defended our rights to the water, drove off the shepherds, and even watered our flocks, so here we are! Egyptian or not, Jethro the Midianite priest is now aroused to his native sense of desert hospitality, and rather fiercely demands to know where this man is. Why he has not been invited to their dwelling?! And he sends the daughters off to invite him for a meal. Again, the text only leaves us, as readers, room to contemplate, without overstressing the point: notice how different is the generous response of Jethro the Midianite priest, who invites Moses into the hospitality of his family, from the response of the *Hebrew*, who openly mocks and rejects Moses, though both received the same bid by Moses for justice.

All unnecessary details are once again passed over in sovereign neglect and silence. Only the crucial points matter. Moses does come to stay with

Jethro. In the course of time, he is married to one of Jethro's daughters, Zip-porah, and they have a son. The name of the son, Gershom—which is related to the Hebrew word for foreign migrant—is a reminder that even while in Jethro's home in Midian, Moses belongs to another people, and to another place. We are not to think of his stay in Midian as an ending, but only as a new beginning. Still, in the first episode, Moses is fleeing from the home of his birth; in the second, Moses finds a new home thanks to the hospitality of a gracious family of Midianites. We wonder at the strange ways of God!

The third and final narrative moment in this section continues the concentration only on the essential. Time passes, and we are carefully re-minded that while Moses is in exile in Midian, the condition of the people Israel in Egypt has hardly improved. They continue to cry out in the agony of their oppression. But two things do change. The Pharaoh who pursued Moses into exile dies; the slate is, at least on an earthly level, wiped clean. Yet far more important, a new era, a new beginning, occurs in *God's* time. The cries of the people are now heard by God, who listens, notices, and now turns toward the affliction of his people. He remembers his covenant with the patriarchs—with Abraham, Isaac, and Jacob—and now is set to act for the good of his people, according to his promise. In God's time, suddenly we are made aware that something is about to happen not only for the redemption of Israel; indeed that love of God is aroused which is grounded in the eternal sovereign redemptive purpose of God. Nothing can, or will, ever be the same.

We are born connected to our fellow humanity by the gracious promise of God in Jesus Christ. However, we are called to make good that connection through *active* solidarity with others. Christian discipleship requires active solidarity with the weak and the vulnerable, with the community of faith at large, and indeed with the global reality of humankind under God's gracious care. Solidarity is a choice we make—identical with the decision of faith it-self—that manifests itself in the manifold and fluid decisions of daily life in the world. It certainly begins with active awareness of the needs and vulner-abilities of our neighbors, both across the street and across the planet. We must leave behind the comfort of our assumptions, our circumstances, our preconceptions, and engage the world on its own terms. Simply to step out into the world and learn the truth of our neighbor in need is the beginning of a life of service to the other. But it does not end with awareness; it is completed only in concrete action. We can truly see only as we act, we can truly act only as we see, the reality of our neighbor in need. There is no set formula; there is no guaranteed success; there is only the joy of service that carries our efforts forward in common with all who serve the risen Christ.

The right of God in Jesus Christ is the one norm by which the human rights of every person on earth are fully established and revealed. That is not to deny the realities of class, of gender, of race; of religious difference, of national and regional location; indeed, of personal bias and limitation. Rather, transcending every category of division is the one reality of *God's* right that gathers every human person on earth under the protective shield of universal human right. As followers of Jesus Christ, we embrace and celebrate human rights everywhere. Where the poor are oppressed by the rich, we are there to protest, and to stand in solidarity with the poor over against the rich. Where the powerful would push aside the weak, we stand with the weak to insure the just and equitable purpose of God for every person on earth. Where racism runs rampant, we join the march against this scourge upon the record of human justice. Where women and men are not treated with equal dignity and respect, we will not stand idly by, for human rights are coequal to all people. Where immigrants are shunned aside as second-class citizens, we remind ourselves that we too are immigrants, as was Moses in Midian, as was Jesus in Egypt, as have the people of God been time and again throughout their history, indeed as are we all, immigrants on this earth awaiting a new kingdom to come. Our point is not to identify human rights with the will of God, for that is to turn the biblical witness upside down. Our point, rather, is to recognize that God himself identifies his right with the outbreak of human rights in the world, for that is the revealed will of God as attested in Holy Scripture. The measure of truth in the Bible is not any form of human self-realization, but rather God's own just claim upon the whole creation, which cannot be evaded.

The act of Moses in killing the Egyptian is neither condemned nor affirmed in the Old Testament narrative; it is presented with careful attention to the inherent ambiguity of the deed, and the nexus of complications in which it is imbedded. Clearly Moses is acting out of a just sense of outrage at the horrific violence shown by this Egyptian—by all Egypt—against the enslaved people of Israel. He kills to prevent murder. Yet clearly even for Moses the act holds inherent nuances.

Why does he so carefully carry it out in secret, if it is a just act in the cause of freedom? Moreover, there is another social context in which the act is imbedded, which is not at all clearly positive, in fact just the opposite. For the enslaved people of Israel, the murder of the Egyptian by Moses appears to be just another instance of one power-hungry individual usurping unjust authority from another unjust power. Regardless of the good intentions of Moses, there is not the slightest acknowledgment that the violence of Moses establishes the rightful freedom of the people of

Israel, far from it. There is rather the cynical point that power has gone to Moses' head, and he had best be careful.

Finally, there is the theological context in which the act is carefully inserted, though that context will take time to unfold. For now, we as readers can only conclude that the act leads to nothing positive; that indeed God's way will appear in time, but it will certainly be a very different way than that imagined now by Moses the self-designated liberator. So, what are we to conclude, now, in our time, about revolutionary violence? The issue is not at all whether unjust oppression needs to be overthrown. It does. The issue rather is the genuine means by which that oppression is best now and forever defeated. Is it by violence? Or is it by nonviolent, active, civil disobedience? If nothing else, our text is a warning that violence must always be viewed in a variety of contexts, and that the wider the angle in which it is evaluated, the less persuasive and effective it becomes.

Human beings make plans, but God directs our steps. Moses comes to realize from the beginning that he has a purpose in life: to lead the people Israel out of bondage from Egypt. But God intervenes to lead him along the path, step by step, which will lead him to that divine destiny. And as often happens in the Bible, it leads in a profoundly different direction than Moses envisions. Which of us draws a straight line to map out our lives, and then walks that line from beginning to end? There are interruptions along the way, sometimes even profound disruptions, that often enough cast everything into doubt. There are new circumstances seemingly forced upon us that would apparently contradict everything we thought we knew about the divine purpose for our lives.

And yet, somewhere along the way, we begin to realize that our horizons are beginning to expand. We are seeing a world around us that until now has been beyond our understanding, even beyond our vision. We meet people that we would otherwise never meet in a million years, and it is from these very people that we learn priceless lessons of discipleship we could learn nowhere else. We learn that the mission of the gospel, while it goes forth from the people of God, is not limited to the circle of the church, but encompasses the whole world, indeed the whole creation. We think we lose God when our plans go astray. Instead, what we discover is that God himself disrupts our plans in order that he alone might be Lord of our lives, the one source of every comfort and joy, every truth and insight. Never be too sure that your life is off-kilter; sometimes that is exactly where you need to be in order to realize that finding God is really about God finding you.

4. The Burning Bush

Exodus 3:1–15

THE CALL OF MOSES is recounted in a brief narrative section that brilliantly combines narrative opposites. The familiar everyday world is suddenly interrupted by the extraordinary and inexplicable; the present stream of daily life is emphatically left forever behind by the claim of the utterly new; the sovereign divine commission, grounded solely in God's will, is nevertheless recounted side by side with a human response of individual personality. Indeed, to probe even deeper, the very *being* of God is announced in such a way that his acts make it known, while his *acts* are thrust forward as nothing less than the articulation of his eternal being. All of this in fifteen verses! The commissioning of Moses as the one who will lead the children of Israel out of bondage in Egypt is rightly celebrated as one of the great call stories of the Bible, with features comparable to the call of David, the prophets, and so forth. Yet somehow, the call of Moses at the burning bush stands out in memory as archetypal, not only of the biblical call stories in general, but of God's call to each and all of us who enter even now into the service of the risen Christ.

The account begins by describing the ordinary, even mundane, existence of Moses, who now lives the life of a shepherd in the semiarid desert steppe of Midian. He is going about the customary day in and day out routine (as the verbal form of the Hebrew reinforces) of seeking suitable pasture for the flocks of his father-in-law Jethro. Whatever is about to occur, we are certainly not in the presence of a human quest for religious self-transcendence! Indeed, we are given no information at all about the inner psychology of Moses, who is simply doing his daily job the best he can. And his life as a shepherd leads him to make a fateful decision: he leads the flock out of the wilderness area toward Mount Horeb, looking for suitable forage for the animals. So far, we are witnessing the humdrum of ordinary life.

Until suddenly everything changes in a moment. The text summarizes everything to follow in a single narrative heading: the angel of the Lord appears to him in a flame of fire. Now, suddenly, the ordinary gives way to the absolutely extraordinary, the unspeakably astounding. Now, suddenly, the life of the shepherd and his flock is forever left behind in the past, and the absolute *new* of a called servant of God emerges in its place. Now, suddenly, God himself directly encounters Moses, with sovereign freedom; yet Moses too remains a distinct personality, whose curiosity and struggle are included, not excluded, in the encounter with God.

Moses turns aside and notices an ordinary sight; a common desert bush is on fire, hardly a cause for interest or concern. But he suddenly notices something about the scene that is inexplicably mysterious: the bush continues to burn, but it is not consumed by the flame. How is this possible, he wonders? A burning bush I understand; but a burning bush that leaves the bush unscathed is impossible. I must at the very least leave aside my tasks and investigate. Moses abandons for the moment—it will turn out to be for a lifetime—the task of finding fresh pasture for the sheep, and turns aside to see this strange and marvelous sight. How can the bush be on fire and not burn up?

The narrator then shifts to the divine perspective, that of God, who from now on takes the initiative. God sees that indeed Moses has turned aside to investigate the marvel before him. And God calls to Moses, by name, from out of the burning bush. Moses responds with a ready willingness to hear God. God tells Moses to remove the sandals from his feet, for he is now standing upon holy ground, for this is none other than Horeb, the Mountain of God. Where God is present, the earth is shattered; silence and wonder alone are worthy of his majesty. Stillness is required; life cannot, must not, go on as usual; take off your sandals, your old life is now ended. You begin a new life at this very moment. God then identifies himself to Moses as the God of the promise, the God of Abraham, Isaac, and Jacob, the God who has made a covenant with his chosen people. Moses is terrified in the majestic presence of God. He does more than take off his sandals. He hides his face. He is afraid of God, not the surface emotional reaction of fear, but the deep and total personal reaction of profound reverence and soul-shattering awe.

God then announces his plan and purpose to Moses, and commissions him as the agent of his coming deliverance. God is not remote in the heavens, however it may at times so appear. In fact, God has directly observed the sufferings of his people Israel under the hard bondage of their Egyptian taskmasters. He does not simply observe them, he knows them, understands them, takes their struggles to heart. That is to say, the God of heaven and earth understands the suffering of his people from the *inside*, not the outside. And now the time of deliverance has arrived. It is not a change in the calendar; it is a change rather in God's own unfolding purpose, God's own time, which now turns directly toward the deliverance of his chosen people from bondage in Egypt. Even more, the deliverance has a goal: to bring his people to the land of promise, the land flowing with milk and honey. I will move my beloved people from suffering to hope, from bitter despair to a new land of promised fulfillment; and you, Moses, will be the one to lead them for me.

It is of course an astounding divine statement. Moses is not treated by God in the biblical narrative as a passive instrument of deliverance, far from it. As the call of Moses proceeds, the first reaction—then the second, the third, and so on—is to offer a series of reasons why he most certainly is not suitable for God's call! Who am I to announce to Pharaoh that you are going to deliver your people from bondage? I am just an exiled shepherd here in Midian, cut off from Egypt for all this time, living the life of the wilderness, in an occupation hardly suited to lead anything or anybody. Who am I? God does not reject the resistance of Moses, but rather offers an assurance, and a sign. The assurance is profound and basic: God's presence will be the decisive factor, which will overcome every human objection, including yours and ultimately Pharaoh's as well. But also, a sign: to assure you that the matter is certain, I will lead you and the whole people right back here to this holy mountain, Horeb. Here on this mountain, you will worship God.

Moses objects again: when I return to Egypt and announce that God has sent me, they will ask your name, which involves your intention, your new plan for their lives. We know what the God of the fathers once wanted, but what does he want now? What should I tell them? Once again, God does not dismiss Moses' objection but uses it to guide Moses further along the path set before him. Human personality is not canceled out by the divine call, but included within a sovereign purpose and plan that encompasses all reality.

The answer God gives to Moses is justly famous. He first directs the answer concerning his name to Moses himself. The name he announces is both an answer to Moses as well as a refusal to answer: I will be who I will be. This is not a meaningless repetition of phrases, far from it, nor is it a philosophical assertion of pure self-containment. Who is God? Well, who God is will be made clear in his future acts, which for now he refuses to reveal. God will make himself fully manifest on his own time, in his own way, by the decisive acts he performs; yet the God who acts in the future will be the same God as the past. I will be who I will be; only for now, you must wait in hope.

Then God tells Moses what he must say to the people. Moses is not charged to declare now to the people Israel the ultimate purpose of God for intervening in their lives at just this time. God will make that clear only by his fresh action of deliverance; God will be, only as he does. Yet Moses is the one God has called as messenger, through which this ultimate divine purpose will work itself out in their lives. Nor does this new divine intervention in their lives give them only temporary insight into the reality of the divine. God's name, known now in his coming act of deliverance, is the name by which God will forever be known in service and worship. This God is God forever.

We stand back now and consider the call of God in Jesus Christ in the light of the call of Moses. Three points are essential. First of all, the call of God is not the completion of a spiritual or moral journey we undertake. Quite the opposite. The call of God radically intersects our lives from above and brings all human moral and spiritual projects to an end, calling our lives into being, as it were, from the dead. Discipleship is newness of life. We have plans and projects that we hope will lead us forward to a divine dimension of ourselves and the universe. The call of God does not complete these plans and projects, but thrusts them aside, opening before us the broad vistas of his ever-renewing love. We have political and moral agendas that we are quite certain originate in a divine impulse to better the world, and follow them in order thereby to find God in the world. The call of God does not sanction or underwrite these agendas, but overthrows and subverts them. God alone is God; he will not be included within any moral or political agenda. To encounter him is to step onto holy ground, where he alone confronts us not to our destruction but to our ultimate redemption. To follow the call of God is to leave the projects of life, the moral and political and personal agendas we have constructed, however pious they may sound, forever behind. Jesus Christ is risen from the dead; to live with him is to follow the exalted Lord in the new world that he himself has brought into being and rules. We continue to live in this world, but our lives are now forever grounded in the call of God, not in the inner resources we bring or receive from life as we have always known it. We are made new, because the God who calls us brings a new world into being through the resurrection of Jesus Christ.

And yet, second of all, precisely here the biblical witness offers a sharp corrective to any one-sided view, as the call of Moses so brilliantly illustrates. From the moment God encounters Moses at the burning bush, we begin to discover ever fresh elements of his personality. And these are not only not ignored or discarded by God, they are taken seriously, enveloped, and included within the eternal divine purpose. God does not call us as passive vessels of his will, but as active agents of his purpose, whose deepest desires, fears, hopes, and dreams are embraced by the divine mercy. The Bible offers no explanation for this mystery of grace, as if there is some philosophical principle of providence at work. It is simply so: God call us as human persons into his service, and knows our inner and outer lives better than we know them ourselves. We find our deepest desires met far beyond our ability to articulate them by the simplicity of his command. We discover our furthest-reaching dreams abundantly fulfilled by the direction he leads us, now here, now there, until we can only look back in wonder. Even our struggles are not subverted but taken seriously by God, who gently leads us time and again back to the path he has set before us despite our many doubts and misgivings. The Bible has no conceptualization of types of human personality, an invention of Greek philosophy. Rather, the biblical narratives present a vast array of individual characters in all their unique emotional, intellectual, and physical possibilities and limitations. Ultimately, we cannot know, even ourselves, as we are known by God, who does not turn aside our uniqueness but shapes it into his glory.

And a third point, so clearly brought out in the story of Moses. The call of God in Jesus Christ is not a general principle laid down once and for all, the same for all time. It comes always in the unique historical moment of the present. We may and should admire the figures of the early church for their service to Christ; but we live in a very different time, with very different needs and resources. We may give our deepest respect to the great figures of the Reformation, who faced unspeakable challenges with enormous brilliance and success. But we face different challenges, and are called to a different path of faithfulness. To embrace the call of God is to live fully in the present moment. Nostalgia for the past is a trap of disobedience, however much we may learn from those who have gone before us. The God of Abraham, Isaac, and Jacob called Moses to a different task; the same God even now calls us in a new time and a new way to serve the risen Lord in the present for the sake of the future. We can but trust him, who always leads us forward and never backward.

We also learn from this extraordinary passage spectacular insights concerning the biblical witness to the living reality of God. God's reality is clearly not discovered by Moses; it is revealed by God. God makes himself known to us; we do not find him by human cleverness, however advanced we may pretend to be in our postmodern world. Modern technology may build fantastic new castles of ingenuity, but they are no nearer to God than an ancient ziggurat. The God we come to know is a God who lives, first of all, in the fulfillment of his love and freedom. God is free to love his people by coming to meet us where we are. He does not love us from a distance. He meets us, calls us by name, and invites into the covenant of grace that comprehends the past, present, and future in the one reality of his merciful kindness. God turns toward us in love without reservation, giving himself fully to us, binding his very identity as God together with his commitment to our well-being. And yet, not in contrast to, but in complete fulfillment of that love, God remains free to be God in his own time, and in his own way. He gives himself to us, but he does not give himself away. God acts only according to his own sovereign plan, which he shares with no one. We are called to follow him, certainly not to lead him, not even to equal partnership with him. God's genuine love for all humanity is crowned by his freedom to be God in his own time and way; yet God's freedom to be God is only fully expressed by his total and complete commitment in love that surrounds and upholds the whole creation.

God lives, second of all, in the dialectic of being and act, as expressed in the name he reveals to Moses: I will be who I will be. God is not pure being; God is not discovered, as was once often affirmed in theology, by the analysis of being itself. God is not the mysterious ontological secret of the universe, the ground of reality. Nor is God pure act, if by that is meant that we do not know who God is, only how he acts toward us. Again, it has often been declared that the limits of our knowledge of God are such that God's true reality is beyond our awareness; we know only his relation to us, not his true being.

Both of these false assertions—pure being and pure act—are set aside by the sovereign majesty of the biblical witness, which refuses to be painted into a philosophical corner. God's being—his true inner reality—is made known *only* in his act, in the event of his saving love. That is one truth, upon which we can fully depend. Yet on the other hand, it is God's *own* true being—not a mere projection of God—that is declared to us in the act of his kindness and mercy. What is declared to Moses is in fact fulfilled in the incarnation. The incarnation is the event of God's entry into the world—as act—in such a way that God's true reality is not only fully manifest, but fully present among us—as being. "God was in Christ reconciling the world to himself"; that is the final word of being and act, act and being, in which God is known among all humankind.

God lives, third of all, by taking human suffering upon himself. He knows human suffering not from the outside (as sympathy) but from the inside (as empathy). He takes it to heart, knowing our struggles even better than we ourselves can fully name them. God not only shares our suffering, he illuminates it, by bearing it, and lightens it, by bearing it away. God hears the cries of us people, whether they are gathered as one or scattered, alone in the silence of hardship. God hears, he listens, he understands, and he draws near to save.

5. Passover

Exodus 12:1–20

AFTER MOSES RECEIVES THE call of God in the wilderness of Horeb (Sinai), and is told by God the name by which he is forever to be known among his people, Moses is joined by Aaron and they return to Egypt for the great confrontation with Pharaoh. Moses is reassured by God that the outcome will indeed be the liberation of the entire people from bondage, but not before the mighty hand of God acts throughout the land according to his sovereign and mysterious purpose. From a human point of view, it does not go well; Pharaoh refuses their declaration of God's challenge to let his people go. And as a result, the plagues of God descend upon Egypt: blood, frogs, gnats, flies, disease, boils, hail, locusts, darkness. The plagues ascend in their destructive force, yet Pharaoh in every case fails to see the divine meaning hidden in the suffering. His heart is hardened; that it is to say, he will not see the signs indicated by these terrible events visited upon his land and upon his people. Yet from the point of view of God's unfolding plan, God's glory is now being displayed, as he makes his signs and wonders multiply in terrible and awesome judgment. Yet, more is to come.

God informs Moses of one final, tenth plague, the most terrible of all. It will strike the Egyptians without regard to station or wealth, and even Pharaoh cannot avoid the consequences and the meaning of this last awful moment of judgment. At midnight, God will strike down the firstborn of everyone in Egypt, including all people and animals. Yet no harm will come to the children of Israel whatsoever; it will be clear in a final and definitive way that God does indeed make a distinction between Israel and the surrounding people. Only then will Pharaoh let the people go.

It is at this point in the biblical narrative that the Passover is instituted. We will briefly describe the elements of the event itself, then summarize several themes emphasized in its celebration.

God himself carefully describes the ceremony of Passover to Moses and Aaron. Passover—and the divine event of liberation of Israel from bondage that it forever commemorates—is not to be understood as one event within the onward flow of time. Rather, Passover is a celebration that forever alters time itself. It is a new beginning *of* time, not just a new beginning *within* time, and so the calendar itself must change to reflect this divine alteration of the life of the people. Everyone in Israel is to celebrate Passover, without exception; it is a special celebration of the whole community. The unit that undertakes the celebration is to be the family. This is not a gathering of tribes, or of friendly associations, or of like-minded individuals; this is for families, bound together within the one community of faith. Each family is to select a kid, whether a sheep or a goat. If a single family is not able to consume an entire kid, then it is entirely permissible for two small families to join forces and share an animal together. Everyone is to contribute their fair share in order to purchase the lamb or goat.

The animal itself is precisely described. This is no ordinary meal. The animal is to be a year old, male, and without blemish of any kind. It is to be selected and then kept back for four days before the actual feast of the Passover. On that day, at twilight, each family of Israel is to slaughter their animal, and sprinkle some of the blood on the doorposts and lintels of the houses where they are staying. The animal should be roasted over the fire, then eaten with unleavened bread and bitter herbs. The entire animal is to be roasted, and cooked only in that way, over the fire. And, the entire animal is to be eaten, with nothing left over to the next day; anything not eaten is to be incinerated.

Only now in the description are we given a more refined indication of the purpose of this extraordinary meal. For it is to be eaten fully clothed, sandals on the feet, staff in the hand; it is to be eaten in a hurry, as if the people are ready to leave in an instant. For on this night, God will carry out the terrifying judgment of the tenth plague, passing through the land and killing every firstborn in Egypt. Yet the blood on the houses of the children of Israel will be a sign to God and to them that he will pass over their houses, leaving them safe inside, free from the plague let loose upon the entire country of Egypt. Only unleavened bread shall be eaten during this time, for Israel is set apart from the divine judgment on the one hand, and ready to make haste to follow the redemptive love of God for his chosen people.

Several features of the Passover celebration stand out. First of all, there is the extraordinary tension between the past and the future, between memory and hope. Clearly the Passover looks forward in hope, for it is the beginning of a new time in God's history with his people, indeed in God's redemptive purpose for the world. There is hope because God in his love mercifully rescues the people from cruel bondage by destroying the destroyer, the Egyptians, in such a way as to preserve the lives of the oppressed children of Israel. The future is now open before them in a gift of divine freedom that is absolute, and grounded solely in the freedom of God himself. Yet there is also memory, a celebration of this one event from the past that never truly recedes in its astounding significance. Each new generation, henceforth, learns just how amazing the love of God is, in passing over the Israelites while enacting his terrifying judgment upon the Egyptians. Each new generation remembers the fearful awe of this night, eating a meal that binds them together with that first generation for all time to come. Hope for the future is grounded in this very memory of the past, while memory is kept alive by hope; and both are ultimately grounded in the one God of all life, the one source of past, present, and future, for Israel and the nations.

Second, the Passover is a celebration of the entire people of God. While the detailed arrangements are organized by family units, the accent is on the whole people gathered at once for the sacred meal. Nor is this a statistical statement, as if the point is to add up all the smaller units, until one can be assured of the largest possible unit of assembly. The accent is clearly theological in nature. Unlike, say, later Roman Catholic and Protestant debates, which had trouble envisioning a holistic community of faith that is at the same time spiritual in nature yet visible in form, the Passover event assures that the fundamental grounding of Israel's existence is precisely that: a single visible, spiritual congregation. Right from the beginning of its liberation from Egyptian bondage, the people of Israel is a people of God, called by God into existence as a unique people dedicated to his service alone.

Third, the account of the crossing of the Red Sea—which will come next in our exegesis, as it does in the biblical narrative—is prefaced by the instructions concerning Passover, and is followed by the celebratory Song of Moses. Put simply: the event of exodus is bracketed on both sides by the meaning of that event. There is no unedited, unmediated description of the exodus from Egypt; the depiction is a witness of faith from beginning to end, rendered in such a way that it is treasured forever in a religious community that indeed is forever linked to it. Now, modern historians— whether maximalists or minimalists makes no difference—will inevitably want to dig behind the biblical witness of faith to determine "what really happened." Regardless of their concern, the biblical witness itself, and the community of faith which treasures it even now (both Jewish and Christian), recognizes that such a move runs exactly counter to the very heart of the testimony of Scripture. We can gather to celebrate exodus; we can sing of exodus; but one thing we cannot do is find the "route" of exodus on a map. The effort to dig behind the witness of faith to an uninterpreted "fact" is closed off by Scripture itself. Nor is the point to suggest that the subjective actualization of exodus is the real focus of the text, for as we will see, it is certainly not. God liberated a people from bondage by wonders and miracles; the focus is on God's own miraculous intervention in human life for good. But his footprints can be seen only from the vantage point of faithful celebration, even today.

We consider now the biblical witness to Passover from the standpoint of the subject matter to which it refers, its theological referent. Without question, based on the witness of the New Testament, Christian testimony is univocal: Jesus Christ himself is the true fulfillment of Passover. He is himself the paschal mystery, which even now gathers his people into celebratory feast; he is the pure and spotless Passover lamb, indeed the lamb of God who takes away the sins of the whole world. In the community of faith in Jesus Christ we are thus compelled to reflect theologically upon the relation of the old and the new. It is essential, however, that we move in both directions. On the one hand, we understand Passover in the light of the gospel; that is, as a shadow whose substance is Christ himself. On the other hand—and this second theological movement is sadly often missing in traditional Christian exegesis—we also only truly understand the gospel in the light of Passover. Passover remains promise even in the church, whose true significance fleshes out our full understanding of the reality of Christ for church and world.

Jesus Christ himself is the one true Passover lamb of God, sacrificed for the sins of the world. To understand Passover in the light of the gospel is truly to meditate upon the cost to God of the redemption of the world. God did not command a sacrifice for sins to placate himself. God himself entered our world, becoming human without being any less God, in order to die on the cross as an expiation, a covering, for our sins, for our sake. Even before creation itself, Christ was destined by God as the pure and spotless lamb to take away the sins of the world. Christ himself broke the power of sin once and for all, by his death on the cross. God in Christ reconciled the world to himself—by suffering, by dying.

We too are called as disciples of Christ to suffer and die with him. We are called to leave one life behind—the life measured by success and triumph—and to live a new life with him—a life conformed to him, in faithfulness and service. We are not called to rule over our enemies but to help them, to pray for them, to walk with them along the same path of human need and divine blessing. We are not called to seek out victory over others as a way of life, but summoned rather to the constant focus of putting the needs of others before our own. We are not called to fulfill ourselves, but to master ourselves, that we might truly see others in their own legitimate quest for genuine human fulfillment. We are called to leave one world behind—an exodus from bondage—which is the world of self-realization, self-actualization, self-enslavement; and to step forward into a new world, a new creation, formed according to the image of Christ in life lived for others in mutual love and heartfelt friendship. There is no going back; we never stop struggling against the old life of sin and bondage, but neither do we ever lose our focus on the new life of the risen Christ that draws us forward.

The change of time is once and for all. The old is gone, the new has come. The death and resurrection of Jesus Christ are not simply the beginning of something that will be completed by us, not at all; Christ himself is already now the one true beginning that forever transforms the whole creation. We do not build his kingdom, for he himself has already established it now and forever, through the cross. We live under the sign of the cross, we are conformed to the image of the cross, we suffer to complete the agony of the cross, but in no sense whatsoever do we advance the work of Christ by our own efforts; for Christ himself has already accomplished the redemption of the whole cosmos. The newness of life in which we live and move is his gift to us, not our accomplishment before him. Our faith and hope are set on Christ alone.

We now move in the second, reverse direction of theological interpretation. That is, we ask: what is the meaning of the gospel in the light of Passover? The question is essential for contemporary Christian theological reflection upon Scripture for three reasons. First, it is necessary to retain the confessional affirmation of the ontological—not just historical—bond between the Old and New Testaments, which profess one eternal purpose of divine grace for the redemption of the cosmos. Second, it is crucial to affirm the continuing validity of the communion between the synagogue and the church, between the celebration of the Jewish Seder and the Christian Eucharist, as two parts of the one people of God. And finally, it is necessary to the full understanding of the subject matter; that is, we simply cannot truly understand the paschal mystery of Christ unless we move in both directions of theological interpretation of Scripture, for the sake of the gospel.

We learn from Passover, first of all, that God in Christ saves a people, not individuals. Of course, God knows us each by name, calls us each by name, even before the world was made. We are not specks floating in an undifferentiated mass of humanity, but persons established by the divine will in all our uniqueness. But that does not change the fact that God calls us all into community with one another. That happens in families, as we recognize the self in relation to others, coming to know our very existence as human persons only as we grow in responsibility for those nearest to us. It happens in the community of faith, whether the particular congregation in which we worship, or indeed the universal church that, while an article of faith, is nevertheless visible throughout the earth in all its fragmentary dependence on God's grace alone. It happens in our responsibility to society, by which we participate in the ever-expanding search for the common good, a search from which Christians can never shrink, but in which Christians cannot pretend to have the right answer to every question. God saves a people; that is the message of Passover that enlightens the gospel to glory.

Second, however much we rightly understand the gospel as a personal struggle against sin and evil, a striving toward the goal of the risen Christ, we must necessarily recognize in the light of Passover that the gospel is political. I do not mean that the gospel favors one political party over another; only God knows which party he belongs to. But I do mean that the gospel works in the world in such a way that on some issues sides are necessarily taken, that choices are made, that votes are cast, even that activism is necessarily embraced. We move from bondage to freedom when we celebrate the risen Christ, from enslavement to a new birth of justice for all, especially the weak and vulnerable. That is biblical theology, not party politics. Whoever reads the story of Passover, which prepares us for the event of exodus, knows full well that God at times takes sides against the unjust power of the bully and the tyrant, the oppressor and the autocrat. And God moves in the world to set free those who have labored unjustly at the hands of a cruel and systemic barbarism. The church cannot stand idly by in such times. To embrace the gospel—as instructed by Passover—is to take a stand against oppression, and for the full civil rights and dignity of everyone.

Third, while we affirm without reservation that Christ is the final, definitive divine event of reconciliation for the whole world, we yet await the complete manifestation of that event. God's final victory is yet to come; God's final consummation of his purpose is yet to be accomplished. And so, in the meantime, we live lives of readiness, waiting and watching in the world, not getting distracting or weighed down, but keeping our eyes fixed upon the glory which is to be revealed at the last day. Our feet are shod; our loins are girded; our bread is unleavened; our meal is already prepared and eaten in haste, standing and not sitting; for we know that Christ is coming soon in grandeur and triumph.

6. The Miracle at the Sea

Exodus 14

THE ACCOUNT OF THE miraculous crossing of the sea is yet another example of poetic narrative in which the confession of faith is central to the biblical witness. Yet it is crucial to observe the extraordinary elements of narrative skill that guide the retelling of the story. Rather than speaking in the voice of an omniscient narrator, the biblical witness here unfolds by shifting from one perspective to another, thus not only expanding the parameters of the event, but most certainly heightening the theological tension that guides it. While we may have learned of the great crossing of the sea long ago, even as children, it is essential to relearn the biblical witness again and again, if we are fully to appreciate the heart of divine grace.

The narrative of the miraculous crossing is introduced in 13:17–22, by pointing directly to the majesty of God's own self-declaration. God has his own sovereign purpose, and he manifests his purpose according to his own gracious and unrestrained will. Having delivered the people from Pharaoh, God does not lead the people of Israel on the most direct route from Egypt to the new land of promise. If he were to do so, they might very well balk at the threat of military engagement with the dreaded Philistines. So, God leads them on a more *indirect* route. Notice: from now until the people enter the land in the book of Joshua, God is *leading* them, even as they wander through the wilderness, indeed everywhere they go. The indirect route however forces the people up against a clearly insurmountable physical barrier, which is the Sea of Reeds. They do leave ready for action, one way or another. They leave permanently, taking the bones of Joseph with them for final burial in the land of promise. God leads them in a pillar of cloud by day, and in a pillar of fire by night, both guiding them and giving them light to travel. Whatever happens will happen according to the sovereign purpose of God. But the reader is unsettled; how can this possibly work out for the good? Is this not a self-evident trap, an epic blunder?

At this point, Moses is brought into the narrative. God tells Moses at least some of his sovereign purpose, though not all. The people are to encamp in front of the Sea of Reeds, hardly a propitious choice from a military perspective, pinned against an unfordable sea. God tells Moses of the purpose and thoughts of Pharaoh, who will conclude from the change in their direction that the Israelite people are hopelessly confused and lost in the wilderness. And rightly so, we might add! He will regret his decision to let them go, as God hardens his heart. And he will pursue them with all his army. The Egyptians will then know that God is indeed Lord of all reality. The primary theme for the narrative is thus set. *God* has his sovereign purpose; yet *Pharaoh* has his own kingly purpose. And these two purposes are diametrically opposed to one another. Recall from the opening verses of the book of Exodus that this conflict has been paramount. The future of the people of Israel is at stake, as the reader now must watch what happens when God's promised purpose and Pharaoh's purpose mount a direct, head-on collision. How God will in fact enact his gracious purpose is not yet clear, to Moses or the reader.

First God, then Moses, and now Pharaoh is the focus of the narrative, like voices in a majestic fugue. Pharaoh learns that the people of Israel have indeed left the land of Egypt. He gathers the leading courtiers around him, and together they express utter regret at what they have done, giving the Israelites their freedom. What have we done, letting Israel leave our service? Regret turns immediately into action. Pharaoh orders the entire Egyptian army, including its picked troops and charioteers, to engage in hot pursuit of the people of Israel. But notice already as the narrator hints at what is to come. Pharaoh thinks that Israel is confused and wandering aimlessly in the wilderness; in fact, they are led by God exactly where he wants them. Pharaoh thinks that the people of Israel are little more than prisoners of the desert; in fact, they are walking out in bold defiance of their previous servitude, heads held high. Subtly, the narrative focus is shifting. It is not really a contest between God's purpose and Pharaoh's purpose. We are beginning to realize that Pharaoh's purpose is already *included* within the divine purpose all along. Only one true purpose guides this event from the beginning, and that is God's.

The final narrative "voice" in the narrative fugue is now introduced, which is the Israelite people. A summary sets up the scene. The people of Israel are now pinned against the Sea of Reeds on one side. And on the other side, Pharaoh, together with his entire army, including the charioteers and their picked officer corps, are bearing down upon them, obviously with destructive intent. Given the difference between the slow march of a people, and the quick pace of an army, it is no surprise that the Egyptians overtake them.

The Israelites suddenly look up and glance about them with horrific surprise: there is the fierce Egyptian army bearing hard down upon them! They are completely paralyzed by fear, and soon fall into a pattern that has already set in, and will recur again and again throughout the Pentateuch. That is, in desperation they attack Moses. Why have you led us out of Egypt! Were there not enough burial plots for all the bodies we are about to become after the Egyptians slaughter us? Did you bring us to the desert so the sands could wash over our dead? Did we not tell you that we were perfectly content to be slaves of the Egyptians; so why did you have to meddle in our affairs? We would rather be their slaves than be food for the wild beasts of the desert! Moses does not even attempt to address the wild array of chaotic objections. Rather, he addresses the one thing that matters, which is the oppressive *fear* that lies behind them all. Do not be afraid, he tells his fellow Israelites. You do not have to do a thing. Just stand firm and watch; God himself, and God alone, will accomplish your deliverance this day. Those Egyptians bearing down upon you, you will never see again. God will fight the battle to come, and the victory will be his.

It should be noticed. The reaction of the Egyptians, and the reaction of the Israelites, is verbally quite similar, almost identical. Why did we do this! The similarity is of course more than verbal. Both reactions are based on the failure to recognize God's hidden purpose behind events, shared by Egypt and faithless Israel alike.

The various factors and actors in the narrative have now been fully introduced, and the account drives forward to its astounding conclusion. No one—not even Moses—knows how it is even remotely possible that God will accomplish his impossible purpose. So, God tells Moses to have the people move forward, toward the Sea of Reeds. Moses is to raise his staff, and stretch his hand. The very sea will divide, that the people might walk through the midst of it on dry ground. Pharaoh and the Egyptians will follow, and God will gain glory over all Egypt and his army. The purpose of God will not only defeat the purpose of Pharaoh; the purpose of God will turn the purpose of Pharaoh into an instrument of God's own glorious, redemptive will.

The narrative now allows us to stand back, as it were, and watch in wonder as the finale unfolds, in which all the various fugue-like strands of the narrative are brought together. The messenger of God, and the cloud, stand between the army of Egypt and the people of Israel, allowing their escape. Moses raises his staff, and the sea is parted. The people escape on dry ground through the Sea of Reeds. When the Egyptians are allowed to see what has happened, they are hell-bent on hot pursuit and destruction. The fiery pillar throws them into panic, and God himself clogs up the wheels of their chariots. Until now it was the people of Israel who were afraid; now it is the Egyptians who suddenly realize in terror that God is indeed fighting for the Israelites, against the Egyptians. They try to escape, but the walls of water return when Moses again stretches out his hand, and the army is drowned. Not one is left alive. All that Israel can see on the following morning are the dead bodies of the soldiers who once held them captive in slavery, now strewn along the beaches of the sea. They now have no doubt who has accomplished their deliverance. They now revere God, and trust Moses.

The event of God's saving love in Jesus Christ is of grace, and of grace alone, apart from all human cooperation. The cross and resurrection of Jesus Christ is the one divine event of mercy that puts right the entire cosmos, reconciling all creation to God. Grace, and grace alone, is the way of God in human life. Indeed, God often enough removes one by one the props by which we vainly and proudly would stand on our own feet, sure of our own ability, ready to point to our own achievement. God readily enough puts us in situations in which there is no exit, no point of retreat, no way forward according to any rational calculation. And just here, where all props are removed, all possibilities surrendered, God himself, and God alone, makes a way forward. He suddenly shows us a path that long lay hidden; he suddenly clears away the debris of our lives, and there in front of us is the divine possibility that has been waiting all along. We cannot see it, as long as we are sure of our own abilities. We cannot find it, as long as we rely on the power of our own "positive thinking." God makes a way forward that transcends every human way, negative or positive. Of his gracious mercy alone, he rescues us from the entrapments to sin and folly, from the oppressions to human domination and abuse, and puts us on a new way of freedom and peace. We have but to stand back and watch. We have but to marvel and to praise. We have but to ponder and to pray, and to think gladly upon the glory of the Lord.

Even when God himself in his sovereign care opens up a way before us, we hesitate. Instead of going forward, we complain about the troubles ahead. Instead of seeing with clarity the vision of God's abiding concern, we question the very commitment of God to his own just and constant love. Instead of using the means so readily available to us, we wallow in the difficulties we face, some real, but mostly imagined. Why is it that we struggle to walk on a path so clearly marked out ahead of us by God himself? What holds us back is fear. We simply do not take account of the active and present love of God that directs all things according to his eternal purpose. We see only the petty and jealous purposes of the world (including our own), pursuing the unworthy means and ends of human folly. Surely such folly will defeat the progress and mission of the church! Surely it will defeat the common good of human society! Surely it will defeat my life, which counts for nothing, and less than nothing! There are large and small pharaohs in every age, indeed in every human life; and sadly, these grandiloquent figures steal away the focus of faith on God's eternal purpose alone. Just here, we need to be reminded: *do not be afraid*. God's people have time and again faced circumstances just as troubling, and run up against obstacles just as insurmountable. They have been stopped cold, with no way forward, and no way back. Yet it is in just these circumstances that a new way, a better way, a miraculous way, suddenly opens up in front of them, not because they are clever and wise, but because God is eternally committed to our welfare. In times of struggle, pray and watch, and see the salvation of the Lord.

Perhaps nowhere is it more clear in the Bible—certainly in the Old Testament—that we are not redeemed by God because of our faith. There is not the slightest indication that the people of God put their trust in the Lord's redeeming love as a *condition* for its fulfillment. Quite the opposite; they continually express their complete *lack* of confidence in God's ability to accomplish his promise right up to the very moment of its glorious design. God's love for us, and for the whole world, is not grounded in our ability to trust in him, for indeed we have no such ability. The reverse is true; our faith is grounded solely in God's love. Faith itself is part of the gift of redemption, not a precondition for it. Rather, God's redeeming love is grounded solely in his own eternal reality. God loves because he is himself a relationship of love; God loves because he elects to form a relationship of love—a covenant—with humankind, which in fact expresses the free affirmation of the other in unity that God himself defines.

That is not to say that faith is irrelevant, not at all. Faith itself is part of the gift, and exercising that faith is required among those who enter into the loving embrace of God's redemptive will. Where there was fear, now there is confidence. Where there was denial, now there is open wonder. Where there was sadness and misery, now there is the joy of song and celebration. Where we once doubted God's ability to accomplish his eternal promise, now we see that the mystery of that promise is hidden from the powerful and the mighty, and revealed only to those who know where to look. Faith, in the biblical world, can come before, during, or after the miracle of divine grace; but it is always a divine *gift* of that miracle and never a human condition for receiving it.

Just as the people of Israel moved from slavery to freedom by walking through the waters of the sea, so we too move through the water of baptism, leaving one life behind, and embracing the new life that is to come. Baptism is the sign of our real unity with Christ the crucified and risen Lord. As surely as we receive the water of baptism, so surely is one life now washed forever away. A life in which buying and selling, owning and grasping, striving and winning, dominating and securing, head up the list of our priorities; those priorities are now forever in the past, buried with Christ in the grave. As surely as the water of baptism washes us clean, so too do we now live with the one priority of the rule of God in Jesus Christ. Serving rather than being served; casting stones away rather than gathering them together; looking out for the good of our near and distant neighbor rather than seeking our own way in the world; pointing to Christ through word and deed rather than exalting ourselves. That is not to say that the political freedom of exodus is a mere trope for inner transformation. Not at all. But it is to say that political liberation without the knowledge of the gospel leaves us no nearer to the truth than we were before. To know Christ is *always* to act, and to act decisively for freedom and justice in the world; but that is not to say that to act for freedom and justice is at the same time to know Christ. Christ alone shows us the way, because Christ alone is the way.

We are reminded by the miraculous crossing of the sea that God works in ways beyond human comprehension, both extraordinary and ordinary. Moses raises his staff and the sea parts; yet a wind blows, separating the waters. Moses raises his staff again, and the sea rushes back together; yet the wheels of the Egyptian chariots are mysteriously clogged, blocking their escape. A post-Enlightenment idiom would try to divide these dimensions into the natural and the supernatural, debating which, if either, is to be ascribed to the divine. The biblical narrative, with sovereign lack of concern for human moral and theological categories, will have none of it. Both the ordinary and the amazing are ascribed to God, and to God alone. He works his eternal purpose now one way, and now another; but always it is God alone who is working out his redemptive love in the midst of the earth. Faith sees God at work in the amazing and extraordinary. He parts the waters to accomplish his redemptive love. But faith also sees God at work in the daily workings of ordinary life. He turns the world on its axis, and in turning, gives day and night, summer and winter, seedtime and harvest, all according to his own timing. Faith sees God at work everywhere. That is the lesson of exodus.

Finally, the narrative of exodus puts to rest any notion of an ultimate conflict—known to church history as Manicheism—between good and evil. God's purpose alone is sovereign in all things throughout the entire cosmos. Evil may for a time look powerful, may for a time wreak havoc on the earth, may indeed for a time run rampant among the children of

God. But only for a time. Even evil serves God's eternal gracious purpose of love. God's loving will brings good even out of evil. Just as Pharaoh and all his army, in pursuing *their* purpose, serve only to magnify God's *own* overpowering and glorious will, so every human kingdom that asserts itself against God will in the end find itself serving his plan, despite itself. God's kingdom alone knows no end.

7. Bread from Heaven

Exodus 16:1–21

WE NOW BEGIN TO trace a period in the life of Israel that will take them through the wandering in the wilderness. An entire generation—forty years—will be consumed by their trek, for reasons yet to be made clear in the narrative of Scripture. Yet right from the beginning of the wilderness wandering, straight through to the very end, one theme will dominate above all others, and that is the theme of complaint, of murmuring. The people of God, newly liberated from slavery in Egypt, celebrate their newfound freedom by murmuring against Moses, and of course ultimately against God himself. Our passage sets the tone that will dominate throughout this period, and is filled with narrative detail that casts subtle shade and light.

The first point to notice is that the narrator gives a brief geographical and chronological itinerary. Several markers are made clear: they move from Elim, through the wilderness of Sin, and end up at Sinai. In terms of their departure from Elim, the notice is given *spatially*; in terms of their arrival at Sinai the notice is given *temporally* (the fifteenth day of the second month). So, we are not in an alternative universe of the imagination, but in the real world of space and time, the real world we in fact inhabit. That is simply assumed by the narrator. Now, since the advent of modern travel and geography of the holy land by Westerners, concerted efforts have been made to locate all these sites with precision, without consensus. Even the location of Mount Sinai, the geographical center of the Pentateuch, is disputed. What are we to make of the narrator's precision? It is theological, rather than geographical in nature. The point is not to say: go and find these places, using your favorite travel website! The point rather is this: God led Israel wherever they went. Even though they wandered through the wilderness for an entire generation, every single stage along the way was carefully designated by the will and charge of God. They were not a lost generation; they were following God through the wilderness.

While the theme of murmuring, of complaining, will be a constant refrain for the next forty years, the occasion or object of the complaint will change from time to time. Complaining is constant, but the grounds will shift now and again. The theme in the opening narration of the wilderness wandering is the lack of food. Close attention to the narration reveals much.

First of all, the grounds for the complaint are in fact a sham. They accuse Moses and Aaron of bringing them out into the wilderness to starve and kill them, but in fact they have plenty to eat. Yet they would prefer— so they declare—to return to slavery in Egypt, so little does their new life of freedom now mean! They are looking backward, while the narrator is moving the story forward. And their nostalgia for a false past is not only disorienting, but creating false facts. Meat was a rare delicacy in the ancient Near East, seldom consumed even by the very wealthy. Yet these Israelites are looking back to the good old days when meat was to be had aplenty by everyone! Surely you remember those days! Freedom brought them life, but they accuse Moses of fostering their death as a nation.

The narrator clearly unveils the false nostalgia of their backward dreams. Yet the narrative digs even deeper into a hidden layer of motivation. The people of Israel are complaining against Moses. Yet behind their overt accusation against Moses is the underlying issue all along: their unbelief. Despite the radical love of God shown them in the rescue from bondage in Egypt through the miracle of the parting of the waters, they doubt God. It is not their relationship to Moses that is here at stake, despite their explicit accusations; it is their relationship to God. They doubt the very fact that God, in his electing love, has called them into being as a people by the power of his mercy. It will not be the last time such doubt surfaces in the rest of the wilderness journey.

Just as God enfolded the counterplan of Pharaoh into God's own all-encompassing purpose for the liberation of the people of Israel from bondage in Israel, so now God enfolds the purported testing of God by Israel into God's own testing of Israel by God. Indeed, the God of the Bible has a way of turning the world of human experience upside down. To begin with, God utterly ignores the complaint of Israel concerning their hunger. Rather than respond to a false narrative, God creates a *new* narrative, indeed a *true* narrative, a new *reality*, by the giving of his promise. That promise is the giving of bread from heaven, which will now begin and accompany Israel throughout the long wilderness wanderings. The gift however comes with precise conditions that are laid out for Moses; and it is those conditions that constitute God's own test of the people.

The bread will come from the heavens—like the dew, in the ancient picture of the world—beginning with each new morning, a divine miracle of food. Each new day the people of Israel are to venture forth and gather just enough food for the day, no more and no less. On the sixth day, twice as much bread will come, and twice as much should be gathered. As Moses and Aaron explain to the people what is about to unfold, Moses makes the divine stakes crystal clear: "Your complaining is not against us but against the Lord." The gift comes on God's initiative alone, it comes on his conditions alone, and it comes on his timing alone. Israel is to receive an inexpressible divine gift, but in receiving it the true quality of their faith is at the same time exposed, for good or ill. The gift of the promise in fact exposes their unbelief.

The narrative then points to the sudden self-manifestation of God amidst the people. The story of the wilderness wandering will be repeated in many different contexts, but it is always the same. The people murmur against God, a constant refrain with only the minor change in topic from one episode to the next. There is a disputation between the people on the one hand, and Moses and Aaron on the other, as if the leadership of these two is the real issue. But finally, God himself steps forth to resolve the matter by showing the glory of his will. He does not honor their grumbling. Nowhere in this account does God suggest that the people really do need food. Rather, grounded solely in his redemptive love, God provides food in order to make known his loving-kindness, which is his very being. The people are to learn who God is through his gracious care for their well-being, throughout the entire wilderness journey. God makes himself known to Israel by supplying all of their needs, and indeed far more than they need.

The fulfillment of the promise of food comes the very next morning. When the dew of the morning is lifted, there remains across the surface of the desert a flaky substance never before encountered by the people of Israel. It can only be described in terms of what it is like; it is like coriander seed, and tastes like wafers in honey. It can be gathered each day, but it cannot be stored. When each person goes forth to gather and brings their manna—for that is the new name—back to their tent, they discover that each has exactly the same amount, no matter how much they gathered. No one has too much, no one has too little. The promise of God provides for the needs of the day, but not for the needs of tomorrow; tomorrow will take care of itself.

Of course (of course!), there are those who immediately put the promise of God to the test, and gather an extra amount to be aside, for future storage. They find on the next day that it has been fouled with worms. Similarly, the manna does not remain on the ground all day long, but burns up with the morning heat. God's promise is not *timeless*, but meets the needs of the moment. Nevertheless, when the people obey the command of God and gather the manna each day, they find that they have exactly enough to eat to fill their needs. And the manna does not stop from one day, to the next, to the next; in fact, it continues for *forty years*, for an entire generation, throughout the wilderness journey. The promise of God is all-sustaining in its mercy, just as Israel is dependent upon God, day by day, for its very existence.

We live in a cultural world in which enough is never enough. The sense that "more" is always required to be more fully human is of course reinforced by a multitude of messages from the world of marketing, as if we simply *cannot* live another day happily without coming into possession of this service, or that product, or this latest iteration of a technological advance. We are barraged by such messages on every conceivable media platform. But it goes beyond mere marketing. We live in a social world in which the very definition of our humanity has come to rest on what we possess. We are considered—and consider ourselves—more human, the more we possess, and less human, the less we possess.

Far worse, there is afoot in the religious world—indeed the Christian world—a notion that the role of God himself is to supply the greatest number of possessions to those who please him the most. The insidious "prosperity gospel" is not limited to any one denomination or theological movement, but is in fact widespread in our time. And of course, it is false. God gives *enough*. In his bountiful love, he gives exactly what we need to flourish, and far more; but he does not waste his goodness. The culture of excess, which can never say enough, is a fundamental contradiction of the gospel. The inability to say, I have all that I need and far more besides, is a catastrophic loss of basic faith in the living reality of God. The threat of the prosperity gospel strikes not only at the heart of Christian truth, it seriously jeopardizes the health of God's good creation, contrary to his will, and threatens the equality of all peoples and nations, in direct contradiction to the living command of God our savior. The prosperity gospel is false faith.

The inability to say "enough" is the root of inequality in our world. God gives enough to feed and supply all peoples, in all nations of the earth. That is simply a fact. But instead of *using* the goods and gifts of God for the purpose for which he intends them, we *hoard* them. We take for ourselves far, far more than we need, and in so doing we deprive others of the most basic needs of human life. God gives to each according to their need, and requires from each according to their ability, according to Scripture. But we twist and distort his good purpose. We hoard his gifts, not according to need, but simply because we can. Far beyond use, far beyond even desire, we gather and gather and gather even more, until we no longer even know what we have, stored away from sight, never to be seen or used again, and even pay for the privilege of storing our junk. Meanwhile, down the street, or across the planet, live our fellow human beings who lack the basic necessities that make human life human. There is a direct *connection* between what we have over-gathered and what they lack. The bounty of the earth under the gracious hand of God produces enough; hunger is not an *agricultural* problem, but a social problem, a political problem, indeed a *moral* problem.

Indeed, from a Christian perspective, hunger is a theological problem. God causes the earth to produce a bountiful yield, more than enough to feed humankind. We gather far more than we need, thus depriving the ability of others to find even the basic fulfillment of human need, for one simple reason: we do not put our trust in God. God and God alone is the source of all life. God and God alone is the source of the sustenance by which we live. We do not live simply by eating food; we live by knowing God. To know God truly is to put our active trust in him in the very center of our existence. We do not need to gather more than we require, for God alone is our strength; God alone gives us the gracious gifts by which we live. We do not need to hoard wealth and so deprive others of the basic goods of life, for God alone is the supreme good of our being, the one true fulfillment of every need. We *can* say that enough is enough because God is God in our lives. We can live a life of abundant simplicity because the living God truly lives in us, and is the very center and heart of our existence. We can accept joyfully and willingly the limits of human possession because God himself has made us his own, God himself has given us the unlimited joy of his electing love, without restriction.

As we consider the witness of our narrative in the light of the gospel, we remember the stricture of Deuteronomy: humankind does not live by bread alone, but by every word which God himself speaks. And who is the Word of the Father? Who is that bread, by which alone humankind gains true sustenance, in this life and in the world to come? Jesus Christ himself is the true bread of life, the true manna from heaven, the one true promised gift of life. To partake of him by faith is already, even now, to inherit eternal life. To share in this one true bread is not only to find the one true fulfillment of all human existence, though it is that. Christ and Christ alone is the peace we seek, the joy we crave, the satisfaction of every need we feel deep in our innermost selves. Even more, to partake of this one heavenly bread is even now to pass from death to life, from this world that is passing away to eternity that is to come, and that in Christ is already here. Eternal life does not begin when we die, it begins when we believe; and Christ the true bread of life is the food that even now feeds our very being for eternity with him. This food alone brings true life; all other food brings death. To partake of this food in faith is to pass from death to life, from the old world which is passing away to the new world which is to come, and in him is already here, ruling even now in the midst of the earth. Christ alone sustains us along the way. Christ alone gives us strength for every trial of life. Christ alone enriches our enjoyment of everyday life by his presence, daily renewing our sense of wonder and joy. Feed on him.

Only in him do we learn the true meaning of contentment. There will be times in life when we have more than enough, and in such times, we are called by him to share what we have with those who have little. But there will be other times when we too, like the children of Israel of old, must journey through the wilderness. A sure thing suddenly collapses; a well-made plan suddenly crashes to the ground; human frailty suddenly becomes glaringly obvious, whether in our own lives or in those we love. We come up short. We, who perhaps once had plenty, even more than we needed, now must struggle to get by. It is crucial not to spiritualize our text; it is vital not to try to be more spiritual than God. For the fact is, God gives the children of Israel real bread to eat. But he gives only what is needed, no more and no less. And that is the secret of contentment. We learn to appreciate every morsel of daily sustenance as a direct gift from God. God breaks through the façade of a dependable causal nexus of work and reward, to remind us that every single possession we own is his gift, every meal of which we partake comes down from his overflowing love for us. Contentment means recognizing the hand of the Giver in the gift, and so realizing that as long as we know the Giver, we will never be without. Whether in plenty or in want, God is with us still.

But he does not dispense his grace as a lifelong endowment upon which we can draw on our terms, on our conditions, on our timetable. Rather, God's promise of abiding care comes on his terms, his conditions, and his timetable; and that means it comes one day at a time. God's mercies are new every morning. He may use the wonders of miraculous intervention, or he may use indirect means of which we can scarcely even be aware, but either way God and God alone is the one true source of our daily bread, our daily existence, in every dimension of human need and enjoyment. We must surely emerge from our tents to gather; passivity is no substitute for genuine faith. But we gather because God himself and God alone provides our every need one day at a time. Give us this day our daily bread, we are taught by our Lord to pray. Not, give us a lifetime of bread that we may divide up in yearly dividends; simply, give us this day what we need for the day, and let tomorrow take care of itself. There is a kind of holy, carefree Christian *minimalism* that follows the gospel wherever it goes, as we wander through the wilderness of this world.

8. The Education of Moses

Exodus 18

FOR SOME TIME NOW, the narrative of Exodus has focused upon the extraordinary miracles of God's wonder, accomplished for his people Israel through his servant Moses. Now, suddenly, the narrative takes a surprising break, both in substance and style. In substance, it shifts back to an earlier phase in the life of Moses, when he was yet to be called by God to the momentous task in which he is now engaged; a time when he was fleeing the wrath of Pharaoh into the land of Midian. There he was welcomed with embracing hospitality by a Midianite priest named Jethro, and would eventually come to marry one of Jethro's daughters. As readers we have come a long way since then; indeed, Moses has come a long way, since that time of wandering alone in the wilderness, fleeing in terror from Egyptian might. Yet suddenly here we are now once again in the presence of this very man, Jethro, who once again enters Moses' life, seemingly from out of nowhere. Why? We are reminded in this amazing chapter that, while Moses is the called servant of God, named by God himself as the deliverer of the people Israel, Moses remains an ordinary human being, which in the Bible certainly centers on his life in a family. So, the chapter shifts the style, slowing the narrative way down, giving time for Moses the human person to reconnect with his family even if only for a brief interlude. And while he does so, he comes to realize an invaluable lesson. His life as an ordinary human being still has something to teach him as a called servant of the living God.

The chapter naturally divides into two sections, the first being the blessed reunion of Moses with his father-in-law Jethro, his wife Zipporah, and their children (1–12). The narrator takes care to reintroduce Jethro to the reader, lest anyone miss his importance, relating his calling as priest in Midian, and underscoring his familial role as the father-in-law of Moses, an exalted position in the ancient Near East. Zipporah as well is reintroduced, as are their two sons. Their Hebrew names are stressed. Gershom means a foreigner, or a migrant; Eliezer means that God alone is my help. The children of Moses are a constant reminder that his homeland lies in front of him, not behind him, and that only God alone can draw him forward. No earthly power can accomplish this. Yet Jethro comes to greet Moses precisely because he has heard of all that God has done for him even already. It is a chance for Moses the human being—and for the readers as well—to pause for just a moment and realize the enormity of what has already happened. God has brought the enslaved people Israel out of Egypt, and they are now free, despite utterly impossible human obstacles.

And so, the father-in-law and the son-in-law; the husband and the wife; the father and his children; for just a brief interlude reconnect on a human level now in the wilderness, with Egypt long behind them, and with the land of promise still ahead of them. There is a blessed moment of greeting, and an invitation to enter into the tent of Moses. It is worth reflecting: only now do we realize that Moses has his own tent! It is obvious that he must. But the narrative has been so focused on Moses the called servant of God that it has left little room for Moses the ordinary human person. Moses sleeps too, just like everyone else. He obviously has a tent, just like everyone else. Yet here we are, far into the story, and we only now hear how he lives from day to day.

Moses relates to Jethro the scarcely believable events of the deliverance from Egypt. All the focus is on what God alone has done. Jethro in turn is overjoyed at the divine bounty shown to the people of Israel. Indeed, Jethro— a Midianite priest—makes the confession that his understanding of God has been altered by what God has done for the people of Israel. This God, the God of Israel, is greater than all gods, he tells his son-in-law. There are sacrifices offered, and there is feasting to celebrate this beloved family reunion. Moses, the human person, is filled with heartfelt joy, even in the desert.

The narrative continues at the same slow pace, as if to make fully clear that the life of Moses the human person is not left aside even when the account quickly shifts to his official duties. The human person simply cannot be separated from the office, as Moses will soon find out. The indication of time—it is simply "the next day"—recounts what follows as a kind of accident, a happenstance with beneficent result in the end. And while the action centers on Moses and his official duties, the perspective is all on the outlook of Jethro, the priest of Midian, and what he can and will contribute to the education of a liberator of God's people Israel.

The day after Jethro and the family of Moses arrive, Moses engages in his official role as *judge* of the people. Jethro observes the action throughout the day, as it unfolds the entire day long, from sunup to sundown, an exhausting stretch of time not only for Moses but for the crowds of people who come to be heard, and who must each wait their turn. The role of judge is not as yet clearly defined, but it is evident that Moses is tasked with the role of adjudicating every matter of controversy, large and small, civil and religious. One man, and all these people with their myriad problems; therein lies the extraordinary tension of the scene. It is exhausting pandemonium from dawn until dusk.

Jethro is a quiet and humble teacher, but he is not shy about intervening for the good of his son-in-law. He asks a simple question: why in the world are you alone trying to accomplish such an enormous task? He is not really seeking an explanation of fact; he is seeking rather to draw out of Moses insight into his own situation. And Moses responds with overeager alacrity. He explains that it is his bound duty to decide every single matter of every single situation among the entire body of God's people, no matter how long it takes, no matter how long people must wait until the task of the day is finished. It is exhausting even to hear the explanation! Even as he describes his situation it is quite clear that Moses is describing an impossibility, a prescription for failure on multiple levels. What he has not yet achieved is valid discernment concerning a solution to the problem he is facing.

And that is exactly what Jethro offers. He does not mince words. He states without exaggeration that the situation as it now exists is completely intolerable. Moses is not only exhausting himself by taking on an impossible task; he is exhausting the people who come to him, and who must stand around all day long waiting their turn. The fact is, Jethro tells his son-in-law, you are not really doing a good thing here, no matter how it may appear to you now. And the reason is actually quite obvious, if you think about it. You alone are attempting a task that should actually be done by numerous qualified people, thus saving your strength, and expediting the process of ordinary social and religious life for the people. You have to change your approach.

And so Jethro makes a proposal for a rather dramatic change in the life of the community of Israel. You are certainly the representative of the people before God; you bring the needs of the people *as a whole* to God, and teach them God's will. But when it comes to the daily grind of social and religious dispute, you need help. Choose a set of people, all of whom show characteristics of integrity, honesty, and trustworthiness, and let them judge ordinary day-to-day cases. Only the hardest cases need to be brought to you, and you can decide only them. Moses hears the advice, accepts it, and puts it into practice.

Two points need to be stressed. Both Moses, and the biblical text, clearly identify the advice of Jethro with the will of God. Yet it is also clear that Jethro is a priest from Midian, a foreigner, certainly not an Israelite! There is no attempt to account for the apparent discrepancy; good advice is good advice, no matter its source. And second, the will of God and practical need are both at stake. It is in the practical needs of the moment that God's will is found; and it is only through God's will that the stresses of the day gain clarity and resolution. Jethro leaves, and Moses has found a new direction and new energy.

There is a long-standing, persistent misconstrual of the Christian witness—so persistent that it can only be considered ontological—and that is this: that the Bible offers the Christian community a closed system of truth by which every question can be answered, every position made secure, every secret of the universe fully known. Today that closed system is called a "Christian worldview" but it has gone by many names in the history of Christian thought. And right here in the middle of the Pentateuch we learn that such a view is in fact unbiblical, and therefore false. There is no closed system of truth in the Bible; there is no Christian worldview; Christians do not have the right answer to every question. No less a figure than Moses himself receives guidance from the priest of a foreign religion concerning the heart of Israel's life under God, simply because the guidance is wise and true. To be sure, God's word is always to be kept, God's command always to be obeyed. But the living will of God is not for the Christian community to be separated off in self-isolation from the world, but to engage the world in a posture of fundamental openness. To be faithful to the God of the Bible is to be *fully open* to the surrounding world.

We learn from the Bible that the world belongs to God, and not to us. Our faith in God the Creator is an article of faith. But we learn from modern science both the beauty and frailty of the planet upon which we live, and the vast open spaces of the universe in which we live and move and have our being. Science is not an enemy of faith, nor does science lead to faith. For the Christian community, science is a tool of exploration in the universe that God has created and called good, nothing more but certainly nothing less. Christians who oppose science in the name of piety are contradicting the biblical word. We learn from the arts the depths and heights of human experience in the world. The Bible certainly affirms the reality of what it means to be human; and we are lucky to have artists of all mediums to teach us the mysteries of human experience in ways beyond our knowing. We learn from philosophy the skills of human reasoning. Again, philosophy does not lead to faith, nor does it lead away from it. But for the Christian community, the variety of schools of philosophy can be an exercise in human reasoning that supports the call not only to believe, but to think through what we believe. Education in the most basic sense is not a threat to faith but always and everywhere to be affirmed and supported by those who know and love God in the world. Public education—open and accessible to all, free from constraint by political manipulation—is a gift of a free and democratic society, supported wholeheartedly by the gospel, for there is nothing to fear from growth in learning wherever it takes place. In every respect, and in all realms of human endeavor, the basic posture of the Christian toward the surrounding world is one of open willingness to listen and to learn, in order that genuine faith might grow into the living reality of Christ the risen Lord.

Yet as Christians we are pragmatists in the best sense of the world. God's will does not hover above the world in the clouds, untouched by the realm of genuine human life and experience. God reaches down where human persons live out the everyday, ordinary life of human existence, in the most concrete ways possible. We are always open to the world; but look especially for those aspects that touch humanity in ways that can be seen, even measured, and certainly felt by the day-to-day constraints of being alive on this earth. We do not measure the content of ideas by the impact they have on the world, but we do insist that valid ideas have such an impact, not just on the world in the abstract, but on the daily life of ordinary persons, especially the weak and vulnerable in our midst. Does it contribute to the goodness of life for those who are struggling and hard-pressed by life in our global society? Then it is probably an idea whose time has come. Does it detract from such a boon for the world? Then it can be safely set aside, or even actively resisted. Stiff, uncorrected, stubborn allegiance to a set of truths without regard for their living contact with the real world is not a biblical stance.

The present passage can hardly be characterized as political in nature in the modern sense of the word. And yet, neither can it be denied that theological reflection on the substance of the passage opens up the realm of human political interaction in society. More specifically, two points are worth stressing. First of all, the advice of Jethro, and the way it is embraced and carried out by Moses, could hardly be a sharper biblical rejection of contemporary populist authoritarianism. If ever there were a figure in the Old Testament who could lay claim to a populist mandate of absolute authority, it would be Moses; and yet right here in our passage he not only declines, but accepts and devises a system that undercuts that very authority. Human authority is to be *shared*, not hoarded. No ruler is perfect; no one can do everything; no human person has the right answer to every question. To be wise in the way of God is to recognize limitation, not to embrace unlimited rule. Indeed, when Moses recounts the new arrangement of shared authority in the book of Deuteronomy, he makes it fully clear that the *people* choose their own leaders (1:13). These are not handpicked oligarchs, ready to rubber-stamp the will of Moses; these are independent judges chosen by the people to exercise right judgment in the way of human wisdom. We can hardly stress too fully: when the church in our time follows and supports populist authoritarian regimes—whether in the name of the God of the Bible or not—the church is contradicting the will of God made known in Holy Scripture. The church in such cases is failing the full confession of the gospel, to its own profound detriment. It can only repent, and be renewed by the living word of God.

The second "political" point is equally clear in our passage. Leaders who exercise the role of critical discernment and judgment over the lives of the community must display public *character*. There can be no excuse, whether on the left or the right. We cannot say: ah, but this or that leader has done so much good! This leader is a fighter! This leader is on God's side, even if his or her personal life is a shambles! Jethro stresses; Moses affirms; and the biblical word today rightly makes clear: true political leadership is built on personal character and integrity. Those who habitually tell lies are not the leaders the church should ever support. Those who bully, and cajole, and threaten, and demean, are not living the life of integrity that the church supports, in any way whatsoever. Those who abuse others sexually have no place in political leadership, according to the will of God made known in the divine word. There will be conservatives and liberals, traditionalists and progressives, in the large tent of God's holy house; but none will vote for people without personal character and integrity wherever the gospel truly holds sway.

Finally, we are instructed by the example of Moses to reflect upon the rich and complex reality of Christian discipleship. On the one hand, Christ the risen Lord calls us to leave everything behind in order to follow him. All ties of family and culture, values and religion, are forever cut, binding us directly to Christ the risen Lord. Each of us stands alone in solitude before the marvels of the burning bush. Yet on the other hand, even as called disciples we remain fully human; indeed, the call of the gospel enhances our humanity, it does not cancel it out. In particular, we come to know the beauty of family love, and therefore our true selves, as if for the first time. Parents and children, aunts and uncles, nephews and nieces, husbands and wives, all are taken up into the new world of God, which is the world of friendship and love. Here we learn lessons of life and wisdom we can learn nowhere else. We are not two different persons, disciples and human beings; rather our discipleship draws our humanity forward toward a new divine goal, while our humanity grounds our discipleship anew in the beauty of God's good creation. In all things, God alone surrounds and upholds us.

9. The Great Apostasy

Exodus 32

THE STORY OF THE golden calf is of course one of the most profound and memorable narratives in the entire Old Testament. The brilliant techniques of Hebrew narration are on full display. The scene shuttles back and forth between the heavenly realm of the mountain above, where Moses meets with God, to the earthly realm down below where the people are quickly dissolving into open idolatry. The suspenseful buildup is even accentuated by the clever use of sound, as the cries of the people down below are heard quite differently by the youthful ears of Joshua halfway up the mountain, and the more experienced ears of Moses, who realizes just what they mean. The entire episode unfolds as a series of encounters centered on Moses: with God, with Joshua, with the people, with Aaron, with the Levites, and finally with God again; Moses, who now emerges not just as a prophet who speaks the commands of God to the people, but as the one who stands as the mediator between God and the people. Yet the story is not told simply for its narrative fullness. It stands at the beginning of Israel's history as a sign of all its ways to come, a history marked by apostasy again and again. Indeed, the New Testament will bear witness to the same reality in the life of the church; and experience confirms that the church is constantly threatened by the selfsame idolatry of the golden calf. The temptation is always with us, and all too often the people of God, even today, succumb.

Moses has now been on the summit of Mount Sinai for forty days and nights. There he has received the law of God, centered in the two tablets of the Ten Commandments, written in stone by the finger of God himself. The account of the golden calf opens down below among the people. They are impatient; they gather, not to Aaron (as some translations have it) but *against* Aaron. They refer to Moses with cruel abuse as "this Moses," as if he meant no more to them than a throwaway hack. They ask Aaron, clearly

and decisively, for a new leader, a replacement for Moses. Indeed, their re-
quest strikes even deeper, into the heart of Israel's relation to God himself:
"make us gods who will go before us." The demand is without ambiguity: it
is open rebellion against the living God, and the open embrace of rank human idolatry. According to the Scriptures of Israel, God created all things;
now Israel, the elect people of God, would in turn create God. Israel has
chosen the way of utter depravity and ruin.

Aaron's response introduces a certain religious ambiguity, which in
certain respects makes matters even worse. He commands the people to
bring items of gold, and the widely positive response is immediately forth-
coming. Aaron then fashions a golden calf out of the molten metal. The
people respond with religious rapture: these are your gods, O Israel, who
brought you up out of the land of Egypt! There is not the slightest ambiguity on the part of the people, who are in open rebellion against God, and
have lapsed into crude idolatry. They have made with their own hands the
gods they now worship. Yet the ambiguity is introduced by Aaron, who
seeks to incorporate the *calf* into the worship of the God of Israel! The calf
is not an idol (according to Aaron), just another avenue to true worship
of the one God! But the people will have their final say. The next day, after
the idol is constructed, the entire camp breaks out into a religious orgy,
offering their sacrifices to the golden calf made with human hands, eating
and drinking in revelry.

In the second scene of the narrative, we are suddenly transported to the
mountain above, where God is meeting with Moses. The narrative contrast
between the realm below and the realm above is stark and deliberate. Indeed,
it is precisely this contrast that strikes at the heart of the episode of the golden
calf as a whole. God has *just finished* delivering the two tablets of the law to
Moses, when the orgy breaks out down below. The serenity up above is shattered with an urgent divine summons: go down at once! God tells Moses that
your people—notice the pronoun—are in open rebellion.

Yet how else can God describe those who have surrounded the golden
calf with their adoration, these are your gods O Israel!? God's own election
of Israel as his beloved people is quite clearly at stake. They have abandoned
him for a god of their own hands; why should he not now abandon them?
Again, only the reader is now aware that while the people are dancing stu-
pidly and chaotically their very fate as a people is being decided, far beyond
their awareness; neither the people nor Aaron have the slightest clue. But with
profound consequence, and in common with other biblical passages, God
sets a condition for the erasure of his relation to the people of Israel: Moses
has to agree! Let me alone, he tells Moses, that I may destroy them.

But Moses will not let him alone. He makes three arguments to persuade God to continue his electing love for—not the people of Moses—but *your* people, O God (the battle of pronouns begins). First of all, he reminds God of the sheer miracle of Israel's existence, why they are a people at all; namely because *God* himself rescued them from bondage in Egypt. Second, he convinces God that the Egyptians would mount a public relations campaign for their own benefit, proving that God only rescued Israelites to destroy them all along, thus proving the rightness of the Egyptian position all along. And finally, Moses appeals to the free and unmerited promise of God to Abraham, Isaac, and Jacob, a promise that has been guiding the existence of this people from the beginning. The prayer is effective. Despite the chaos of idolatry, God is indeed merciful and gracious, though he will not overlook the sheer heinousness of human pride. Only God can make the future a reality.

As Moses descends the heavenly realm of the mountaintop to the earthly realm down below, the tension of the scene ascends to a shattering climax. He stills carries with him the tablets of the divine law; the covenant of God is yet intact. Halfway down the mountain he meets Joshua, and together they hear the sound of shouting arising from the camp below. To the young Joshua it sounds like battle cries, perhaps in response to an attack by bedouin marauders. But to the experienced ears of Moses the cries could not be more awful, for they are the shouts of orgiastic rebellion. Sound is replaced by instant recognition as Moses approaches the camp. There it all is, dramatically displayed in a moment before him: the reveling, the dancing, the singing, and above all the idolatrous golden calf. With enraged fury, he hurls the tablets of the covenant to the ground (a scene immortalized in art by Rembrandt), breaking Israel's sacred relation to God as surely as the tablets are shattered into fragments. He grabs the hated calf, burns it with fire, grinds in it into powder, scatters it on the water, and forces the people to drink it. Where is this hideous god of yours now!

Then Moses turns to Aaron, whom we will recall has sought a different relation to the idol than the people at large. How does Aaron fare? Moses is unrelenting in demanding an explanation. Why did you let things come to such a horrific conclusion? Aaron first offers the explanation that it was, after all, typical of Israel to turn away from God, as Moses well knows. His own role is all but left out of account; this is the fault of the people, not mine! Then Aaron gives the excruciating description of the actual production of the idol. He had requested gold, thrown it into the fire, and this calf just sort of popped out! In other words, Aaron completely exonerates himself, and blames the people for everything. Moses, on the other hand, who had done nothing, defended the people before God, and will do so again.

For in the end, the entire episode is not resolved until the covenant is restored in chapter 34. Moses cuts two new tablets of stone, ascends Mount Sinai, and God once again writes on them the words of the Ten Commandments. Despite the heinous act of idolatry that just for a moment destroyed the covenant relation between God and the people of Israel, God himself restores the covenant afresh. God indeed declares to Moses his true name: "The Lord, the Lord, a God merciful and gracious, slow to anger, and abounding in steadfast love and faithfulness . . ." (34:6). Aaron could not hold the people back from idolatry; Moses holds God back from abandoning his promise.

Apostasy is a perennial threat in the life of the church. From the very beginning, we seek to make our own gods. We do not want a god upon whom we must wait; we want a god who must wait upon us, who is on call to our needs and desires, our personal, cultural, and political plans and projects. We resist and reject the very notion that God remakes us in his image, and instead remake god in *our* own image, a god we can therefore predict and control, a god indeed we can manipulate for ourselves as we please. Deep in the very heart of humanity is the desire, not to be like god, but to make god like us.

In such a religion, to believe in god is the same thing as to believe in ourselves, a most potent object of human religious devotion. Such a god will not say: come unto me all who are weak, and weary, and carry heavy burdens. Rather, the gods we create will say: blessed are you who are strong enough to stand up for yourselves, for in so doing you yourselves become strong in my strength! Blessed are you who fight, for I will conquer all in your way! Blessed are you who help yourselves, for I will fill up to the last measure the fruits of your conquest! No, the idols we create are not for the weak or the vulnerable; not for the outsiders or the marginalized; not for the helpless or the dying. The gods we create celebrate the greatness that is humanity itself, and magnify that grandeur. These are truly gods of gold.

We see such idolatry around us; we see such idolatry in ourselves. And perhaps we wonder: why can't we just go back to a time when things were so much more clear, so much more pure, in short, so much better? Why can't we go back to the time of the Reformation, or the early church, or the New Testament? Surely if only we could immerse ourselves in one of these worlds from the past, God would reach down and touch and bless us. And indeed, there is no doubt that each of these worlds has much to offer us still. But we learn from the episode of the golden calf that *nostalgia itself* is an idol. We cannot go back to any beginning that is pure, for *from the very beginning*, there is idolatry. There is no golden age in the Bible, no golden age in the church. The very notion of retreating backward into the past is yet one more attempt to chisel out of gold another calf that we can control, manipulate, supplicate, and call our god, though it is lifeless and worthless. We only find God when he comes to us on his terms, in his time, in his way. Nostalgia is an escape from God, not an embrace of him.

We make yet another profound mistake when we equate apostasy with the rejection of religion and the affirmation of secularity, a particular temptation of modern Christianity. We are true, pious believers; you are secular worshippers of a pagan god! We must separate from you into our own world of religiosity, or we will be stained by your secular idol worship! So we commonly hear, but what does the Bible say? Clearly, in the passage before us, it is *religion itself* that is the means for idolatry! The people do not turn away from religion but embrace it! Aaron does not reject the true religion of the fathers, but *uses* it to rename the gods of the people! The worst forms of idolatry do not arise from within the old world that is passing away, but from the threat of temptation in the life of the people of God. We are impatient for change, and so we rename a new "god of change" and call it holy.

Our lives seem empty, and so we rename a new "god of self-fulfillment" and write our songs of praise and worship. We want power and recognition in the world around us, and so we create our new "god of politics," whether in the shape of a donkey or an elephant, and bow down to worship. We cannot bear the thought of being left out of the great discussions of our time, and so we create a "god of relevance," and name that god a "worldview," and thrust it into the public space demanding respect. And in all these ways, we lose the one thing that matters: God himself. God is not the essence of change, or the source of self-fulfillment, or a political project, or a worldview. God is *God*. We must choose; either to know, love, serve, and trust him as he is, or to turn away to idols of our own manufacture, and thus to lose him.

The mediating position of Aaron—which is now more popular than ever, both on the religious left and on the religious right—forever seeks to combine the gospel with the changing fads and customs of culture and society. But we must be relevant, we hear. We must keep up with the times, or we will lose our audience! We are holding to the core principles of our belief, but we are also embracing the necessary changes to keep ourselves relevant to these new circumstances! After all, so it said, the world is losing touch with traditional family values (whatever that means); surely Christianity not only celebrates the gospel of Jesus Christ but also the teaching of traditional family values! Surely, we embrace the core principles of our faith, but we also insist that people choose the candidates we endorse because they too promise influence and power if only we will stand by them! If we can only elect our own "Christian" candidates, then they will be beholden to us, and then we will be at the center of national attention, we will hold the reins of power, we, the pious leaders of the country and the world, will gain the influence that is rightfully ours! And all without abandoning our core beliefs! But of course the project of mediating theology is a crass and ridiculous illusion, as crass and ridiculous as a calf crafted of molten metal, named "god." Those who chase the idol of influence and power in the name of their core beliefs not only lose their core beliefs, they lose the One in whom they believe. At what price does the church gain influence and power in the world, when it loses its own soul? At what price do leaders in the church gain the notoriety they crave, when in doing so they lose the faith they cherish? The project of mediating theology, from the perspective of Scripture, is the very definition of theological madness.

We see, in the contrast between Aaron and Moses, the difference between a pious leader and a true mediator. The pious leader is glad to lead the crowd astray, as long as he can lead from the head of the pack. But when the final accounting comes due, he stands by the wayside, pointing fingers at others, justifying only himself. I was not one of them! I was only doing the will of God, but they were perverting the cause I was trying to teach! He sells out the people, to save himself.

The true mediator, by sharp contrast, seeks to save the people in the sight of God, by joining their side, even in their folly. He prays for them, even when they go astray. Without joining their ridiculous and heinous idol-worship, he nevertheless stands with them before God, petitioning their ultimate acceptance by God, despite their foolish ways. The true mediator maintains his solidarity with the people even in their desperation, knowing and believing that God is able to overcome their folly and make right what human beings do so badly. In the light of Scripture as a whole, we confess: Jesus Christ is the one true Mediator between God and humankind. When we all—we all—went astray, he did not stand apart in pious pointing of fingers; he joined us where we are, becoming sin (yet without sinning), that he might remove our sin from us. In Christ God himself took our side when we sinned against him, that he might reconcile us to himself, and make us whole once again.

Our only hope in life and in death is the forgiveness of God. In the end, we have no claim upon him. We have all strayed, not once but countless times, like lost sheep, right from the beginning. We are with God, because he in his sheer kindness and mercy alone has decided to be with us, has chosen not to abandon us, has graciously acted to embrace us and gather us unto himself. There is only one covenant in the Bible, and it is a covenant of grace, pure and free. We are not partners in that covenant, coequal allies with God in a cause greater than the divine or the human. God is God; and his promised mercy alone keeps us in living relationship to him. His love is a miracle, which creates our lives anew each day. Our whole existence is nothing but gratitude for his loving-kindness.

III. Leviticus

1. The Day of Atonement

Leviticus 16

THE DAY OF ATONEMENT described in Leviticus 16 continues to be central to both Jewish and Christian affirmation, yet it is observed literally by neither. In Jewish practice, the Day of Atonement—Yom Kippur—is the high holy day of the Jewish calendar. In Christian understanding, the atoning death of Jesus Christ for the reconciliation of the world to God is the central affirmation of the New Testament gospel, in direct correlation with the text before us (as well as Isaiah 53). Both communities affirm the eternal significance of atonement together, thus surely in some sense confirming their unity as one people of God. Yet each community interprets the significance of Leviticus 16 in very different ways, thus at the same time demonstrating the tension within that larger community. We cannot here resolve that tension, but we can at least point out that the passage before us binds together in God's sovereign purpose what no human being dare tear asunder.

A few points need to be stressed before we describe directly the ritual of atonement and its mysterious significance, as outlined in this chapter. First of all, despite the protest of modern sensibilities, there is no distinction in the Pentateuch between the ritual and moral dimensions of God's revealed will. God makes known his will in sovereign freedom, and the content of his imperative is grounded solely in his gracious reality. Both the command to love neighbor (as we will see) and the sacrificial system of Israel are included in the book of Leviticus, which is shaped as a record of the laws given by God to Moses on Sinai. There is one law; the Day of Atonement is simply part of that divine plan for the life of Israel.

We can even go further. The Day of Atonement is absolutely central to the book of Leviticus. In the opening chapters, the various sacrificial offerings are described: burnt offerings, grain offerings, offerings of well-being, sin offerings. Then the priesthood of Aaron and his descendants is inaugurated with a ritual of ordination. Almost immediately there is a profound breach in observance. Aaron's two sons, Nadab and Abihu, fail to observe correctly the divinely willed protocol of incense offering, and are killed by God. We recoil at such an event, but we are forced rather to contemplate: violating God's holiness is a direct affront to God himself. Religion is not the free invention of spirituality, but rather the guided service of God. After the institution of the priesthood, various distinctions between the pure and the impure are outlined, once again grounded solely in God's own decision, not in human health regimens.

Following chapter 16 on the Day of Atonement will come a series of laws concerning proper human conduct in community. These laws will govern both the ordinary and the sacred life of the community, which are not separated—God is one, and his command rules and overrules all things. In the pages to follow we will turn to these laws of life in the presence of God. So, observe: the Day of Atonement comes, as it were, as the fulcrum between the offerings that God's people bring to him, and the offerings they bring at his command to neighbor in society. In that sense, atonement is the central theme of the book of Leviticus. We will return to the question of what that tells us about the book, and more specifically about the revealed will of God to which it attests. But first, we need a brief description of the day itself and its mysterious significance.

The ritual of the Day of Atonement can be concisely described. It is to be repeated once a year in perpetuity, on a precise day, and is to be celebrated by every member of the community, including resident aliens (immigrants). On this day the sins of the community during the entire previous year are to be expiated—forgiven—before the Lord. A bull, and two goats, are chosen for the sacrifices of the holy day. There are three elements stressed in the description, with ever-widening circles of inclusion. First of all, Aaron, the high priest, is to present the offering of a bull as a sin offering for himself and the priestly family. Some of the blood of the offering of the bull is to be sprinkled over the mercy seat. Thus, the high priestly family acknowledges its own sin, and presents a sacrifice for expiation.

Second, one of the two goats to be sacrificed is presented as a sin offering for the sanctuary. Even the sacred place of the sanctuary has been polluted by the sins of the people during the intervening year, including both ritual and moral violations—though biblical law does not really distinguish between the two. One of the goats is chosen by lot as a sin offering, and the blood is smeared and sprinkled upon the altar of the sanctuary. Even the altar itself, which bears the sacrifices of the people before God, is to be cleansed by the blood of this offering, for the altar too is compromised by the sin of the people. Atonement concerns not only people but institutions, and that is because (as we shall reflect below) the power of sin reaches beyond people to infect the religious structures in which they worship.

And third, and perhaps most dramatically (as if what has already occurred is not dramatic enough), the second goat is brought forward, still fully alive. Aaron lays his hands upon the head of this second goat and confesses all the sins of the people during the previous year in what is clearly a solemn act of supreme, communal confession of sin. This second goat is not killed or sacrificed. Rather, it is released into the wilderness. It carries with it all the sins of the people, taking them off the people into the barren regions where it wanders in a solitary place, inaccessible to humankind, the goat and the sins it carries banished forever. After all three of these rituals are observed, then the animals (the bull and the first goat) are offered as sacrifices on the ritually cleansed altar, and the remains are taken outside the camp. Sin has now been removed from the people, the priests, and the sanctuary, before God; a new reality is created and confirmed.

We consider now the significance of the ritual of atonement. While never delivered in the biblical witness in systematic form, and grounded solely in the mystery of the divine will, certain features are clear and worthy of close consideration. Perhaps most important of all is the simple fact that at the heart of the book of Leviticus is the *promise of forgiveness*. While often neglected, or even derided as a late production of legalistic Judaism, the book of Leviticus not only contains objective laws by which human life is guided by God's presence, but an objective means by which human failure is both forgiven and restored into God's life-giving presence. Human moral failure is certainly deeply felt, and the remorse of guilt is real. But humankind is not left without remedy, not thrown back on their own resources of self-definition in relation to God. God provides the very means to lift the burden off human shoulders, setting them free to a joyous life in his presence, set free once again from the guilt of the past, renewed in vivifying relation to God by an objective act of divine restoration.

It is precisely divine grace of restoration that exposes the crippling dimension of human sin. Sin is exposed as a power of destruction that far exceeds the limits of individual moral failure. Sin is a destructive force that sweeps away the humanity of both the individual and the community, destroying the moral integrity of both at the same time. Even further, the power of sin destroys the legitimacy of the very religious institutions established by God himself for human well-being, the institution of worship.

Atonement is the work of God; God himself acts to restore humankind through his gracious mercy. God is not the object of atonement; God is not atoned, not propitiated. God is the *subject* of atonement; God atones for human sin, by providing a way of propitiation to cover human sin. The sacrifice provided is in the form of substitution, though how that takes place is never defined. By God's will, the sins of the individual and the community are transferred to the sacrifice, which in being destroyed destroys the sins that it carries. Sins are not punished; atonement carries no hint of punishment in the Bible. Sins are *broken*, carried away, abolished, by a gracious divine act of providing an atoning sacrifice to bear them away from the sinner, and cancel them out forever. The power of guilt is removed, and life is restored under the divine forgiveness.

Perhaps this is a good place to drive home a crucial point in theological exegesis, which is this: it is simply false to imply—as Christians have often done—that the Old Testament is a book of law and the New Testament a book of grace. On the one hand, Jesus himself summarizes the very heart of the divine imperative by citing the Old Testament itself, including the book of Leviticus. Jesus did not come to abolish the law, but to fulfill it. Yet on the other hand, here right in the heart of the book of the law, is the central witness to divine grace, the day of atonement. Human beings are in the wrong over against God, and as a result the most fundamental relation to God—the covenant of grace—is disrupted. There is no possibility at all of restoring that relation from the human side. No moral act, no religious transformation, no mystical enlightenment, no social self-transcendence, can in any way whatsoever bridge the gap created between God and humankind. It is a great gulf fixed. With humanity it is impossible. Only with God does it become possibility in the reality of the event of grace itself. The grace of atonement creates the promise of forgiveness, the promise of forgiveness is fulfilled in the grace of atonement.

It is only in light of the scope of divine grace that we recognize the universality of sin. The entire community, from the high priest and his family to the families of all the faithful, are required to participate, for all have sinned and spurned the mercy of God. The Bible does not teach, anywhere, that here on one side are the faithful righteous, standing in pride and power, and there on the other side are the sinners, to be warned against and ultimately defeated. If we do not recognize the universality of sin—and that means recognizing ourselves as sinners—then we do not understand the free gift of the promise. We have all seen how hate divides and conquers the common life of humanity, leaving broken lives and bodies in its wake. We are all aware of the petty cruelties of daily life, whether they are practiced in the halls of power, or on the streets of our cities, or sadly enough in our homes. We have all watched as the tiny minority have risen to the very top, a pinnacle so high that it is out of sight, while the vast majority have sunk so low that it is difficult to imagine how recovery is even possible; watched, and done nothing. We have wished for ourselves what we have denied to others, offered to others only the second-best choice, not the first, taken the highest seat in the banquet and left others to fend for themselves. We are all sinners; all guilty; none are able, in our own power, to rise above the human condition that the promise of grace alone both reveals and sets right.

We are tempted to view sin puritanically, which means moralistically, and therefore individualistically. We must relearn to view sin biblically. Sin is not an act of an individual, though it effects those acts. Sin is rather a malignant power, a hideous impossibility that nevertheless even in its cancellation by God exerts distorting force on the world he has created. Sin affects individuals and communities. Whole peoples sin. Nations sin. Individuals, too, sin. Sin can become structured into the very fabric of the common life of society. Worst of all, sin can become structured into the community of religious life itself, including the Christian religion—maybe even at times especially the Christian religion. Only God can heal individuals, nations, Christianity itself, by the sheer promise of his mercy. It does no honor to the truth of the gospel to deny that Christianity itself can at times harbor the worst tendencies of human frailty. Even Aaron, the high priest, and his family, needed forgiveness, as well as the very sanctuary of God. Far better is it to recognize: judgment begins in the household of God, and we who believe in the gospel are first in line to admit that we, too, are frail sinners who live by grace alone, perhaps we most of all.

To what then, we now ask, does the Day of Atonement refer, as to its true theological substance in the present? According to the Christian confession of the gospel, the death of Jesus Christ on the cross is the true subject matter of the atonement, prefigured in the Old Testament witness, enacted and announced to all the world in the New. We do not understand the death of Christ on the cross in the light of the Old Testament; rather, we understand the Old Testament witness in the light of the passion of Christ. Once there were bulls and goats as a sacrifice to God. Now, in the fullness of time, God himself entered our world, becoming human without being any less God, and himself went to the cross as the one true atoning sacrifice for the sins of the whole world. Once the sacrifice was repeated year after year. Now, again in the fullness of God's eternal purpose, the death of Jesus Christ on the cross happens only once in God's own time, in which the past, present, and future of all time is contained.

The atoning death of Christ happened in time and space, yet it happened once for all, circumscribing all time and space, all nations and all peoples. Once, a priest and his family, year after year, offered the sacrifices not only for the people but for himself and his family, for there is no one righteous before God. Now, Christ himself, the one true high priest, offers *himself* on the cross, and having risen from the dead is exalted to glory, where even now he ever intercedes for his beloved church, and for the whole world. Jesus Christ himself is the true reality to which the Old Testament Day of Atonement points as a sign.

Yet if Christ is revealed fully only in the New Testament, he is indeed concealed—truly—in the Old. Therefore, we also view the atoning death of the cross from the vantage point of the book of Leviticus. God alone is the subject of this event, not its object. God is not propitiated by the cross, as some in the Western theological tradition wrongly assumed, but is the one who covers human sins through the grace of his self-giving love. Again, against elements in the Western tradition, there is no hint of punishment here. Christ is not punished by God on the cross. Rather, Christ himself *becomes* sin; God *condemns* sin not by punishing it but by *destroying* its power, by abolishing it forever. Christ *defeats* sin by taking it to the cross, and therefore putting it to death. Again, we are speaking of an objective reality, an alteration of the human situation before God effected by God himself. Sin is broken and the gulf between God and humanity introduced by sin is overcome by God, and God alone, apart from all human cooperation, through the cross of Jesus Christ. And again, the cross of Christ does not create a new human possibility, but a new human *reality*, universal in its scope. God and humanity are reconciled through the sacrifice of Christ on the cross. Peace with God comes through the cross of our Lord Jesus Christ. Christ died for the sins of the whole world; God was in Christ reconciling the *world* unto himself.

We are, perhaps, not so accustomed in our time to hear the call to sacrifice, but it is essential to Christian discipleship. Those who follow Christ are summoned to share in the sufferings of the cross. Just as he went outside the city, scorned and rejected, so too we are often in situations where our faith collides with the social realities of our time. Just as his body was broken and crucified, so too at times our bodies bear the marks of Christ. Just as he faced his death in the loneliness of Gethsemane, so too we often enough find ourselves in the loneliness of solitude, whether we like it or not. In following the way of sacrifice in the service of Christ, we are not to be troubled. Christ himself draws nearer to us in struggle than he does at times of ease. And the very God who made the universe and all that it contains, cares less for a billion galaxies of worlds than he does for a single cry of pain and distress from the least of his children.

2. The Divine Imperative

Leviticus 19:1–18

THE LOGIC OF THE divine imperative receives its central theological definition—both in form and content—in this remarkable chapter of the book of Leviticus. In many ways, it is the central moral chapter, not only of the book of Leviticus, but of the entire Pentateuch, one could even argue of the entire Old Testament. Indeed, according to the attention given to it by Jesus himself, one could certainly argue that it contains the central ethical imperative of the entire Bible, a subject to which we will return in our concluding reflections. In short, the church neglects the book of Leviticus to its own peril.

"I am the Lord your God." The phrase is repeated *eighteen* times in this single chapter. We come to ethics not through a system of moral virtues or values, traditional or modern, but only through the living reality of God. Indeed, already God has rescued for himself a people from bondage in Egypt. Already he has elected and called them through the grace of his merciful love. Already, despite their willful rebellion in the wilderness during the episode of the golden calf, God has claimed this people for himself through the divine act of forgiveness. God's grace alone is the basis for the divine imperative.

"I the Lord your God am holy." The divine imperative is grounded solely, completely, and exclusively, in the sovereign activity of God alone, and can be derived from no other source. There is no ethical *worldview* in the Bible. There are no moral principles, no moral system, no abstract moral values or agendas of any kind whatsoever. God is *God*; and he continues to communicate his living and active will to his people: that is the sole basis for the imperative. Grace lays a total and complete claim upon humanity, and that claim is never given over into the hands of human manipulation, but is reserved always and only for the divine purpose alone.

The answer to God is either obedience, leading to wisdom and life, or disobedience, leading to folly and death.

"Be holy as I am holy." God's grace lays claim upon a people as his own. God has already established his covenant of grace. Indeed, God has already separated a people for himself, and sanctified them as his own. The call to holiness is not therefore the call to engage in a process; God has *already* made his people holy by delivering them from bondage in Egypt. Only God makes his people holy; only God sanctifies those whom he claims, by grace, as his own. When the divine imperative is spelled out more clearly in the book of Leviticus, the point is not at all to chart a path by which Israel can become something that it is not. Rather, the point is to show Israel the way to manifest in life what in reality it already is: holy unto God.

The challenge for the people of God therefore is to *be* what God has already called and *made* them: a holy people and nation. That is true, in relation to God, in relation to each other as a community of faith, and indeed in relation to the surrounding nations of the world. God himself is the sole norm by which all holiness is measured; therefore, the people of God are called to reflect the very nature of God himself in the world. Keeping the commandments of God has no other moral agenda than this: to show forth in the world the divine majesty. The people of God are called away from the bondage of any and all systems of human obligation, including religious systems, to live in the freedom of God's sole rule over reality, that they might reflect his very nature.

To live in the service of God does not make the people of God holy. God's own electing love has already set a people apart for himself. God alone makes a people holy. Yet refusing to serve God in obedience to his commandments can trade away the divine summons of grace, leaving only catastrophe. The call to holiness is serious not because it can gain a status with God, which comes only through grace, but because through human failure to respond to the call the relation to God can be ruptured and compromised.

With respect to the content of the divine imperative, there is no attempt to distinguish between what we would today term ritual and moral dimensions; both together are incorporated in the one will of God for his people. The command to show deep reverence for parents runs along the same moral plane as the command to observe the sabbath. Both intersect human life directly from above, and command ultimate allegiance. Both promise abundant life. There is throughout this chapter—and indeed throughout the book of Leviticus—a clear respect shown to the sheer physicality of human existence. The commandments are external, and while they reach deep into the heart of human experience, they likewise show an immediate concern for the well-being of human bodies. Nothing is more characteristic of the biblical view of the person than this holistic apprehension of human unity as constituted by created order. To be sure, that is not to say that emotion is left out, for even grudges are forbidden, uncontrolled rage ruled out, distorted anger to be abolished, for toxic emotion is itself a violation of God's rule of peace.

Surely what characterizes the moral imperative of this chapter most clearly is the radical break it imposes upon the given social order of society. In ordinary social worlds, like associates with like. Slaves, widows, families, the wealthy, the prominent and powerful, each have their field of operation, each have their mutually reinforcing connections, each have their rules of social inclusion and more importantly exclusion. Whole social worlds are built upon this basic system of caste, which self-evidently operates both formally and informally in the contemporary world all around us. What is remarkable is that the divine imperative of Leviticus shatters—literally breaks into pieces, like a potter's vessel—the heart of this caste system. Divine care does not focus on the center of society, thus maintaining the social order, but rather on the edges of society, turning the social order inside out.

Commands are concrete and obedience is pragmatic. Growers are instructed not to harvest the crop to the very edge of their fields, nor to gather the gleanings, but rather to leave some produce for the poor, the helpless, the immigrant. God has taken up into his own care the weak and vulnerable in society, and now obligates those with the means to do so to extend special care to those in need. Day laborers are to be paid at the end of the working day; for without any other source of income, they need payment in order to care for their families. There can be no ridicule, no abuse, of the disabled, the helpless, the indigent, the underprivileged, the neglected. God is their keeper, and those who insult the helpless insult the Almighty himself. All justice is to be genuinely impartial, and it is not just in any way to defer to those who hold power in society. God himself is the true source of all justice, the true measure of all judgment; therefore, defense of the rights of the poor is required in obedience to him. Immigrants, strangers, foreigners, are to be treated with the same dignity as fellow citizens, since all Israel were once immigrants in the land of Egypt, rescued by the mighty hand of God alone. There can be no neutral standpoint in the face of injustice. God is just; therefore, all are commanded to act justly, and not to stand idly by when human well-being is threatened.

We have argued that there is no larger conceptual framework in the Old Testament into which the individual commandments are placed. God is God; that alone suffices to ground the divine will. Yet suddenly, a new note is heard. It is still a concrete command, still a divine imperative whose force is derived solely from the being of God himself. And yet, it shines a luminous glow

on every surrounding command. "You shall love your neighbor as yourself."
Love for neighbor is neither a feeling only, nor an action only, but a comprehensive orientation of the whole person toward the good of the neighbor.
Love suddenly gathers every other command into a new divine light, as it
were. It is not just a central imperative, but the center from which all other
imperatives radiate outwards. Love is the final word.

God's one eternal purpose of gracious love for the whole of humanity
is Jesus Christ, the one content of the gospel, the one true subject matter of
the Bible. There is not one grace in the Old Testament and another grace
in the New, but each in their various ways points to the selfsame identical mercy of God that is Christ crucified and risen. Yet the same Lord,
Jesus Christ, makes an absolute claim upon all humankind; those who are
bound to him in love are called to follow him in obedience. The imperative of God in Jesus Christ is not, and can never become, part of a moral,
political, or cultural system outside of itself. There is no worldview that can
encompass it, most especially a purportedly Christian worldview, which
is a self-contradiction in terms. Jesus Christ himself is the sole source and
measure of God's claim upon the world, just as he is the one true fount of
every blessing. His rule over all reality is the sole power that has already
transformed the whole creation. To do his will is not to build his kingdom,
but simply to live in the light of his hidden glory. Attempts to convert the
imperative of Christ into yet another -ism, whether conservatism, liberalism, postmodernism, traditionalism, and so forth, are all doomed to fail,
for the simple reason that Jesus Christ is a name, not an -ism.

Perhaps we hear a protest: contexts, ideologies, worldviews, provide
the meaning that is necessary to make religious ideas relevant in the present. And the issue of relevance, we agree, is vital, even profound, and we
will return to it. Adding our own theories of context, our own worldviews,
our own ideologies, may help in some small way, but the price paid is far
too heavy. For such impediments severely restrict our ability to hear the full
scope of the divine will in all its splendor and glory. Indeed, such impediments restrict the very movement of the scriptural word into the present
moment, which is the very point at issue.

In short, worldviews and ideologies destroy the freedom of Christian
ethics, grounded in the living word of God. Every new generation of the
people of God is called to live out the freedom of the call of Jesus Christ in
the service of God. And we are called to do so amidst the challenges of our
own time, our own culture, our own place, our own social pressures, our
own resources. If this does not happen through a worldview, or through an
ideological theory, how does it then happen? Scripture is theologically shaped
as a medium through which the risen Christ, through the presence of the

Spirit, makes his will known to every new generation. His call is always concrete, practical, everyday, this-worldly, pragmatic. Yet, how this call comes to us through Scripture is a miracle. The wind blows where it wills. We cannot make it happen; we can only walk with the wind, instead of against it.

The command of Christ, then and now, is the same: you shall love your neighbor as yourself. The reality of the neighbor, already in Leviticus and certainly in the rest of the Bible as well, bursts far beyond the boundaries of convenience and identity. Indeed, the neighbor is not an item on an approved list. I am in fact called by the risen Christ to *act* as neighbor precisely to those who stand in need, precisely to those who are *not* situated close to my identity or personal convenience. In fact, there are no boundaries or limits to the humanity I am called to embrace as neighbor. Love expands well beyond my race, my class, my nation, my social and cultural world however I define it. Indeed, the command of love makes the reality of human need visible, where it would otherwise pass me by. The neglected, the hurting, the poor and vulnerable, the weak and miserable; I am their neighbor, called by God not only to notice but to act, not only to act but to assume personal responsibility. Whether they are Christian or not makes no difference; whether they are friend or enemy is irrelevant; there are no conditions to love for neighbor, which is a distant human echo of God's own unconditional love for the whole world.

There is built into the very fabric of human society, as Scripture envisions it, a profound sense of common mutual responsibility. The notion of a rugged individualism, in which each person claws from existence what is theirs, and bears no responsibility toward the other, is utterly foreign to the biblical witness. On the one hand, everything that comes our way is a gift. No one owns a single possession that has not been first been received from above as a free divine blessing. Any other attitude to wealth is sheer idolatry.

But more importantly here, the ownership of wealth is a divine obligation to the common good, and especially to the weak and vulnerable that crowd the edges of human society. There is built into the very structure of God's design for human well-being a variety of mechanisms by which those who have share with those who do not. Those who are blessed with the goods of the earth are under divine obligation to share those goods with those who lack them. Mutual responsibility for the other is not a choice; it is an obligation. Mutual responsibility is of the very essence of the divine definition of life in community among fellow humanity, and there is no option to ignore it. Now, it should be stressed that this is not an early form of the rule of the proletariat. The passage before us makes clear, for example, that while there can be no bias against the poor in a court of law, nor should there be any bias in their favor; all justice is truly blind. Impartiality in legal matters applies to everyone, rich and poor alike. Yet that does not mitigate the essential point: responsibility for all is enjoined upon the entire community by God himself, and there is no evading it.

We live in an angry, vengeful, bitter age. It seems to have become the height of wisdom—even in certain purportedly Christian circles, perhaps especially there—to identify the other, and then to castigate, demean, and seek to destroy them. Hate of the other has become a measure of piety itself. Based on the witness of Holy Scripture we can only be crystal clear in our witness: those who live lives of anger and hatred reject the gospel of Jesus Christ, and destroy their own humanity. To seek to isolate walls of division between human beings, and then to reinforce those walls with malice, is not the way of discipleship, not the way of the cross, but the way of sheer madness and rejection of God. To harbor resentment and anger toward others in one's heart is to drive out all possibility for the humble life of service to Christ, which rests on kindness and mercy, never on hate and division.

Of course, there is a time for anger, even in the Bible. When we see injustice, we cannot stand idly by; we are right to feel righteous indignation, and to act in the present moment. But that is not the concern of the text before us, which is focused on the habits of the heart. Cultivating bitterness as a way of life—especially as a mode of religious piety—is not only not an option for the Christian community: doing so makes Christian life impossible, and ultimately drives those who foster such anger out of the circle of genuine Christian confession altogether.

We find, yet again in our passage, a profound and fundamental affirmation of the life of the immigrant as an integral part of the community. The immigrant, the alien, is to be loved, and to be treated just as the fellow citizen is to be treated. We live in a world today in which mass migration has become a complex and global reality. There are a variety of national issues, and political responses; but the witness of the Christian community can only be unanimous and heartfelt: welcome the immigrant. Whether we treat immigrants in our world today as a problem to be solved, or as a call of discipleship to be joyfully embraced, has become a fail-safe test of the genuineness of our faith in the gospel. The risen Lord, Jesus Christ, himself meets us in the stranger, in the immigrant. How we treat immigrants is how we treat him; how we dare to mistreat immigrants is how we dare—to our shame—to mistreat him. The stakes could not be more clear on this fundamental biblical issue.

3. Jubilee!

Leviticus 25

IT HAPPENS EVERY FIFTY years, once a generation, a divine revolution in economic justice, setting the world aright. The year of Jubilee begins life anew for the entire community, for all people in all social conditions, and indeed for the earth itself. All life is transformed by the ever-new gift of God, sounding forth in joy throughout the land. There is not one divine concern for the people, and a different divine concern for the earth; rather, God's all-encompassing love renews the entire creation. Jubilee is the radical transformation of the cosmos itself in joyous freedom.

We begin with the profound and fundamental affirmation that provides the theological framework for the proclamation of Jubilee. All that exists belongs to God and to God alone. The entire earth belongs to God; the promised land belongs to God. Israel will come to inherit the land of promise, entering as immigrants, rescued from bondage in the land of Egypt. But what is essential, crucial, to recognize in the explicit witness of the book of Leviticus is that *even after* they enter the new land of promise, they *remain*, forever, resident aliens, immigrants: "for the land is mine; with me you are but aliens and tenants" (Lev 25:23).

They do not enter as immigrants, and convert to residents; they enter as immigrants, and in God's sight—which is their essential truth as human persons—they remain immigrants, forever. The reason is simple; no one owns the land except God, and therefore everyone who travels and lives upon it is an alien, a passing guest. Similarly, all people belong to God. Yes, there are tribes, and families, and individuals, all with a variety of interwoven responsibilities and destinies. But all of these social definitions of human life are radically subverted by one simple, supreme fact: every human person belongs to God alone. All land is his; all people are his; that is the theological background for the radical subversion of established order which constitutes the proclamation of Jubilee.

The basic thrust of the Jubilee year can be briefly described. At the beginning of the fiftieth year, the ram's horn is sounded forth—loudly—throughout the entire land. This signals the urgent divine summons to liberty throughout the entire community, excluding no one, including everyone. The proclamation of *liberty* is the basic message of Jubilee, and the proclamation first of all concerns the health and well-being of the land, the earth itself. There can be no agricultural working of the land; no sowing or reaping, no harvesting of field or vineyard, during the year of Jubilee. The land will, of itself, yield an abundance to feed the people; and what it yields without human intervention may be gladly consumed and enjoyed. It is clear that there is no threat to the life of people or livestock during this Jubilee Year from lack of agricultural production, for God himself gives the growth, as the land enjoys the liberty of rest.

The promise of liberty extends as well to every human person in the community. Everyone returns to property that has been sold, for indeed it remains their own. In essence, no property is ever sold outright; rather, the production of the land is leased, and at the year of Jubilee the land is returned to its rightful owner, who never ceases to be its owner. The point however is not that land belongs to sellers, not buyers; the point rather is that the land belongs to *God*, and to him alone, and therefore he alone determines the conditions upon which property can be transferred and restored. At the time of Jubilee, all property is released to its original owner. To speak in modern terms, God alone owns the title to the land. Moreover, during this Jubilee Year, all debts are canceled, all slaves are set free. The basic principle of Jubilee can hardly be mapped directly onto any modern political or economic system, whether capitalist or Marxist. Since all that exists, land and creatures, belongs to God, and God wills liberty for his creation, the Jubilee Year is a divine event pointing toward the ultimate purpose of God for the freedom of the cosmos under his gracious care. Neither Karl Marx nor Adam Smith had this in mind, surely, though the question of how Jubilee intersects with modern political and economic realities is an open question, addressed below.

The remainder of the chapter in Leviticus describing the year of Jubilee charts the outline of three particular cases in which members of the community have fallen into situations of dire poverty. First of all, there are inevitably some who own land, who through various circumstances fall into debt that they cannot cover. In such cases they are forced to sell their land to cover their debt, which of course means they can no longer make a crop, and therefore no longer generate wealth. The solution is for the nearest relative—called the "redeemer"—to purchase the land and to keep it until the Jubilee Year, at which time it reverts back to the original owner. The land is set at liberty once again. On the other hand, if the original owner is somehow able to come up with the ability to repurchase his land, the price is to be determined by the original sale price, minus the value of the crops harvested since the sale. Jubilee does not mean that fairness is excluded; rather, both the buying and selling of land is to be done with a sense of just price. There are two exceptions to this first case. If a house is sold in a walled city, only a year is set in which the property can be repurchased; after that it belongs in perpetuity to the new owner, even in the Jubilee. On the other hand, Levitical houses may forever be redeemed, and are always to be released in the Jubilee Year. Indeed, land around a Levitical town may not even be sold in the first place.

The second case is even more dire. Suppose a farmer experiences crop failure and is therefore unable to repay a debt. The redeemer of the land—the relative who purchases the land from the owner—is to allow the farmer to work the land to pay off the debt without paying any interest. They may live off the land as they pay the debt, and no profit is to be made from their unfortunate circumstances. Israel remembers full well what it is like to work on behalf of those who profit from their labor, for they were slaves in Egypt. Never again; God brought them out of slavery and gave them the land of promise freely. They received the land as a gift, and must therefore be gracious in relation to those in need.

And third, if things go from bad to worse, a person may fall so deeply into debt that he must give up not only his land, but even the future harvests that the land produces. Thus, he has nothing less to offer but himself, his ability to work. Under no circumstances—despite the custom of the surrounding cultures—is such a person to be treated as a slave. Rather, he is to be accorded the status of a hired worker, treated with respectful kindness, and his wages may be used to pay down the debt. Then, in the Jubilee Year, that person is free from all obligation, and is restored fully to their original property. No member of the community may be servant to another; for all are servants to God alone. All ultimate allegiance belongs solely to him.

It has often been asked whether the various prescriptions of Jubilee were ever actually followed in historical Israel, but the evidence is lacking to decide. More importantly for our interests is the impact of the Jubilee tradition on the growth of the biblical witness. The book of Isaiah announces the promised new time of God's favor in words directly dependent on the Jubilee theme: "The Spirit of the Lord is upon me . . . he has sent me to bring good news to the oppressed, to bind up the broken-hearted, to proclaim liberty to the captives, and release to the prisoners; to

proclaim the year of the Lord's favor . . ." (Isa 61:1–3). In his first sermon
in his hometown of Nazareth, Jesus reads this text from the prophet Isaiah,
and then makes the stunning announcement: "Today this scripture has
been fulfilled in your hearing" (Luke 4:21). *Now*, in the very presence of
Christ himself, the event of Jubilee is fulfilled. This "today" is the new age
of God's redemption, in which salvation has fully arrived in Jesus himself.
The good townsfolk of Nazareth are not impressed; they try to kill him,
clearly foreshadowing the cross.

The Old Testament is revealed in the New. The true reality of Jubilee is
made known in the life, death, and resurrection of Jesus Christ, and according to the Christian confession only there. When Jesus refers to the "today"
of the fulfillment of Jubilee, he does not mean one day only. He is referring
to God's new time, which is identical to the rule of Christ the Lord. The
present, active rule of the exalted Lord, Jesus Christ, is the true meaning
of Jubilee. That does not mean for one moment that the various social and
economic aspects of the biblical witness can be spiritualized and denuded
of their force—not at all. Rather, it means that the vision of social and economic justice that is Jubilee cannot be detached from the living person of
Christ, and converted into an abstract political or social agenda. Christ the
Lord alone sets the prisoners free. Christ the Lord comforts the oppressed,
and liberates them from the bonds of tyranny. Christ the Lord heals the
sick and tends to the wounded. Christ the Lord is present and active in the
details of ordinary life among humankind in every place on earth, in ways
far beyond our awareness, already now, *today*, making real the promise of
Jubilee for all peoples and all nations of the earth.

On the other hand, the New Testament is concealed in the Old. We
cannot truly follow Jesus Christ the risen Lord in the present moment unless we obey his imperative for social equality, economic justice, and political freedom. The reality of Jubilee is not fulfilled by Christ once upon a
time and then set aside; it is fulfilled and therefore established, wherever he
rules, and that means throughout the entire cosmos, throughout all time.
We are not under law but under grace; yet the Old Testament witness to
Jubilee remains a living testimony to the divine imperative for all humanity, and a call to Christians from the living Lord of the church to obedience
and service in the world. God is God; therefore, we are bound to him. The
proclamation of Christ for liberty throughout the land is now a living word
that reaches the uttermost corners of the earth. Liberty embraces the earth
itself, all peoples who dwell in it, and sets on their feet again especially the
poor and vulnerable burdened with care. To follow Jesus Christ means to
embrace the liberty of Jubilee everywhere.

Without any doubt, the call of Jubilee to give rest to the land has an
immediate resonance to church and world in our time. The Scriptures are a

vehicle by which the risen Christ summons every new generation to immediate responsibility before him. There is no question that the issue of global
climate change, and the ecological crisis generally, is a modern problem, not
an ancient one. Nevertheless, there is likewise no doubt that the analogy of
faith hears in Scripture the basic call of Christ to respect for creation.

Since the Industrial Revolution we have seen the earth as a source for
exploitation and extraction. We are now at the point—scientists the world
over fully agree—where those processes of exploitation and extraction are
destroying the habitability of earth itself. No longer is it a matter of geologi-
cal ages, or even of multiple generations. Rather, if radical changes are not
made, and made now, processes will be set in motion—indeed they already
are, quite clearly—that will result in irreversible damage to the earth and
its capacity to foster life, including human life. The earth itself, as the Bible
warns, will extract its own revenge, if human beings do not respect the divinely willed limits of human consumption.

So, what does it mean to declare a Jubilee for the earth? We can no
longer afford to extract and burn coal as a source of energy. It is releasing
carbon dioxide into the atmosphere, and thus trapping harmful radiation,
warming the globe. It has to stop, and to stop now. We can no longer continue relying on oil and natural gas (which releases even more harmful
methane) as fuels, for the same basic reasons. These sources of energy
arose in recent history, and they must disappear in history; there is no
permanence attached to them, other than the self-interest of those who
benefit financially from them. Wind, biofuels, solar power, all are available
in the natural world, all are abundant, all are awaiting human ingenuity
to be captured and used without the deleterious effects of extraction and
exploitation. Jubilee for the earth means an immediate transition to re-
newable sources of energy worldwide in all forms of human life in society.
Scientists are agreed that it is entirely possible. Economists are agreed that
such a transition will provide abundant employment. Our argument here,
on the basis of Scripture, is that from the point of view of the gospel it is a
moral imperative, and therefore nonnegotiable.

The law of Jubilee—which is the law of liberty—without question
directly addresses the highly existential and contemporary question of
inequality of wealth. Within countries, between countries, along racial
and gender lines, there is a measurable and enormous gap between the
wealthy—the super-wealthy, we should say—and the rest of the world. According to the Bible, there should be in place a *regular* cycle in which that
gap is erased. That cycle is set once a generation, every fifty years. Every
debt is canceled, all property is restored to the original owner, all slaves
are released from bondage. Now, some would say that the modern system
of finance would simply collapse if we were to follow the biblical mandate.

Perhaps. Yet on the other hand, if we must then choose between the biblical mandate, and the modern system of finance, our choice is obvious. Scripture alone holds authority in the church of Jesus Christ, certainly no economics devised by human beings, whether on the right or on the left. Others might say that, while the biblical word holds good for private individuals, it does not address the real world of public wealth. But is that true? Is it not precisely the world of public wealth that the biblical mandate covers, indeed without regard for status or privilege? Granted that the imperatives of the book of Leviticus are bound to the living community of faith, do they not necessarily point to the living will of God for the whole world? The whole point of the Jubilee celebration is a public, universal mechanism of restoration of economic and social justice.

But we do not need to decide between an overly literalistic acceptance of Jubilee or a faithless rejection of it. The fact is, the Scriptures are shaped as a vehicle by which we struggle, through the presence of the Spirit, to discern the living will of God for church and world. And we learn the following. Inequality of the sort we are experiencing in the world today is an *offense* to the justice of God. We cannot hide behind our own individual enjoyment of the benefits of Christ when the world itself is bleeding from economic and social injustice of historic proportions. Moreover, there must be mechanisms in place that redress the balance. Private philanthropy is a good thing, but it is not enough. There must be *public responsibility* for the common good invested in the periodic and permanent reduction of inequality. Poverty, debt, and social and economic oppression are threats to the humanity of us all. That system of redress will work best, which on the most pragmatic level ensures that the gap of wealth is permanently reduced, thus fostering the full humanity of every person in the sight of God.

No one knows the right answer to every social, political, economic question, certainly not the Christian community. We all strive for the goals of justice and peace, but how we get there often eludes our best efforts. In the end, the one rule by which to weigh every possibility is the rule of love. Does it set any limits of human concern? Then it is to be rejected, for the rule of love embraces every human being without limit. Does it slide over the real-life concerns of flesh-and-blood fellow citizens? Then it is against love, for love meets people where they are, in the messy reality of everyday life. Does it give others a fresh start in life, setting them on their feet again, pointing them the way forward? Then it certainly accords with love, for love embraces the future, and leaves the past in the past. "You shall love your neighbor as yourself"; what conflicts with this rule is to be rejected, what accords with it is to be fully embraced, for love is always the right answer to the struggles we face.

IV. Numbers

1. The Power of Fear

Numbers 13

THE THEOLOGICAL STRUCTURE OF the book of Numbers is openly concealed in the title of the book, both in the English form, and in the Hebrew title ("In the Wilderness"). As the book opens, the people of Israel are still camped at Mount Sinai; indeed, they will not leave until Numbers 10:11, just after celebrating the second Passover. It has been a year since the glorious liberation from bondage in Egypt. The "numbering" refers to a census of the entire people Israel with which the book opens, tribe by tribe. Thus, we come to know the very names of the generation who left Egypt, and are now on their way from Sinai to the promised land. Yet there will be a second numbering, a second census, in chapter 26, at the end of the book; and we will discover that it is an entirely *new* generation, though the same tribes, the same people Israel. What has happened? An *entire* generation is condemned—by God himself—to wander in the wilderness (the Hebrew title, taken from the opening verse of the book) until all over the age of twenty have perished. It is not a natural transition based on aging, but a *catastrophic* loss of ultimate blessing. The *people* are liberated from Egypt and will enter the promised land; but not the *generation* that left. Only a new generation will experience the fulfilled promise. One generation inherits nothing but failure and defeat; a new generation lives in hope and expectation. One generation dies, a new generation lives. Our text explains why.

As soon as the people leave Sinai, there are already signals that things are going terribly wrong. Once again, the people begin to complain, to murmur, about their terrible misfortune, as if freedom is a burden to carry rather than a gift to be enjoyed. Then it becomes personal; Aaron and Miriam, the brother and sister of Moses, become jealous of his role, and stand in judgment of him for marrying a non-Israelite wife while he was a shepherd in Midian. God dramatically defends Moses as his friend, and Moses prays for both his siblings. Yet somehow, even as the people follow the cloud of God right up to the southern border of the promised land, the sense of exhilarating anticipation and foreboding dread are mixed in equal parts. Something, it would seem, has to give.

And so it does. The writer uses every technique of the narrator's craft to draw out the terrible drama of what happens next. Shades of ambiguity abound, and are left for the reader to notice and to ponder. God commands Moses to send a group of leaders—one from each of the tribes of Israel—on a mission of reconnaissance into the new land, a land that God will give them. From the opening frame of the narrative, we are reminded: the land is sheer divine gift, in no sense is it the result of human acquisition or achievement. The leaders are named, and sent; among them is Caleb from the tribe of Judah and Joshua from the tribe of Benjamin.

The charge Moses gives them is straightforward; they are to navigate their way through the new land of promise, and chart the largesse of the land itself, while at the same time investigating the relative strengths and weaknesses of the inhabitants. They are also to bring back some of the produce as evidence of the bounty of the agriculture. They carry out their mission without trouble, incidentally passing by Hebron, the burial place of the patriarchs, a quiet reminder of how far back the divine promise stretches; indeed, it was in Hebron that the divine promise was first given to Abraham. They discover that well-known warrior peoples—the Anakites—are inhabitants of certain cities, obviously cause for concern. Yet they also bring back some of the astoundingly fruitful produce: grapes, figs, pomegranates, in clusters so large that they must be carried on poles. The mission takes forty days, and they return to report.

It is just here that the narrator slows down the story to make clear the nuances of impending catastrophe about to unfold, so pregnant with disaster for the future of all concerned. The leaders come back to Moses and all the people, and together all the leaders make their initial report, which is straightforward, factual, and mixed. On the one hand, it is quite clear that the land is plentiful indeed, a glorious new land filled with extraordinary blessings for life. Just look at these fruits we brought! The whole land flows with milk and honey, apparently a saying (even then) denoting a land so rich that any life upon it would be a dream. Yet on the other hand, there is a measure of concern, when it comes to the inhabitants. They do have walled cities, which will be a detriment to military conquest. The towns are large, which will make siege warfare difficult. And yes, there are Anakites here and there, esteemed warriors not to be trifled with. The group then lists the various inhabitants by region, including Amalekites, Hittites, Jebusites, Amorites, and Canaanites, all peoples now dwelling in what is after all a rich and fertile area one could scarcely expect to be empty of human population. These are the *facts*, and the entire group sent out on reconnaissance clearly agrees on them. The goal is brilliant; the steps toward it are not easy, but nor are they impossible. Now comes the second question introduced by the narrator: what is to be the *opinion* formed by the people (and the course of action that opinion leads to) based on the facts?

Four responses are given, in an atmosphere of sharply escalating crisis. The first to give his opinion is Caleb—he is later joined by Joshua—who urges the people to immediately enter the promised land and defeat the inhabitants. There can be no doubt of the outcome, Caleb assures the clearly shaken people of Israel gathered around; it is a wonderful land, and it is ours for the taking. The grounds for his confidence are spelled out with crystal clarity before the people. Caleb measures the obstacles to be overcome in reference to the *unlimited* sovereignty of the divine good pleasure, which has already freely given the land to the people. They cannot lose, because God is infinitely greater than any obstacle they might face; now is the time to enter and possess the land! So, Caleb (and Joshua).

The remaining spies give their opinion next, and here again the narrator brilliantly depicts the shifting tones of rhetoric. For while they are delivering an *opinion* based on an agreed set of public facts, they couch their opinion in the form of a *new* set of facts. That is, they change their story, to match their opinion of what should happen: the very essence of malign, ideological propaganda.

They had said—in agreement with Caleb and Joshua—that the land was bountiful, and even brought proof in the form of produce; now they declare that the land is some sort of wild, primeval forest, a fairy-tale nightmare that "devours its inhabitants." They had admitted that there are notable warriors living in various cities, clearly a military challenge to be weighed; now they turn these warriors into giant mythological creatures known as Nephilim, half human, half divine, so tall that ordinary mortals are in comparison the size of tiny grasshoppers! How awful! It is a bravura performance, subtly substituting sheer fantasy for public reality in order to convert an opinion into a new version—a false version—of alternative factuality. Clearly, they measure the obstacles in front of them, not in reference to the divine promise, nor even in reference to the human capacity of the Israelite army (which is considerable), but in reference to hysterical *fear*.

The people come third, and it is hardly surprising by now how they respond. They were already shaken; they only needed to hear from the SPY news network in order to confirm their worst fears. They complain and murmur against Moses and Aaron. They boldly state that they would rather *die* in the wilderness than fight against giants and people-devouring forests. They blame God for delivering them from slavery in Egypt in the first place, and decide on the spot to choose a new leader to guide them back to the land from which they only recently escaped. The narrator leaves us simply to ponder. In a sequence of just three speeches, we have moved from a virtual paradise to be claimed, to a hideously irrational desire to return to certain death as slaves at the hands of the Egyptians. Such is the power of fear, and the human folly that gives into it.

People talk, prevaricate, manipulate, revolt; but always in the Bible God himself gives the final verdict, here in the fourth speech. The glory of the Lord appears, and God himself declares his will. Thanks to the intercession of Moses, God will not destroy the entire people for their utterly faithless disregard for his promise. But he will give this generation—the adults who came out of Egypt—exactly what they asked for. They would rather die in the wilderness? So they shall; they will wander for forty years in the wilderness, just as the spies traveled forty days through the land, until they die. Only the new generation will enter the promised land. God is slow to anger; but he will by no means clear the guilty. Only Caleb and Joshua shall enter the new land of promise.

As we reflect on the subject matter of the biblical witness, the Christian community confesses: Jesus Christ is the true content of the divine promise. In his life, death, and resurrection, in his exaltation to eternal glory, the promise given to Abraham is now completely fulfilled. The redemption of the cosmos is complete; the reconciliation of all things is now a reality, through his cross. That truth is the one source of our confidence and strength, anchored not in the daily changes of earthly existence, but in the eternal constancy of divine love, which cannot and will not fail.

Yet, we must add another point in the dialectic of biblical faith. As the living church of Jesus Christ we live out our lives on earth; we struggle still through the sufferings of change and time and worldly resistance to the realm of God, including our own resistance. In short, though the promise is certain and secure, we who treasure it nevertheless wander through the wilderness of this world, even as the eternal promise of God unfolds through time in stages. There are joys here to be cherished and remembered, but also dangers to be avoided, and regrets we would rather forget if we could. There are challenges to be confidently faced, but also failures we would gladly avert, if only they were not so menacing and apparent. In short, we live *between the times*: between the already fulfilled eternity of God's promised hope in Jesus Christ, and the unfolding challenge of life amidst the ambiguities of the world around us. We must not let go of absolute trust in the promise; yet our faith is in God, not in the power of positive thinking. We are familiar with struggle.

One option needs to be quickly and forthrightly discarded, though it is widespread. Some would argue that God's promise in Christ is not yet fulfilled, that it is still an open future. There is a timeline yet to unfold, a biblical list of "prophetic events." In the meantime, there is an absolute struggle between good and evil, which battle for the soul of the world. This view is based on fear, not on faith, certainly not on biblical faith. Such fear demonizes opponents as enemies of God; takes every opportunity to turn challenges into crises; magnifies differences of opinion into absolutely incompatible worldviews.

The gospel in fact shatters all worldviews, including the false worldview of dualistic fear. Such fear is not grounded upon the sure word of God found in the Bible, but rather uses the Bible as a pretext for standing in judgment over perceived adversaries, many of whom may very well be friends of the truth. Such fear loves crowds, loves masses, loves hysteria; it hates reason, hates conversation, hates dialogue. Fear usually works behind the scenes to whip up support, and then strikes when the frenzy is at a fever pitch. It never takes the times to ask: is this really true? Is this an accurate picture of the world around us? Is this a true explanation of the biblical word that we profess to believe? Is this indeed God's will for church and world? We necessarily live in the tension of faith, which the Christian life can never fully escape until the blessed day when time itself shall cease; but fear is in no way whatsoever the proper response to that tension. Prophets of fear are false prophets.

We cannot and must not give up our absolute trust in the promise of God in Jesus Christ; yet we continue to live our lives in the ambiguous tension of the unfolding world all around us, muddled as it sometimes can be. How are we, as faithful disciples of Jesus Christ, to navigate our way? The answer is to cultivate the gift of true objectivity. Perhaps the most difficult vision of all is simply to see the world around us as it is, neither with the blinders of fear, nor with the false hopes of positive thinking, but with the realistic image of true objectivity. We can attain it only with help.

We need to listen to experts who know what they are talking about, and eschew advice that comes from sources with an obvious prejudice built into their obstructed understanding. We need to compare our own conclusions with the conclusions reached by other well-meaning people in the public realm of give-and-take, and not withdraw into a world of private religious fantasy. On the other hand, as people of faith we can attest to the world that there is always hope; that there are ways forward, even when we must look diligently to find them, for God never leaves us without a way ahead. We can point out that sometimes the solutions are found in the most unlikely places, for God takes pleasure in hiding his treasures where few would think to look.

Above all we can fight fear with the calm of objective discussion, for absolute faith in God's promise clears a space in the world for true realism.

Every generation of the church faces different challenges, summons up different resources, navigates upon unique circumstances. Of course, often the church succeeds marvelously in facing the demands of the time, and we are all the beneficiaries of the brilliant blessings handed down from age to age, whether in hymns and prayers, in theology and exegesis, in mission and discipleship. But it would seem that just as often, perhaps more often, the church fails miserably to meet the challenges before it. We come up to the very edge of the promised land, and instead of crossing over, we fail to lay hold of the one thing needful, the truth of the gospel as it is revealed through Scripture in our time and place.

What accounts for the church's failures? In the end, there is no adequate explanation; the only true freedom is a faith in the promise which moves forward, and any other option is no freedom at other, but meaningless, chaotic, self-contradictory bondage. Yet without explanation it happens, and often enough follows the pattern of our passage. A generation sees the future promise of God shining brightly before it, yet it retreats into the past, clinging stubbornly to the familiar and comfortable, unwilling to let go of the guarantees of safety and security it falsely finds in the surrounding world. It forgets that God alone is our comfort; God alone is our safety and security; God alone is our past, present, and future, whose presence even now is the fullness of time. The church fails when it seeks a God whom it can control, by conforming God to its own expectations and experience, a God whom it can name for itself, choose for itself, a God who is willing to partner in a joint enterprise of religious piety. It forgets the awesome truth that God alone is God who made the heavens and the earth, who rules and overrules all that exists. He cannot be controlled, but controls all things in the sheer constancy of his love. He cannot be manipulated or chosen, but chooses us by the sheer electing love of his merciful grace. We do not name him; he himself gives us his name in baptism, and claims us as his own, and by claiming us set us free to be ourselves for the first time. He has no partners, but himself lives an eternal relationship of love, a relationship he condescends to establish in his gracious covenant with all creation, even with us, his church, whom he calls by his name.

Every generation of the church faces the challenge of the gospel in a new way, some with extraordinary blessing in faithfulness, others careening wildly from the one path ahead that leads to the promised land of divine mercy and love. Yet God never leaves himself without witnesses. Even in defeats, whether many or few, they shine like lights in the world.

2. The Waters of Meribah

Numbers 20:1–13

THE NARRATOR EXPERTLY SETS the scene for what will develop into one of the most dramatic episodes of the Pentateuch, and certainly the most tragic in the life of Moses. The setting is the same as the account of the sending of the spies into the promised land, which is Kadesh in the wilderness of Zin, on the southern border of the new homeland. The place is the same; but the time could not be more different. *Forty years* have elapsed. In those years, an entire generation has died off, the first generation of the people rescued by God from bondage in Egypt. Only five are left: Caleb and Joshua, the two faithful spies, and Moses, Aaron, and Miriam. As the account opens, the narrator briefly and soberly records the death and burial of Miriam, the sister of Moses and Aaron, just outside the new land of promise. And so, there are four. What began with such enormous hope a generation ago has now come to this; and even this pitiful remnant will sadly, and soon, diminish further. One generation begins in hope and ends in tragedy; the new generation, we will see, begins in tragedy, but will thankfully end in glorious hope.

The whole congregation is now encamped in the desert wilderness on the southern border, just outside the land of promise. It is a new generation, not implicated in the fears and faithless rejection of God by the old. But they are still in the desert, and some of the old problems reappear, above all the lack of water to drink. The narrator—not the people—records the simple fact: there is no water to sustain the life of this great people whom God has brought forth to be his own.

Their reaction is entirely predictable. The people complain to their leaders, Moses and Aaron. The litany of complaints is all too familiar, and echoes the theme of murmuring in the wilderness that is a constant refrain in the biblical portrait. They wonder why Moses and Aaron brought them out of

Egypt in the first place; notice, not God, but these all too human liberators. Why let us and our cattle die here in this wretched desert? Sure, we saw the produce of the promised land, the figs, vines, and pomegranates, but where are they now? And where is the water? Without water, they wish that they had died when the rest of the people died during the wilderness journey.

It is of course an almost stock response by now as the people react to hardship. An entire generation has already passed away in the wilderness having made exactly such responses in the past. We can be forgiven perhaps if we assume, as readers, that we are faced here with yet another in a familiar pattern of faithless Israel, and if we steel ourselves for the divine judgment that is sure to follow. In fact, such an assumption, however familiar, is wrong. There is not divine judgment on the people. There is not divine reaction to their response. The reason has already been supplied by the narrator. Their complaint, however poorly couched, is legitimate: there is no water. They will die of thirst here in the desert without something to drink. The reaction of God is different this time; tragically, it is the reaction of *Moses* that follows the familiar pattern, and we will watch in horror as the power of false assumption destroys his chance of entry into the promised land.

Moses and Aaron proceed as they have so often during the wilderness wandering. They retreat—apparently under enormous pressure from the vehemence of the assembled crowd—to the tent of meeting, in order to supplicate God. They fall on their faces in humility and reverence, and the divine glory appears to them. Now, once before a similar situation has evoked a similar response. It was while the first generation of the people Israel were on the journey from Egypt to Sinai. At Massah, in Rephidim, the people lost any access to water, and they characteristically complained loudly to Moses, demanding something for their thirst. God commanded Moses to take the rod that he had used during the great plagues of Egypt, and in full sight of the elders of the people to strike the rock designated by God, and water would flow from it. Moses obeyed, and the water flowed.

This time, a full generation later, though in similar circumstances, God once again commands Moses what to do. God does not offer general ideas or ethical principles in the Bible. Instead he provides concrete commands in response to historical situations. God is a living God, who lays claim upon human life in the immediacy of the moment. And this time his command is unique and different. He tells Moses to take up the rod, the same rod used before at Massah, the same rod used before in confrontation with Pharaoh. This time, Moses and Aaron are to gather the entire assembled people. There is, this time, no mention by God of striking the rock with the rod; rather, Moses is to verbally *command* the rock in the sight of the people, and the waters will flow miraculously from the rock. They will have plenty to drink, as will all their animals. There is no mention of judgment of the people by God, only exact instructions on how Moses is to carry out the task of supplying them with life-sustaining water in a dry and thirsty land.

What starts out as an account—apparently—about the testing of the people, turns out in an instantaneous flash to be a terrible test of Moses himself, a test he will fail with catastrophic effect.

Thus far we are following a narrative sequence that has been sadly repeated a number of times in the wilderness, with the sequence of complaint, gathering against Moses and Aaron, meeting with God, and the divine response, now well established. It is only now that Moses himself breaks the pattern, and shatters the very hope of the divine promise. He does so in three ways, told in quick succession.

He takes the staff, as the Lord commands, and with Aaron gathers the people in front of the rock. So far so good; he is following the instructions given to him by God. Then he makes his first terrible error. He speaks to the people with deep bitterness and accusation: "Listen, you rebels!" There is nothing in the divine command to warrant such an attack on the people. The narrator has made it clear from the beginning that the fundamental complaint of the people is fully legitimate. They will die without water. Neither does God condemn them. Yet Moses takes it upon himself to accuse them of rebellion! He has, until now, during all the extraordinary twists and turns of the wilderness journey, done nothing less than put his own life at stake in order to act as intercessor for the people with God. Now, with no undue provocation, he suddenly snaps, and turns against the people, no longer their intercessor, now their adversary and judge. Who made Moses judge over all the people Israel, we are given to ponder? Is that not God's role alone?

Moses then asks a fatal—and boastful—question: "shall we bring water out of this rock?" Regardless of the exact emotional nuance of the question, which probably has a range of meaning from taunting to boasting, the main point is that Moses has once again exchanged his customary role as an *agent* of the divine will for the role as the very *source* of miracle among the people. Ordinarily it is fully clear; God works *through* Moses and Aaron. But now Moses unaccountably suddenly aggrandizes to himself and his brother the role of quasi-divine miracle workers and providers for the people. It is entirely out of character; but that is just the point. This is not the Moses we know and expect, yet it is Moses who makes the terrible mistake.

And finally, while it was made abundantly clear that he is to speak to the rock—as God commanded—he instead taps it with his rod, as he once did before at Massah. It is as if Moses simply stops listening to God, and goes on his own merry way, doing what he has done before, rather than obeying the clear command of the living God. Indeed, he taps the rock twice; as if to make it petulantly clear that he will do it his own way this time.

God indeed causes water to gush out for the people. But his judgment of Moses and Aaron is swift and definitive. They failed to put their trust in God; they failed to honor his holiness before the people, his inherent right to be God in his own way, according to his own good pleasure. And so neither Moses nor Aaron will enter the promised land. Now there are only two, Caleb and Joshua.

We are all called in the church of Jesus Christ into the ministry of intercession for others. Our role is to pray, not only for family and friends, for church and community, but even for enemies, perhaps especially for enemies. It is not an easy calling, but that is irrelevant; it is the calling to which the risen Christ himself daily summons us, and so it is the path of discipleship we are required to follow. Yet it is so terribly easy to lose our bearings in relation to the gospel, and to fall into the trap of the world; that is, to suddenly see our enemies as adversaries to be opposed, rather than fellow creatures of God to be loved and cared for. It is utterly irrelevant to our calling as disciples of Christ whether others may consider us enemies, or may treat us in less than friendly ways; how they treat us is not our problem but theirs. Our challenge is how we treat our fellow human creatures, all of them. Human religion often sets boundaries between human beings—including, sadly, the Christian religion. But the gospel of Jesus Christ tears down those boundaries. Our prayers are to follow the gospel as it gathers into one the entire human family under the divine care, who makes the sun shine and the blessed rains fall on all peoples of the earth. Where your prayers stop, your love stops; where your love stops, your faith stops; and where your faith stops, your grasp of the gospel falls short of the sheer grandeur of God's all-encompassing mercy.

The great temptation of religion—again including the Christian religion—is to assume a human partnership with God. It is one thing to believe that God in his rich mercy works in and through the lives of his children; it is quite another to suggest that God and his children together form a partnership of cooperative labor in redeeming the world. God and us together, standing up for traditional values, saving society from its degradation! God and us together, working revolutionary change building the kingdom of God! The point is not to deny that God freely enters our world, freely uses our lives according to his sovereign and gracious purpose, freely and mysteriously weaves into the very fabric of human existence patterns of divine love. All these things are true. Yet they come to us as miracle, as grace; we receive them with gratitude and joy, not with proud boasting that we are the ones who bring the divine will into effect on earth. God works his will in our lives in ways far beyond human understanding. It is cause for wonder, never for boasting.

Judgment of others brings anger against others, and it is that anger that causes false assumptions to cloud our understanding. Anger keeps people—even well-intentioned people—from seeing the legitimate needs of others. Perhaps people may not always express themselves perfectly; but the fact is there is a basic human need for adequate food and drink, for adequate housing and access to healthcare, for the fundamental rights of free citizenship without fear. Anger towards others can only stand in judgment over the way those needs are *expressed*; but the God of the Bible time and again throughout the entire Scriptures clearly and abundantly affirms the *validity* of those needs without any ambiguity whatsoever. There is no water; they need to drink. There is no food; they need to eat. They are not well; they need to be healed. They have nowhere to live; they need shelter and care. If we focus solely on the way people express needs, rather than on the needs which are expressed, we fail the test of the gospel. If we listen through the frustration to the underlying anguish being declared, we are in a position to help, and that alone is what truly matters.

There is no indication anywhere in the Bible that God's eternal will changes over time. God's commandments are firm, established in the heavens. Yet God is a living God. His commandments do not express abstract moral principles that can be systematically grasped and arranged, and then applied according to a so-called biblical worldview. There is no such worldview, least of all in terms of biblical ethics. God alone commands; ours is to obey the concrete word of his commandment. He may command this at one time; and now that at another time. We are not invited to seek a higher moral unity, nor are we compelled to obey blindly, but rather with intelligence and imagination we are summoned to carry out the concrete summons to obedience that is even now the living claim of God upon human life. To be clear: just because it was done that way in the past, does not mean that it is the will of God in the present. We cannot simply ignore the clear command of God in the present moment, and simply repeat the past as if we know better than God the truth of his will. At every moment, our hearts and minds are open to the fresh hearing of the word and claim of God upon our lives.

And indeed, times change, whole generations change. Customs that were once familiar to parents and grandparents may be deeply unfamiliar in church and society to a new generation. Ways of tackling social and cultural issues that were once neglected or shunted aside may be so common among a new generation as to be taken for granted. The biblical narrative is not unaware of the power of generational change. To be sure; it can happen both for good and ill. At times, a new generation arises that forgets the most basic lessons of divine worship and service, and catastrophic disaster is the result. But at other times, a new generation comes along with a fresh start, an open horizon ahead, and the arc of the biblical witness pulls it forward into the future rather than back into the past. We simply cannot treat every generation as if they are the same. We must not force each new age of discipleship into the same mold of service to Christ as the one before it, nor carry forward assumptions that are no longer operative, effective, or even particularly relevant. Time is not an empty container through which generations move, in the Bible; rather, generations carry forward the passing of time itself. It is through the passing from one generation to the next that time moves, and with time the onward thrust of the eternal divine purpose.

If even Moses commits such a terrible mistake; if even Peter and the remaining disciples quite clearly misunderstand the most basic lessons of Christian discipleship; we can be sure that no one, really no one, is perfect. We have all done things we regret. We have all said things we instantly wished we could take back. Our faith has been challenged, and we have quivered in fear. Our confidence has been shaken, and we have lashed out in anger. We make false assumptions about the people we hold most dear in this world. We leave untended the needs of others, when offering our best would otherwise be so simple. We take things personally that really should be left alone, and leave to fester wounds it is within our power to tend. As we will see, even in judgment, there is grace for Moses; he will not enter the new land of promise, but he will be the first to see it from the mountaintop. We all receive grace upon grace, even in our weakness. Yet as we wander through the wilderness of this world, it is well to be reminded that we are in good company when we realize our common frailty. It is not an excuse; but it is a comfort to remember that we are all alike as sinners, all alike in need of divine love, all alike in being upheld solely by the sheer mercy of God Almighty.

3. The Daughters of Zelophehad

Numbers 27:1–11

WE BRIEFLY SUMMARIZE THE narrative arc of Numbers, in order to set the context for this extraordinary passage. Recall that the book opens with a census of all the people of Israel, the entire generation whom God delivers from bondage out of Egypt. God leads them stage by stage from Sinai, where they receive the sacred law of God in covenant grace, to the very southern edge of the new land of promise. Spies are sent across to scout out the land and the inhabitants. And then catastrophe. The people pull back in fear and mistrust, misled in part by the outrageous lies of the spies, in part by their own sheer unwillingness to put their faith in the divine word of promise. What began with such great expectation quickly descends into bitter loss, as an entire generation is condemned to wander aimlessly in the wilderness until they pass away.

Meanwhile, a new generation begins to arise, those who were twenty years old and younger when the people refused to enter the land, and therefore took no active part in the rebellion, not being yet of age to go into battle. They come of age in a time of deep uncertainty and loss, wandering through the desert, but in the end will find themselves poised to claim the cherished divine word of hope. Slowly the losses mount, as first Miriam dies, then Aaron dies, and Moses is told by God that he will not enter the land of promise either because of his failure to give God honor and glory at the fatal encounter at Meribah.

Once again, the new generation is on the move, generally from the southern border of the promised land, around to the eastern border. The Moabites, the Midianites, and the Amorites are defeated, as the people move to the Transjordan, the area on the eastern bank of the Jordan River, from where they will one day soon launch their crossing into the new land (as told in the book of Joshua). Even still, there is disaster awaiting, as the final remnants of the old generation mix with the population of the Moabites, including the worship of their god Baal-Peor. The worship of an alien god is the last act of apostasy for this first generation; a plague from God runs through the camp and destroys the last remnants of those who were rescued from Egypt. Twenty-four thousand die; the old generation is now gone. In the midst of life, there is death.

Yet in the midst of death, there is new life. As soon as the final plague snuffs the life out of the old generation because of their worship of an alien god, the narrative of Numbers suddenly turns to a new chapter in the history of God's people Israel; that is, the second census, recording the new generation, is given in the very next chapter (26). They are now located on the plains of Moab, just across the Jordan River from the city of Jericho, when the census is taken. Of the old generation, now only Moses, Joshua, and Caleb are left; Moses has been told that he will not enter the promised land, and Joshua will be the leader chosen by God in his place. There is clearly a sense of extraordinary anticipation as one by one the various tribes are listed, with their clans and families. After the full listing of the people comes the ominous proclamation: there is not one left of the old generation, except Caleb and Joshua; all the rest have perished. This is a new generation of the people of God.

A careful reading of the census, though, yields one anomaly. The sons of Joseph are Manasseh and Ephraim, and among the descendants of Manasseh is Machir, head of the clan of the Machirites. So far, everything is normal for the time. Tribal and clan identity passes down from one generation to the next through the oldest son, in a patrilineal system very familiar to the ancient world. Machir's line passes through Gilead; and Gilead's line passes through several generations until it reaches Hepher, whose eldest son is Zelophehad. Here the text records the fact which will provoke an ethical crisis: Zelophehad has no sons, only five daughters: Mahlah, Noah, Hoglah, Milcah, and Tirzah. The fact is left unremarked, but not unnoticed, in the census of the new generation. In fact, it will be these five women who will take the initiative in raising the untidy facts of real life to the level of a creative new solution in moral reflection.

In our passage, the five women come forward and stand before Moses to present their case. The act in itself is not unusual; often enough, matters large and small are brought to Moses by the people, and he either answers the query directly, or he consults with God in the Tent of Meeting in order to know the divine directive. But in this case, the act is surrounded by several unspoken assumptions that will need to be drawn out explicitly as the extraordinary scene unfolds. And the first such assumption is that these five women are crossing a line. In a patriarchal society such as Israel, simply coming forward *at all* is an act of courage. Yet they hesitate not one bit. Before not only Moses, and the priest Eleazar, the priests, and the leaders, but before the gathered congregation of the people, these five women exercise their voice as members of the community of faith. Nor does the biblical narrative censor them in any way; on the contrary, as we will see, their efforts are in fact rewarded in the end. At least for a moment, female initiative has a place alongside its male counterpart in Israel.

They present their case. Their father, Zelophehad, died during the wilderness wandering, one of the lost generation now consigned to the past. He was not implicated in any open rebellion; he was simply one of those who did not step forth in faith to grasp the divine promise. Now, he died before he had any sons; implied is the fact that his wife has also died. Only his five daughters remain. What is to be done? Two more assumptions are at work, actually three.

First, land is passed from father to son. The legacy of a family—the "name" of the father—is handed on from one generation to the next in perpetuity through this mechanism of insuring that landed property is always kept secure in the family line. We are not just describing here a custom, but a divine law in Israel, which is intended to ensure that the promised land about to be inherited remains in the tribes and families to whom the living God gives it, and not expropriated. That is the second assumption. All land remains in the tribes, the clans, and the families, to whom God gives it. The purpose of patrilineal descent of property is to reinforce the security of property within the tribe and clan, while the security of property depends upon the mechanism of patrilineal descent.

So, what happens when there is a contradiction between these two assumptions? That is the issue raised by these five extraordinary women. If property can only be handed on to a son, and there is no son, then property will perforce be removed from the legitimate realm of the family. If on the other hand, in a family without sons, should property remain within the family, it can only happen if it passes through the daughters. The women must inherit the land in order to preserve the family legacy; and that is what they petition Moses for.

Moses does what he has so often does; he brings their case before the Lord, presenting the matter in the Tent of Meeting, and awaiting the divine verdict. This is God's law, and therefore God's decision, not Moses'. And God decides that these five daughters are exactly correct! They should possess the property of their father. God himself overturns, in this instance, the principle of male inheritance of property. Indeed, God turns it into a new principle of divine law; whenever a man dies without a son, the property passes to the daughter. Women can own property in Israel henceforth.

I spoke of a third assumption that needs to be noticed. These five women are raising the issue of dividing the land well before there is any land at all to divide! The people are still on the wrong side of the Jordan River! These women are looking forward in full anticipation to the new land of promise, in such great contrast to the spies, and the old generation, which turned aside, and turned back. Hope creates expectation, and expectation creates the possibility of creativity. God's promise reorders all life.

The Apostle Paul boldly declares: Anyone who is in Christ is a new creation; everything old has passed away; see, everything has become new! The cross of Jesus Christ is the death of the old; the resurrection of Jesus Christ is the final victory of the new. Christian life unfolds in turning away from the old that is passing away, and turning toward the new, God's new creation, God's new world, which though hidden is already here. To live with Christ is thus to walk in radical newness of life.

For you, the question is not: *can* you change? Jesus Christ has already changed your life; he has indeed already changed the whole world. The only question is: *will* you live the new life that Christ has even now made for you? That means first of all a life of anticipation, of expectation. You may be absolutely certain that you know what your future holds. You have added up every possible element, weighed every possible factor, and there is up ahead a destiny that is locked in, with no uncertainty remaining. If so, you could not be more wrong. God's eternal promise has already created a new reality in your life, and in the world around you. But it comes only to those with eyes to see and ears to hear, only with those eager to know the true beauty of God breaking anew into creation from above. It is a promise far off, but also a promise near; it is a salvation yet to be revealed, but also a salvation very near at hand; it is a day for which we wait, yet today, even today—the day of salvation.

Anticipation engenders genuine courage. Courage does not see a situation and simply try to struggle our way through. Courage sees a situation and seeks to imagine a way fundamentally to change the stakes that hold us, and all people, back. Courage does not simply keep time; courage realizes that God himself has changed time by the eternity of his presence, and therefore steps forward into a transformed future. True courage takes imagination: not simply seeing the world the way it has always been, but taking the time to imagine a world that might yet be, and constructing the path that leads us and others to a new goal. Creativity requires genuine boldness. We cannot delegate imagination. We either take the time to use our own creative resources or we fail the task at hand. We cannot say: someone ought to fix this problem! Rather, ours is to say: there must be a way, for God himself leads us forward; where does he lead? Nor can we always know the end when we strike forth at the beginning. All we can do is to take the initiative in hope, and then wait and watch as God himself renders the decision. In the end, all change is in his hands, not ours. That is our true freedom, not our loss.

We do not strive for creative change for ourselves, or for ourselves only, but for others. There is certainly our own immediate family, which constantly requires the minor and major readjustments of life in a changing social and economic environment. True love is dynamic, not static, and nowhere is this more true than among those closest and dearest to us.

There is second of all the church, the community of faith throughout the world. Just think for a moment of the changes you have noticed in church life throughout your life, and you will realize that the church is no stranger to divine transformative love. Some will only want to hold those changes back; others will seek change merely for its own sake; but the heart of the church is change that results from faithful service to the risen Christ, who ever breathes new life into his people through the gifts of his living Spirit. Participate in and foster those blessed changes. And there are changes in the human family all around you. God does not keep the world in perfect immobility; immobility, complete and total rest, is death. The world is not dead but alive, for it is in God alone that we live, and move, and have our being.

How do we discern the living will of God in the world today? The answer of course given everywhere and always by the universal, confessing church of Jesus Christ is to search the Scriptures. It is through the medium of Scripture that God makes his will known to the church for the sake of the world. Yet the passage before us allows us to be more precise. We can quickly rule out several options. Scripture is not a set of unitary, coordinated propositions; God's will is not a system of moral truths arranged according to logical canons. We know that because our passage presents us with two biblical norms, both valid, which clearly conflict with one another. God alone is the norm, not a logical system. God's living decision is the ultimate truth, not a human judgment of rational moral rectitude. It is not God's will because it is right; it is right because God wills it.

But nor, on the other hand, does Scripture present us with a conflicting agon of moral voices, from which we must now decide which to follow. Yes, there is clearly a moral problem to be solved in our passage, of momentous consequence. But it is not presented as a dissonant conflict of moral visions, nor is the ultimate moral truth a consequence of human consciousness or perception. Finally, our text does not envision moral wrestling with God in term of ahistorical images left free to depend upon reader response to define moral direction. In the end, moral enquiry on the basis of Scripture is reasoned, engaging heart and mind in the presence of the living God, who guides us from the texts of the Bible finally to the truth of his will.

There are some moral issues in the Bible where hard boundaries are established. There are, for example, no texts in Scripture that permit adultery. But there are several issues in the Bible where there are a range of witnesses—often a wide range—which must be carefully mapped along ethical and theological coordinates that reflect biblical usage. Scripture is not a flat given, but a dynamic witness, which points to a living God, before whom we must wrestle, often long and hard, to hear the truth of his will in obedience and service to others. Legalism is not helpful; issues of fairness and human well-being clearly come into being; sometimes simple justice trumps abstract rules held in place simply for their own sake. We can never abandon the Scriptures as the one source from which we seek to hear the living will of God; but so also must we ever remain flexible and open to the new realities that God himself speaks through these very Scriptures, as he alone guides the church for the sake of the world.

Consider the role of women in the church, still a major unresolved topic in many parts of the ecumenical church. Yes, the Bible certainly, on a horizonal level, ascribes to the patriarchal rule of life that everywhere ruled the ancient world. No rewriting of Scripture can change that. But that is not the only moral voice in Scripture. Our five women constitute only one of numberless passages that intersect that horizontal plain vertically, as it were, from above; in which women have equality with men in roles of leadership, ownership, and full participation in the community of faith and social life. Deborah is a judge; Huldah is a prophet; Esther saves her people; Ruth is the one true exemplar of a faithful Israelite, even though she is a Moabite by birth; and on and on. All of these vertical lightning flashes are summed up in the Pauline confession, that in Christ there is neither male and female.

Now, we repeat, nowhere in Scripture does the vertical replace the horizontal. But now, in our time, history has in fact *eliminated* the horizontal from the moral universe of humanity. It is now a moral dictum of humanity: men and women, women and men, are equal, in every respect. The horizontal plane of the Bible is gone; the patriarchal world of ancient times is now in the past; only the vertical remains. And so we ask: is it truly the will of God that we, in the church, *erect* the horizontal plain in the church when it is absent in the world? Are we to insist on the *inequality* of women in the church when the world has recognized their *equality*? Or, are we rather to recognize that the vertical dimension of Scripture—which insists on full equality, as in our text—has in fact reigned triumphant as the living will of God for both church and world? I think it is time for the universal church fully and completely to recognize, on the basis of Scripture, that the latter is the case, and never again to look back.

V. Deuteronomy

1. No Other Gods

Deuteronomy 5:1–6

AFTER THE MANY YEARS of wandering in the wilderness, the new generation of God's people Israel finally arrives at the very edge of the land of promise. Still in the wilderness; just across the Jordan River, now forty years after the exodus from Egypt; poised to cross the river, yet still in the plains of Moab; God commands Moses to speak to the entire gathered community. It will be his last speech. At the end of it, Moses will die, as God himself already told him, following his disobedience at the waters of Meribah. The speech he gives has one goal in mind, set out at the beginning: to explain the divine will, the divine imperative for the new generation of God's people. The book of Deuteronomy comprises this speech—really an extended sermon—that Moses gives, now that they are about to cross the river and inherit the promise.

They face a new situation, unlike the generation who came out of Egypt, which died in the wilderness. For this generation will now enter the land, occupy it, settle it, and live in it. The will of God remains eternally the same; yet it now applies to a different set of circumstances, and indeed addresses an entirely new congregation. They now live between promise and fulfillment. The promise has already begun in their midst, and the power of that promise has brought them to the very edge of the Jordan River, ready to cross over. Yet they are not there yet. A future remains. The entire Pentateuch will end with that hope still intact, the promised grace of God already apparent, yet final fulfillment still pointing forward toward the future. The book of Deuteronomy seals the whole Torah in hope. Indeed, the book of Deuteronomy serves to render the whole Pentateuch accessible for every future generation of God's people, evoking fresh commitment to the one God of all creation. Like any good sermon, it is both timely and timeless,

engraving the power of the living God in the written word to evoke unrestrained commitment from every new listener.

Our passage opens as Moses continues to address the entire gathered
congregation of Israel on the banks of the Jordan River, within sight of the
promised land. It is essential that the whole congregation is involved. Yet nuance is clearly if subtly implied. There is only one people of God, Israel, from
the exodus from Egypt to the very present moment. Yet there are now *three*
generations envisioned: the original generation that perished in the wilderness because of its unbelief, the new generation that is even now standing
before Moses hearing his words, and the generation yet to come, which will
inherit the land and live by the will of God written in the law of Moses.

A dialectical relation is clearly set up: there is only one people, one law,
one land, one leader; yet there is now a new people, a new entry into the
land, a new formulation of the law, and a new leader (Joshua) about to be
inaugurated. There is only one covenant for all time; yet that very covenant
claims every new generation with a fresh set of challenges, measured not by
circumstances per se but by the living claim of God upon human existence.
The direct, immediate, existential claim of God is caught in the opening
words of Moses in chapter 5: "Hear, O Israel, the statutes and ordinances
that I am addressing to you today; you shall learn them and observe them
diligently. The Lord our God made a covenant with us at Horeb." With *us*; not
just with our parents, or our remote ancestors, but with us.

Indeed, Moses stresses the point by piling Hebrew words on top
of one another so quickly as scarcely to be translatable into meaningful
English. Here is a literal translation: "It was not with our fathers that the
Lord made this covenant but with us, we, these here, today, all of us, alive."
Everything rests upon the direct, immediate, contemporary, existential
claim of God's will upon those who *now* listen to the divine word. God's
living word is not somehow buried in the wilderness along with the previous generation, or with any generation in the past. Rather, the living God
continues to speak his word in the contemporary moment precisely to this
generation, addressing the new situation they will face as they cross over
into the land of promise and inherit the land.

God's word is always present, not because of any human ability to
close the gap between one generation and the next—a feature utterly foreign to the text—but rather because God is living, and always acts in the
present moment to guide his people in every new circumstance they face.
To make the point hermeneutically: contemporaneity and actualization
are not an added feature to Scripture, but are rather clearly built into the
theological shape of Scripture from the beginning. God's covenant does
not need to be made contemporary, so much as God's people need to

respond in the present moment to the living claim of God that is ever new and fresh. Indeed, the function of the book of Deuteronomy is to render the whole Pentateuch in such a way that it becomes, in written form, a *permanent* guide by which the living reality of God instructs every new generation of his people in the living truth of his will.

Moses begins his summary of the divine will, the commandments of the Lord, by grounding them firmly in the grace of the covenant. In no way whatsoever does obedience to the will of God constitute Israel as the people of God. Rather, only the freely given covenant of grace, initiated by God alone according to his own sovereign and mysterious purpose of love, constitutes and establishes that relationship. There is no moral achievement, no national quality, on the part of the people; indeed they spectacularly lack any such qualifications, as Moses will soon remind them: "It was not because you were more numerous than any other people that the Lord set his heart on you and chose you—for you were the fewest of the peoples. It was because the Lord loved you and kept the oath that he swore to our ancestors . . ." (Deut 7:7–8). God's love is electing love, grounded ultimately in the very nature of God himself. Any attempt to reverse that relation—as if obedience to the commandment of God constitutes a rationale for the divine love for Israel—flies directly in the face of the very heart of the gracious promise of God.

Yet grace commands a response, and that response is summarized in the book of Deuteronomy in the Ten Commandments ("ten words" in Hebrew). It is crucial that these commandments are addressed to the entire gathered community, as if to make it fully clear that this particular summary of the divine will applies without restriction to all, at all times. The commandments are laid out by Moses in a way that is comprehensive and straightforward, with no need for explanatory additions or circumstances. Indeed, Moses reminds the new generation that these words alone God himself spoke "with a loud voice" and wrote them down on tablets, with no need for Moses as an intermediary. Yet despite the enduring quality of the Ten Commandments, they are not given by Moses as abstract moral principles, an idea of the European Enlightenment foreign to the Bible. They operate within a community that is bound to a living God by a gracious covenant, which generates a unique history of a people with its God, who brought them out of bondage in Egypt and now stands ready to lead them into the land of promise.

The first commandment is a guide to the whole, indeed a guide to the Law itself: you shall have no other gods before me. Three issues resonate within this profound and all-encompassing command. God is making an absolute, exclusive claim upon the allegiance of his people, which will brook no compromise whatsoever. Only God is to be worshipped; the worship of anything or anyone else is utterly forbidden. Moreover, the exclusive claim of God upon the lives of his people is personal, even existential, in nature. It reaches beyond the mind to the very heart of their being, claiming the whole person in the most practical decisions of life. There can be no theoretical affirmation of God's exclusive reality when the life of the heart and will wander aimlessly among the idols of the world, free to grasp and to be grasped. Finally, there is not only an exclusive affirmation of God, but an affirmation of the uniqueness of God. God alone is God, and he is God in his own way. God alone defines who God is. God is not "the divine"; God is *God*, this God, who make his living reality known solely through his word, and who rejects every attempt to halter his truth with the surrounding gods of the nations.

Jesus Christ is God's one eternal covenant of grace with all humankind. We do not understand Christ in the light of the covenant; we understand the covenant of grace in the light of the death and resurrection of Jesus Christ, for he alone, the true word of God, gives meaning to every word of Scripture. The covenant of grace binds the entire community of faith into one, leaving out no one, embracing everyone. It gathers into one, not the righteous and the powerful, but sinners and the weak, the foolish and the helpless, the wayward and the lost. It casts aside those who stand their ground on their own moral and personal achievement, and reaches out to the guilty and the oppressed, the troubled and the confused. The covenant of grace gathers into one the people of God from all the earth and sets them free to live for Christ, and for him alone. We have no goal but Christ; we have no desire but the risen Lord; we have no life but his life, which is in us and among us and with us always. The seal of that covenant is our baptism into the name of the triune God; the joy of that covenant is our eating of the bread of life, and sharing in the cup of eternal life. God's covenant of grace in Jesus Christ is always present and active among the life of his people, for Christ is risen, and even now is present, alive, here, today.

Every new generation of the church faces a unique set of challenges, opportunities, resources, possibilities. It is as true for the individual congregation as for denominations, as it is for the universal church from one age to the next. The most instructive thing we can learn through careful study of the history of the church is not how to retreat into the past, but rather how the generations of the past faithfully and responsibly rose to the occasion of facing the *present* moment from one age to the next. Always there emerged a new voice, a new trend, a new vision, a new direction; always there settled in a fresh appropriation of the word of Scripture to meet the exigencies of the moment, however promising or discouraging it might have seemed. We do not learn, for example, from monasticism that we today should withdraw from the world into enclaves of piety; we learn rather the joy of singing the faith, the importance of concentrated reading and study of Scripture in the life of the community, the call to humble service in the world, even if it invites ridicule and disdain. We do not learn from the Reformers the need to break away from the mainstream church; we learn rather that every age of the church lies immediately open to the reforming power of God's Spirit, that the Bible alone is the sure and certain guide to God's living will for church and world, that the challenge of passing on the faith from one generation to the next is an all-consuming passion. We cannot retreat into the past. Instructed by the past, we can only meet the horizon of the future that greets us even now in the present moment.

God calls us to speak and to live the truth of his word in a world that celebrates untruth, often enough in the name of religion. We are called, in a world fractured by division and hate, to be peacemakers, reaching beyond the divisions of society to embody the new humanity that Christ himself has already formed among us. We are called to proclaim, in word and deed, the gospel of free grace, in a world consumed with self-assurance, self-advertisement, self-display, self-advancement, self-worship, again often enough concealed under the guise of religious devotion. We are called to stand with the hurting minority against the proud and disdainful majority, even when—especially when—that means putting our own comfort on the line. We are summoned by the living Lord to affirm our faith in words that matter, in words sanctioned by usage and sealed often enough by the blood of martyrs; yet not only to affirm that faith but to live it, and so in our own lives to be faithful witnesses echoing here below the great cloud of witnesses above who forever proclaim the glory of Christ. We are called to know Christ and to enjoy him, whether it is convenient or popular or not, regardless of the cost.

You shall have no other gods before me. The point in the first commandment is not primarily to censure a direct denial of God. Rather, it is directly opposing the religiously motivated attempt to link any earthly motives, projects, agendas, with the living reality of God. In our time, obvious examples all too quickly come to mind. Nationalism is the attempt to link the experience of belonging to a nation with belonging to God, as if the two forms of life are on the same or similar plane. They are not. The living reality of God cuts radically across all ties, all boundaries—of nation, of culture, of family, of state—and binds us to him alone. Any attempt to elevate the nation to the realm of the divine—not necessarily by directly worshipping the state, but by implying the divine preference for one state over another state—is utterly forbidden to those who follow Jesus Christ. On the one hand, in comparison to the exalted reality of the risen Christ, no nation, no state, belongs to Christ; no state is a "Christian nation." There is the risen Christ, exalted in glory, on the one hand; and there are the finite nations of the earth, all together but a single drop in a bucket on the other, regardless of their religious demography. Christ alone is King, and *no nation* reigns with him. On the other hand, with reference to the outstretched hand of the gracious Lord of all reality, *every* nation belongs to Christ, simply by virtue of the fact that he holds all peoples, of all nations, in all corners of the earth, in his hands. No nation may claim him, precisely because he has already claimed, already owns, all nations of all times and places. Nationalism is a disease, and the church can only confess against it, never join it.

Not unlike it, and often joined with it, is the disease of authoritarianism. First the integrity and institutions of government are attacked from within. Then, a strongman steps forth as a savior for the nation, the *only one* who can fix the problems that the government can no longer fix. With great shame and repentance, it has to be acknowledged that around the world, in various forms, the Christian community has not only failed to resist the allures of these strongman figures, but has wrapped the mantle of religion around their shoulders, and thrown the prayers and praises of the church at their feet. We can only respond: you shall have no other gods before me. It is absolutely forbidden by Holy Scripture as the word of God for the Christian community ever to fall into the horrific trap of following an authoritarian strongman, no matter how dazzling the promises made, no matter how convincing the arguments may sound, especially the religious ones. Those who confess Jesus Christ oppose all strongmen, whether they appear in the West, or in South America, or in Russia, or in China, or in Africa. Authoritarianism is a denial of the authority of God alone and his word.

We cannot worship God and money. The church is widely misled by the so-called prosperity gospel into believing that belief in God, and acquisition of wealth, are ultimately two sides of the same coin. They are not. To be sure, all wealth comes from God; all good gifts come from God, to both good and evil alike. But God alone is God, not wealth; we came naked into this world, and we will leave it the same way. God alone is the source of joy in life, not a bank account. God alone is our ultimate security, not a pile of riches. God alone is the true treasure of life and joy of the heart, not the things we may accumulate and even forget that we have. Wealth given by God is a tool for discipleship, to be used for the service of others. We are certainly permitted by the biblical word to enjoy the goodness of life under the gracious mercy of God; yet we are also warned that accumulation of wealth for its own sake kills the soul, and in the end renders genuine service of God impossible. We have to choose: God, or wealth. It is either/or. You shall have no other gods before me.

2. Hear, O Israel!

Deuteronomy 6:4–6

THE SCENE REMAINS THE same: the new generation of God's people poised on the very edge of the new land of promise, a land literally "gushing" with milk and honey. The promise is behind them, the fulfillment is in front of them, the living will of God unfolds all around them through his messenger Moses. The first generation has already passed away. The new generation is ready to conquer and divide the land. They will have children, and will come to know their children's children. Yet all will be for nothing if they do not remember the whole purpose of everything, which is the covenant of God's eternal grace that brings them to this moment of spectacular hope and joy. Moses has already summarized the claims of the covenant upon their life in the form of the Ten Commandments, the same commandments given to the first generation. Yet now, in new language found only here in the Pentateuch, Moses suddenly reveals a summary of human relation to God that captures the essence of everything important, without which nothing else really even matters at all. He speaks—for the first time in the Bible—of love for God.

Hear, O Israel! This is not a time for life as usual. Clearly Moses is now about to make a declaration of special significance, even of supreme importance, for the life of God's people. It will become the central theme of the book of Deuteronomy, the primary claim of the divine covenant upon human life, and indeed as confirmed by Jesus himself the most important of all God's commandments. But before the claim comes a declaration, not about the people, but about God. The identity of God alone is the basis for his relation to his people, and for their relation to him. Moses makes two statements, both ambiguous: "The Lord is our God" and "The Lord is one." There are a range of possible explanations for these statements. In my judgment, the best theological solution is not to choose from among the possibilities, but to recognize that the multivalent quality of the text is intentional. The unity of God is clearly presupposed in every possible explanation, but can and should be framed in at least three ways.

Israel belongs to God, and to God alone; and that God has only one purpose for his people, which is his gracious love. There is not a plan A here, and a plan B there, not one purpose governing God's rule in one set of circumstances, and another purpose in other different situations. God has *one*, and only one eternal purpose of love for the *whole* people of God. That purpose is constant and unwavering because it is grounded in the very identity of God himself. God elects a relationship of love with humankind because of who God is. There is no god behind, before, or after that election; God himself identifies his innermost being with the love he graciously gives in unmerited favor to humankind, not based on any claim of merit or achievement, but solely based on the freely given promise.

God is passionate in his commitment toward his people. He is, in the words of Deuteronomy, "jealous," in the sense that he cannot and will not let go of the covenant that he makes with his people. The book of Deuteronomy will leave open the terrible possibility that the people of God can, through ultimate disobedience, cast off the divine covenant by sheer neglect or outright rebellion. But in the end, the passionate love of God will break through the rebellion of his people, for the divine promise is eternal: "yet the Lord set his heart in love on your ancestors alone and chose you, their descendants after them, out of all the peoples, as it is today" (Deut 10:15).

And God is unique, utterly and completely *incomparable* in glory: "For the Lord your God is God of gods and Lord of lords, the great God, mighty and awesome . . ." (Deut 10:17). God can only be denoted, never defined. He can only be understood in reference to himself, according to the majesty of his own self-revelation in his word, never in relation to human religious concepts of divinity, however appealing. God is in no sense whatsoever a projection of human experience, or a correlative or human piety, but rather the true ground of all reality, who will not be enclosed in any human scheme or agenda. All life is gift.

We have spoken of the confession of God's identity; now we must turn to the claim of God upon the life of his people that flows from that confession. "You shall love the Lord your God with all your heart, and with all your soul, and with all your might." These words first appear in the Bible like an ethical lightning bolt, suddenly illumining the whole sky. They are not at all foreign to the rest of the Pentateuch, which after all contains numerous stories depicting passionate devotion to God. Yet there is certainly a luminous quality of absolute claim, of moral beauty, which so shines through these words that both subsequent Judaism and Christianity will understand them as the center of the will of God, around which everything else revolves, the true key that provides the ultimate interpretation in every situation of ethical ambiguity and struggle.

The command to love God is not an additional commandment alongside the Ten Commandments, a kind of eleventh commandment. Rather, it is the one divine imperative that sets every divine command in its proper perspective. Every commandment of God serves one, and only purpose: the love of God with complete and utter abandon above all else. Love for God is not *less* than emotional, but it is not primarily an emotional quality; rather is it the orientation of one's *entire existence* on the living reality of God, without any restrictions or obstructions whatsoever. God, and God alone, is now the very center of all life, the center of every thought, feeling, decision, action, truth, for those who belong to him. To love him is to live in complete and total commitment, utterly undivided by any other loyalty, utterly and completely devoted to him with one purpose only in absolute enjoyment and trust. The totality of existence is involved in true relation to God; that is the meaning of love for God, and therefore of every single commandment in the Bible.

The passage continues by elaborating the profound reach of the divine claim into the very heart of human life, completely relativizing every other moral claim, however worthy it may seem. The point of delineating the elements of human devotion to God is not to divide the self into parts—an anthropology foreign to the Bible—but rather to view the whole self in relation to God from various perspectives. Love is wholehearted, with one complete and unrestricted devotion; that is the sum of the matter, though it can be viewed from a variety of human capacities.

The people of God are called to love him with all their heart. The heart is the human person as viewed from the point of view of human understanding and rationality, but also affection and will. Even memories, life decisions, attitudes, and behaviors are all included in the biblical picture of the "heart." Facial expressions and gestures spring from the same source. To love God with the soul, or self, is to love God with every human desire and emotion comprising the whole person. The self is both individual and interpersonal, tying persons together into families and communities. Human might is the widest range possible of human activity in the public sphere, in which the person shares in the corporate life of the entire community through responsible action, including the use of property and possessions generally. In short, every area of life, intimate and social, private and public, is claimed by God for a love without restriction, determined by passionate and total commitment to him alone.

Hear! The eternal promise of God's gracious mercy comes to us again and again only in the living reality of his *word*. We do not discover God's promise by self-reflection, or self-analysis, or through the projection of self-conscious feeling, or pious inwardness, but through the hearing of the word in faith. It happens once for all; it happens again and again. God's word of promise comes to us when we are so overburdened with the struggles and mistakes of life that we cannot see a way forward. Reason and experience tell us that there is none, that any way of escape is impossible. Yet God always makes a way, parting the waters of human circumstance, whether in the life of the individual or indeed in the life of the gathered community.

God's word does not merely interpret the world, it changes it, so radically that it makes the entire world new, setting us on our feet again and giving us a new future where there was none before. We may be lost in the wilderness of this world, confused and distracted by the temptations pulling us this direction and that. There may come a time in life when the path forward disappears, and we have literally no idea how to take the next step. God's word of promise creates a new path forward, one step at a time, until the future suddenly unfolds toward a distant horizon. God's word does not merely point to the future; God's word alone creates the future, for the future is already enclosed in the eternity of God's living word and will. We may be on the threshold of discovery, yet unable to take just the right step forward for ourselves and for our posterity. God's word of promise creates the legacy we leave behind, blessing us in blessing others.

God has one word for us, and for the world, and that is his word of grace. There is only one covenant between God and all humanity: and that is the covenant of grace in Jesus Christ. There is no such thing in the Bible as a covenant of works, an offer by God to establish our relation to him through works of righteousness by merit. God is one, not two. God is singular and unique, not twofold and double-minded. Before we were born, before creation itself, in the eternity that is God himself, the one covenant of grace in Jesus Christ is God's eternal purpose for the whole world, which encompasses every human person in all times and places.

Are we quick to judge others? We should remember that they too were loved by God before he every made the universe in which we live. Are we so sure that others fall short in their standing before the Almighty? We should remember that in the light of grace, so do we, so do all. Grace shows the whole world our need of God's love, in the very moment that it proclaims that love. Do some insist on their moral standing in the religious and political world? Let them beware, lest they fail to grasp the beauty of grace, which is all-consuming, even as it is all-embracing. God's freely given covenant of grace surrounds the whole creation. How could it not, if God is one, and his grace is one? If that is so, there is no one we shall ever meet who is outside the circle of God's redeeming love. It is a sober thought, a liberating thought, in the end a life-affirming benediction.

In every change, God is constant. God is not Being above, while we inhabit the realm of becoming below; nor is God Becoming below, always moving along with us along the current of change. To pose the problem this way is a philosophical ruse foreign to Scripture. For both being and becoming are human categories of thought, abstract projections of human experience. The Ruler of the entire universe becomes a tiny, fragile, infant, without being any less God; the central fact of the incarnation of the promised Word shatters the categories of being and becoming. God is one because he is *constant*. Despite every human failure, he is constant in the passionate pursuit of humanity. Despite the natural limitations of human mortality he overcomes those limits by entering them himself, dissolving them from the inside, shattering them, and in so doing elevating all humanity to eternal communion with him. We daily grow with him, until one day we will be like him.

The call of the divine promise is love for God with our whole being, without restriction, without restraint, without distraction. To love God truly is to know him fully, just as we are fully known by him. Of course the knowledge of God is never complete in this life. We grow in the grace and faith of the gospel, and that includes our understanding. Knowing God expands our awareness of him (the content of our faith), and at the same time our relationship to him (the depth of our faith). True content causes the depth of faith to expand into every area of life; the depth of faith makes room for greater understanding of the true content of God's revealed will, as we are transformed day by day in the very image of God.

Our decisions in life are no longer oriented toward a variety of factors, with "religion" being one factor among others, perhaps even the highest or chief factor. Religion blinds the will; God illumines true decision. God is not one factor among others in the moral decisions of human existence. God enters human life and *shatters* every other claim to human loyalty. The truth of God's will relativizes every other human loyalty, whether to family, to nation, to culture, or to society. To love God is to lay our lives before him, a sacrifice of thanksgiving and joy, confident that he alone will direct us along the path of true fulfillment. The promise calls us to love God with all our heart, and that means to live with unrestrained joy in his presence. God alone is our best thought. God alone is our one true direction in life. God alone is our finest treasure. God alone is our true satisfaction. In knowing him, we enjoy him; in enjoying him, we come to know him more fully, until we one day behold the vision glorious.

There are of course for each of us a variety of distractions and temptations that draw us away from the true love of God. For some it may be the constant, churning desire to acquire more and more things, until God himself is simply one more thing, one more possession, which is no god at all. For others the constant quest for self-realization may drown out the ultimate truth of the promise that God himself, and God alone, is our highest reach in human existence, the true depth and height and breadth of our being. To know him, and him alone, is to know ourselves for the first time.

Yet for others still, the anger, disappointments, and resentments of the past simply offer a too powerful lure, offering a false self, defined not by who we truly are in relation to God but by what we believe we have lost. For some, the treatment of other human beings as nothing more than opportunities for self-advancement and self-enrichment means the sheer loss of God in the world. Yet love of God is not in the end one requirement among other human requirements; it is the divine promise that *defines* all human existence. The total claim that love for God makes upon our lives is itself a gift of grace. We love, because he first loved us, not just once but again and again; his love breaks through the barriers we erect now and again, until, brokenhearted, we are healed.

It is not we who give the command to love God meaning; rather, the gift of the command gives our lives true purpose, and carries us forward in every change and circumstance. To be sure, we all go through dry seasons. We all at times ask why? How long? Yet it is not we who must somehow carry the passion of love for God through times of difficulty and struggle, but rather, the passionate love for God that flows from his love for us carries us. We reach out to him anew, because he first gathers us again into his arms. We praise and thank him once again, because he readily embraces our lives, broken and wounded though they may be. We sing our songs of joyous love because he himself takes delight in our joy. Love for God is a biblical command; but the command soon becomes permission, then invitation, finally free and open embrace of the One who alone is worthy.

3. The End of an Era

Deuteronomy 34

MOSES FINISHES THE SINGLE, sermon-styled speech to the people Israel on the east bank of the Jordan River overlooking the new land of promise, the speech that constitutes our present book of Deuteronomy (regardless of its lengthy prehistory). A clear transition takes place. Moses turns from speaking to the people, to a series of solemn and carefully orchestrated tasks that conclude his ministry before God (31–33). The first such task is to appoint Joshua as the new leader of the people. The conquest of the land will belong to the time of Joshua, not Moses; yet Joshua will clearly have a different role in the divine purpose. God will lead Joshua, just as he has led Moses; God will give Joshua the same victories, the same strength and courage, the same faithful support, according to the divine promise. Yet Joshua will be guided directly by the word of God revealed through Moses, which will now become the authority for God's people.

The second task confirms the first; the law of God is fixed in *written* form, for all time. God continues to speak; but he speaks through the written word, not apart from it. Indeed, the written word is deposited in the ark of the covenant carried by the Levites, and carefully read at regular intervals to the whole community of the people. The written word becomes the norm by which the people of God are instructed, and through which the people of God are nourished in each new generation. The written word is the vehicle by which the living covenant of God reaches out into the distant future, embracing every new age.

The third task is to teach the people a song, which will be handed on from age to age, until the terrifying reality of its truth becomes evident. On the one hand, the song is a celebration of the sheer beneficence of God, overflowing in abundance: "The Rock, his work is perfect, and all his ways are just. A faithful God, without deceit, just and upright is he . . ." (32:4).

God has sustained his people through every trial, not only in the past, but also in the present and the future. Indeed, from the divine perspective, all time of all ages is filled with the same divine love, which is everywhere manifest. Yet on the other hand stands the contrasting faithlessness of future generations of God's people: "yet his degenerate children have dealt falsely with him, a perverse and crooked generation" (32:5). The reference is not to the generation poised on the banks of the Jordan, but to a distant future, which nevertheless stands under the same, immediate presence of the divine reality that now guides Israel, and acts according to his revealed will. God's faithfulness is unchanging; in time, the disobedience of the people will surely come with incomprehensible perversity. It is clearly not a song of religious triumphalism, but indeed of painful frailty.

Yet finally, Moses offers his final blessing to the people, reaching again from the present into the distant future. Each of the tribes of Israel are blessed in turn, in clear echo of the blessing of Jacob. In sharp contrast to the Song of Moses, the Blessings of Moses surrender the entire people of God, in all times, and in all circumstances, to the all-encompassing rule of God, which is majestic and enriching beyond measure: "So Israel lives in safety, untroubled is Jacob's abode in a land of grain and wine, where the heavens drop down dew" (33:28). In the end, the final word of Moses to God's people Israel speaks solely of the triumphant rule of God, who is gracious and merciful beyond all human measure. Beyond the law, and the miserable failure of the people to keep it, God's final purpose is sheer redeeming love: "Happy are you, O Israel! Who is like you, a people saved by the Lord . . ." (33:29). With these words, and the tasks that they conclude, the ministry of Moses ends. There remains only one final episode that we, the readers, are permitted to witness.

As so often happens in the Bible, first human beings act and react, then God himself steps onto the scene. In this case, the final deeds of God recorded in the book of Deuteronomy are at the same time the last moments of the life of Moses, and indeed the last narrative of the Pentateuch itself. God and Moses are alone together for the bittersweet, poignant scene, bringing to a close a relationship that began—alone, together—at the burning bush. While Moses cannot cross over the river Jordan into the promised land because of his sin, from another vantage point it is clear that his earthly pilgrimage is complete, his life mission entirely accomplished. With his death, the law of Moses literally comes to an end. It will be for Joshua, and the new generation, to engage in the very different task of conquest and occupation; for Moses, the work of liberation and instruction is now done. Only one last earthly moment with God remains.

Moses leaves the steppes of Moab where the people of God are gathered, and ascends mount Nebo, to the highest peak, Pisgah. He is still on the eastern side of the Jordan, just opposite the city of Jericho, the first city to fall to Joshua in battles still to come, on the western side. And there God "shows him" the entire, vast, sweep of the promised land. The narrator slows the pace down as if to register the exalted majesty of the moment, panoramic in its vision from the mountaintop, untroubled as yet by the coming struggles down below. The vision slowly pans counterclockwise, working its way around the sacred geography of the bountiful land, so vast in scope, so lush in beauty.

There in the north is the Gilead range of mountains, stretching forth to the northwest all the way to Dan. West of the Jordan River, his vision now traces the land southward, from Naphtali, to Ephraim and Manasseh, and Judah, all the way to the Mediterranean. Clearly this is not a geography lesson, nor is it a sacred, disembodied vision. This is a divine gift to Moses, the servant of God, a chance to see the promise with his own eyes, before those eyes are closed for the last time. His gaze travels to the far south, the Negev, and then finally comes around to the plain of the Jordan to the southeast of the point just below the summit where he is standing. He sees it all; the entire future promise of God, the same promise given to Abraham, Isaac, and Jacob, yet like them, not possessed by Moses.

And there Moses dies, on the mountaintop. He dies at the command of God. Once again, there is an astounding intimacy in the narration of the scene. Moses dies alone with God, and God himself buries him. The text draws the lesson: no human being knows where Moses is buried, therefore no burial cult can form. Any who wish to honor Moses must honor his written word, the law of Moses, not his gravesite. Yet the remarkable existential quality of the scene cannot be overlooked, reminiscent of God clothing the dishonored Adam and Eve, or remonstrating with Abraham over the fate of Sodom and Gomorrah, or wrestling with Jacob until daybreak. Only God knows where he buries Moses; it is left for the people of Israel to mourn his loss on the steppes of Moab down below. Joshua assumes the leadership that Moses has already conferred upon him according to the command of God.

Moses is not given a human burial, but he is given a eulogy, which closes the Pentateuch. Of all the prophets that arise among the people Israel—clearly the narrative is written from a later perspective—Moses is utterly unique, singled out by God himself, not by any particular merits or characteristics of his own. This man, and only this man, God speaks with face to face, as one friend to another. Through this man, and only this man, does God deliver an oppressed people from bondage with mighty and terrible acts of deliverance. Only through Moses does God show the great and awesome power that brings the whole people out of Egypt, across the parted waters of the sea, through the wilderness, and now at long last to the edge of the promised land. Nothing was not done in a corner; as the closing words of the book indicate (in Hebrew), it was done "in the sight of all Israel." God singled Moses out for a public life, and a private death; and now his work is done.

What is the true measure of a human life? God alone is our home. We come into this world from him. We live in this world with him by our side. One day we all leave this world, gathered by him alone into his eternal embrace. Along the way we all make plans, yet God himself steps into our lives and takes hold, making our lives a witness to his will, shaping our existence according to the pattern of his grace. His blessed teaching marks our path in life, his name our most precious possession, his justice the true way forward in every moment of life. When we falter—as we do, time and again—he remains faithful to his promise, despite our foolishness, refusing to let us go. He sustains and shields us in the midst of harm, cares for us in ways far beyond all possible awareness, guards and guides us through every danger and temptation of human existence. Every good blessing of life comes to us directly from his hand, from the friendships we cherish, the nourishment that enriches and sustains us, the unspeakable joys of life that everywhere surround us. When we are powerless and utterly spent through the burdens and follies that weigh us down, he is our strength, he is our life, he is our protection. When we are wounded, he heals us; when we are dead, he makes us alive; indeed to be fully human is nothing other than to be in relationship to God, for he alone is our life. God himself is the measure of our existence.

The gospel opens wide the door to friendship with God. We do not follow after him blindly, but with open eyes desire the beauty of his will. We do not obey his commandments resentfully, as if taking unwelcome medicine, but with open hearts gladly respond to the gracious call of his love. We cannot search him out; but we recognize that he has searched for us, and found us, and even now knows us better than we know ourselves. And so, we entrust our very being into his gracious hands, fully assured that he himself is our heart, when our heart fails; he is our strength, when no more strength remains. In seeing him, we are transforming into his image day by day. In knowing him, we come to know ourselves as if for the first time. In loving him fully, and alone, above all things, we learn to love our neighbor as ourselves, and so to be truly human. To give this God—who alone is God indeed—glory, is fully to enjoy him, and fully to enjoy him is to glorify him beyond measure.

To be fully human is to live within a tradition, a community with a past, a present, and a future. God's blessing comes to us through the people of God, the church of Jesus Christ. God's rule extends over the entire world, the entire universe, the entire creation; yet he chooses to makes his universal blessing known through a particular people, and to call us into the fellowship of that people, each by name. It is in the context of the worshipping community of faith that we hear the divine word, and learn his will. We come to sing his praises, and learn the joy of his service. We pray in common with all who call on the name of the Lord, and profess our faith in a common heritage which stretches across time and space without limit.

That is not at all to embrace ecclesio-centric triumphalism, a falsification of the gospel. Jesus Christ is the center of the biblical witness, not the church. Jesus Christ is the true content of the gospel, not the church. The church serves Christ; Christ does not serve the political and cultural interests of the church. Yet it is remarkable that the final words on the lips of Moses, the man of God, who after all hardly had an untroubled relation to the people of Israel, are words of blessing upon the tribes of Israel, the people of God. For all its earthly frailty, for all its historical mistakes, both in past and present, and doubtless in the future, the church remains the church. We may languish for a time in the wilderness; we may indeed be thrashed and defeated by the changing fortunes of human society; but for his own reasons, God calls us, and loves us still.

Is death, in the Bible, viewed as the shattering end of life cut short, or the blessed conclusion to life's journey? Certainly, on the one hand, in life we must remember death. The reality of death shatters the myth of success. What does it mean to be a human being in God's world? What does it mean to live an authentic human life? Some answer—even in the church—that human life is measured by the level of success achieved, as if the gospel is a guide to prosperity.

Of all the characters in the Old Testament, the life of Moses stands out for its amazing breadth and scope. Rescued from the Nile where he floats in a basket by none other than the daughter of Pharaoh; called by God to lead the people Israel to freedom; unleashing the plagues upon Egypt when Pharaoh will not budge; raising his staff as the waters part when the chariots of Egypt bear down upon them; receiving the Law of God written by God on Mount Sinai; leading the people through the wilderness to the edge of the promised land; all of this and more is true. Yet even *Moses* can come thus far, and no farther. The promise of God is only one short step away, a *stone's* throw across the Jordan, yet Moses cannot and will not take that step. The fact is, we are each given a unique opportunity that marks the limits of human life. Your life is on loan from God, a gift given to you for awhile, and some day to be taken away. The opportunity does not last forever, and for that reason it is all the more precious, all the more remarkable, all the more astounding. Do not waste time.

How will you live? How will you fill the hours and days you are loaned by God? You can of course chase the idol of success. You can always look for the shortest route to happiness. You can weigh all your dreams on the scale of fame and fortune. You can choose the options in life where triumph is guaranteed. Pursuing success is certainly one way to fill the limited number of days you are given on this earth. Yet according to Scripture, success is surely a false measure of human fulfillment. There is no more important figure in the entire Old Testament than Moses, yet in the end Moses *failed*. The people entered the promised land, Moses did not. There is something far more important to human well-being than success. What is that something?

In the midst of death, we must remember life. To be human does not mean to be successful, but to be *faithful*. During the unique opportunity that your life represents, more important than anything else—indeed more important than succeeding—is that you be faithful to the God who calls you as his own. The gospel delivers you from the tyranny of success, and frees you to a life of genuine service to Christ. There will come times in your life when the only way forward is to embrace the risk of faith. If you measure what you do by guaranteed results, you will fall short of God's call.

There is always an element of adventure of Christian discipleship. We endeavor, not knowing whether we will succeed; we work hard, not being sure of the outcome; we strive, never certain of the final results. In doing so, we learn to derive joy from the effort; we learn to cherish satisfaction from the daily work along the journey; we come to appreciate the mystery of life, so far beyond our control. Whether you succeed or fail is not the great issue of your life; the great issue of life is whether you are willing to take the risk of trying. Your chance to make it count doesn't last forever. You have one opportunity, and that opportunity does not come again. There is no time to regret past mistakes, no time to waste on foolish distractions. Now is the time. Today is the day.

In the end, we are here on this earth for a brief moment of time, a mere point of transition to a new life eternal. We leave in the hands of God the future fruits of our earthly pilgrimage. What God has done through us and in us, he will not bring to completion until that day when he alone is all in all, and all earthly works fade into the shadows before the bright light of his eternal glory.